STORAGE AND STABILITY

Other Books

by BENJAMIN GRAHAM

Security Analysis
   (With DR. DAVID L. DODD)
   McGraw-Hill Book Company, Inc.

The Interpretation of Financial Statements
   (With SPENCER B. MEREDITH)
   Harper & Brothers

STORAGE
AND STABILITY

A Modern Ever-normal Granary

BY

BENJAMIN GRAHAM

*Lecturer in Finance, Columbia University;
Head of Security Analysis Division,
New York Stock Exchange Institute*

WITH A FOREWORD BY

DR. ALVIN JOHNSON

*Director, New School for Social
Research, New York*

FIRST EDITION

McGRAW-HILL BOOK COMPANY, INC.

NEW YORK AND LONDON

1937

1 2 3 4 5 6 7 8 9 0   DOC/DOC   9 0 3 2 1 0 9 8

ISBN : 978-0-07-162631-6

THE MAPLE PRESS COMPANY, YORK, PA.

In 1937, McGraw-Hill published
the first edition of *Storage and Stability*, by Benjamin Graham.
It, along with his teaching, other writings, and a superb record as a money
manager, created a legend that continues to be enhanced rather than
diminished with the passage of time. Graham has become the
most influential investment philosopher of our time.

To commemorate the book's original publication,
and to reintroduce to readers the original ideas and
language of the first edition, McGraw-Hill is proud to
publish this special reproduction of the 1937 book.
This edition contains a new Foreword written
by Irving Kahn, Benjamin Graham's protege
and a renowned investor himself.

This special reprint edition was photographed by hand from the
original pages of the first edition by Jay's Publishers Services,
Inc., Rockland, Massachusetts. A customized vertical camera,
designed to minimize distortion and to prevent damage to
rare books, was used. This edition was printed and bound
by R. R. Donnelley, Crawfordsville, Indiana.

Preface

THE Ever-normal Granary is a Chinese phrase, which has rather suddenly become a central issue in American economic policy. The first and most pressing business of the next session of Congress will be the passage of comprehensive farm relief legislation. By way of offset against the substantial benefits to be accorded by our government to the farmers, this legislation offers an Ever-normal Granary as a safeguard to the consuming population. The Granary idea, briefly, means the storage of reserve supplies of big crop years for use in time of crop failure.

In this study we shall deal not only with the specific Ever-normal Granary proposals now before Congress, but—more comprehensively—with the general possibilities of storage of basic commodities as a source of stability and improvement in our national economy. Most attacks upon the problems of depression may be ranged under two distinct headings: those related to so-called overproduction, and those related to defects of our monetary and credit system. The concept of storage is unique in that it lies at the intersection of these two lines of difficulty, offering at once a synthesis and solution of both.

It is a truism that the proper cure for "overproduction" is increased consumption. But how best attain it? Storage is the intermediate stage between production and consumption. Its function has always been to absorb and level out disparities between supply and demand. In a more intelligent use than hitherto of the storage mechanism there may well be found an adequate remedy for that striking maladjustment between output and effective demand which induces and accompanies economic prostration. Further than that, the storage mechanism might also be developed into the essential preliminary step to an ever higher standard of living. The analogy between storage of staple commodities and storage of water in reservoirs is obvious and by no means deceptive. In both cases storage may be utilized first to prevent periodic disturbance, and then to provide a constantly increasing measure of fruitfulness and power.

Similarly, in the monetary field, storage of basic commodities suggests itself as the most suitable backing for a sound and adequate currency. The unique prestige of the gold standard has been deeply undermined—patently, by reason of the inadequacies revealed since the war; less evidently, by the recent loss of most of the tangible qualities of gold currency and its virtual transformation from physical into metaphysical money. Silver vexes us as a lesser and more questionable gold. The alternative of "managed paper currency" bristles with dangers and difficulties as yet unexplored. A currency backed by, and actually redeemable in, stored basic commodities—on suitable terms—would possess an intrinsic soundness superior to that of gold and immeasurably beyond that of inconvertible paper.

Thus the Storage mechanism, if skillfully employed, offers the solution of our basic monetary problem at the same time that it attacks the underlying maladjustments of supply and demand. Thus, also, it has the enormous practical advantage of being self-financing and self-liquidating. The stored commodities may create the money needed to pay for them—not only for putting them into storage, but also for passing them out later into consumption. Say's law, dear to the classical economist, asserts that production and purchasing power are equivalent. This law, convincing enough in theory, has worked very badly in practice since

1929. A sound plan for monetizing basic commodities held in storage would "put teeth" in Say's law; for a crucial sector of production would then actually create the monetary wherewithal for its purchase.

The storage mechanism, intended primarily to cope with glut and shortage, is vested with the allied function of reasonably stabilizing price levels. Reasonable price stability and general business stability go hand in hand. This is particularly true in the field of basic raw materials, since these exercise a determining influence over the price structure as a whole. It may be demonstrated that the soundest price-control policy would be one that aims at stability of the general level of raw-materials prices over an indefinite period, permitting, however, a gradual decline in the price level of fabricated goods, to reflect improvement in productive efficiency. Concurrently with a stabilized level for raw materials generally, there must be full play for suitable fluctuations in the price of individual commodities in the group, in response to variations in their supply and demand. Our study will inquire whether and how these ideal conditions may be attained in practice.

The idea of storage as a solution of economic problems at least has the support of common sense. It is diametrically opposed to the topsy-turvy Alice-in-Wonderland reasoning that has marked so much of our depression thinking and policy. It rejects the argument that prosperity may be promoted by scarcity; that purchasing power may be showered in a gentle rain of greenbacks from heaven; that collapse due to excessive debt may be remedied by incurring new and larger debts; that our foreign trade may be strengthened by deliberately weakening our currency. The Storage concept leads us away from all these absurdities into the region of the tangible, the sound, and the well established.

For, indeed, no economic policy has a longer and more impressive tradition than the simple and obvious one of storing the surplus of good years against hard times to follow. It was ancient practice in the animal kingdom before man existed. Its written record dates from the Book of Genesis, wherein is recounted the famous storage coup engineered by Joseph in Egypt. If, in Samuel Johnson's phrase, we "survey Mankind from China to Peru," we find in the early history of both of these widely separated lands an elaborate and highly successful storage policy in operation for centuries. And these ancient precedents have been drawn upon in current times as the source of the Ever-normal Granary, projected by Secretary of Agriculture Wallace, and now bound up with the impending legislative proposals for all-risk crop insurance and for comprehensive farm relief.

There are interesting precedents, also, for the concept of basic commodities as the physical backing for currency. Such commodities did, indeed, constitute the earliest money, antedating gold, as our language still shows in deriving "pecuniary" from *pecus*, meaning cattle. Tobacco notes, backed by tobacco in government storage, were legal tender in colonial states in the 1700's. Less directly, but nonetheless actually, the Federal Reserve Act has always provided that "readily marketable staples" held in warehouse should be one of the bases for the issuance of our Federal Reserve notes. Thomas A. Edison, long meditating on the shortcomings of our monetary system, announced in 1922 his currency plan, which provided for the creation of money against deposit of basic commodities held in storage.

In this study we shall deal with a third conception—that of a group, or composite unit, of basic commodities. This group device will be found to overcome the objections that lie against the use of any single commodity (including gold) as the basis of currency emission. Here again we find an abundance of precedent and a well-established technique to guide us. From the days of Jevons, "index numbers," based on groups of commodities, have become the familiar tools of economists. As embodied in the Bureau of Labor Statistics Index of Wholesale Prices, they have already been made a central part of important legislation. Upon them have been based the studies and suggestions of many modern economic thinkers, among whom Irving Fisher deserves especial mention.

Because the storage mechanism offers the natural—one might almost say "the original and only genuine"—solution for basic maladjustments of supply and demand, it is found to yield collateral advantages of great importance. The chief of these has already been alluded to: stored plenty, as the concrete source of an ever-rising living standard for all the people of this land. Related to this highest end is the essential insurance that storage affords against drouth and flood and all visitations of nature. Then again, storage of basic commodities has incalculable value as an element of our military defenses. No aspect of preparedness is more essential and less objectionable than the marshaling of these real sinews of war, including those we must import. As a fourth collateral suggestion, we find that the storage mechanism will offer the simplest and the most advantageous means of dealing with the vexing problems of international trade balances and international debts. Finally, it will appear that some of the underlying problems involved in carrying out the recently adopted social security legislation may also find their best solution by means of storage.

Out of our survey and discussion of the possibilities of storage there will emerge a concrete proposal, which will combine into one concept the three elements above referred to: (*a*) storage as a reservoir to equalize and extend our economic well-being; (*b*) basic commodities as the foundation of a sound monetary system; and (*c*) the composite group, or "commodity unit," as the technical means by which the advantages of a storage system may best be realized. In this synthesis the diverse precedents will have made their several contributions. Confucius will stand beside Edison; Irving Fisher will improve upon the Incas of Peru. It may well be that their combined wisdom offers a clear and effective solution for the paradoxical ills which have beleaguered us in recent years—and which still stand as an ominous threat to our economic and political future.

Benjamin Graham.

New York,
October, 1937.

Acknowledgment

MY grateful thanks are due to Dr. Alvin Johnson for his encouragement and support; to Mr. L. H. Bean for valuable aid in many directions; to Mr. Edward Fitzgerald of Messrs. H. Hentz & Company for a mass of data relating to commodity markets; and to Dr. Frederick C. Mills and Mr. Irving Kahn for their helpful interest. I wish to express my appreciation also to Miss Judith Graham, Mr. James Rosenwald, and Mr. Konrad Katzenelenbogen for their assistance in the research and computation which have gone into this book.

BENJAMIN GRAHAM.

Contents

CONTENTS

PART V. OTHER ASPECTS OF THE RESERVOIR PLAN

Foreword

Very few books in the field of economics are republished after a lapse of 61 years. This book is the exception that deserves reprinting.

Those who have lived through the Depression years of the 1930s can recall the heavy costs both financial and in human terms that our nation suffered. *Storage and Stability* was the result of the indelible impression made on the young Benjamin Graham. He lived through the wild swings of prices and currencies following World War I and their dramatic effects on the state of the world. Over the next seventeen years, Graham analyzed many solutions proposed by economists resolving them into the then-revolutionary recommendation that important currency benefits are achieved by basing the currency on a basket of readily saleable commodities. These stored commodities limit the peaks of inflation and deflation. Building reserves of real assets also supports higher employment. The "commodities basket" will become wider economic policy, and become influential at the start of the twenty-first century as it was at its beginning.

Historically, paper money has had many different kinds of backing—mostly backed by precious metals like gold and silver. But the vast growth of paper currencies have made the use of these metals no longer physically possible. Since the 19th century, many economists have tried to construct adequate reserves for backing their country's currency. Thinkers like Adam Smith, Jevons, Marshall, Hobson, and Keynes have contributed to the search for an ideal currency reserve.

Graham realized that peaceful existence depends upon the promise of adequate distribution of food and lands which grow foods; further, that the three basic human drives for food, clothing, and shelter are always measured in some local currencies. Normally, people accumulate their savings which are the bases for home and equipment ownership. Most currencies feel modest annual effects of some price inflation. But some, like in South America, Asia, and Southeast Asia, have experienced currency swings that are far wider. Without stable purchasing power, savers are denied the benefits of improving their own standard of living. The victims of local inflation grow increasingly limited in their ability to improve their own living standards. Currency swings can lead to wider crises, revolution, and big changes in a country's structure.

The risks of such instability have become greater today. Modern instant communication makes currency trading a 24-hour game with serious social dislocations. One glaring example was Bank of England's loss of over 1 billion pounds trying to support their own currency. While speculators got richer, many English taxpayers got poorer. Currency losses related to normal trades in goods or services are a serious factor in effecting the profitability of normal trade. Currency changes can eliminate all profits made in producing or delivering goods without reference to the value of the goods themselves.

Graham contrasted the conventional savings that individuals and families normally practice and the typical spending practices of central governments. Most countries create or borrow money while their credit is good. They run deficits rather than reduce national debt.

In *Storage and Stability*, Graham sought to make governments behave more consistently by building reserves rather than deficits. He showed how he can increase demand beyond current needs by producing for storage and ultimate use, thus accomplishing two substantial benefits. These benefits include a cut in unemployment and a substantial accumulation of tangible goods for domestic or international use. Graham constructed his reserve based upon the total value of twenty-one major world commodities selected by their prominence in world trade. This total unit or "basket" is representative of total price levels around the world even while individual fluctuations of one or more among the twenty-one could be substantial, the total is more stable and representative.

Graham's first public effort was a group called the Economic Forum, which met at the New School for Social Research in New York. The school's president, Alvin Johnson, had already attracted prominent economists who had fled Germany and Austria. One, Frederick Hayek, subsequently received the Nobel Prize in economics. Graham's group was joined by men like William McChesney Martin, then president of New York Stock Exchange and later the chairman for twenty-one years of the Federal Reserve Bank in Washington, and Congressman Howard Buffett of Omaha, whose constituents had suffered so many losses of farms and bankruptcies in the midwest.

Roosevelt's farm secretary, Henry Wallace, supported Graham, but his department wanted to limit production so prices might rise. The New Deal accomplished many important economic improvements, but was not successful in the area of agriculture or farm products.

Finally, in 1996, the U.S. Treasury issued a new type of treasury linking its interest payments with the Consumer Price Index. The buyer receives higher interest if the CPI increases. Having stable currencies, makes the present disorganized world currency markets far less able to spread to the local currencies.

Our own economy is substantially influenced by its relation to the Consumer Price Index (CPI) as computed by the U.S. Labor Department. A rise in the Index can increase everyone's social security payment and can raise wages when they are tied by contract to the CPI. Another advantage of commodity reserve currency is its ability to limit or even to eliminate the trade cartels which occasionally attempt to monopolize a given raw material. Although cartels inevitably collapse, their effect on the world economy is clearly antisocial.

In the year 1937, when this book appeared, the traditional Commodity Reserve Board (CRB) index was at 194. In 1997, the number of the index was 295, or roughly 100 points higher. This increase is more modest than the actual index for finished goods and services in the same interval of time. At the same time, the population of the world has increased by about 60% (in the U.S., the figure is about 26%). According to the World Bank, 1.3 billion humans exist today on $1 per day. The minimum wage is $40 per day. Narrowing this range is one of the challenges we must solve in the 21st century. The economic issues Graham sought to improve have grown even more critical in both economic and human terms over the sixty years since he published *Storage and Stability*.

Benjamin Graham was a successful businessman as well as an outstanding teacher and writer. In his twenty-five-year career at Columbia University School of Business, Graham instructed and inspired thousands of young finance and corporate students, many of whom have since become prominent. Warren Buffett of Omaha is probably the best known, but he is joined by a long list of other successful partners of banks and investment firms—all of whom freely acknowledge how much Graham's teachings have helped make their own careers so successful.

Benjamin Graham was always open to critical approaches different than his own. He was flexible enough to realize that conditions change, and that his plan should be modified to meet new conditions. With the reintroduction of his classic, today's readers can now re-examine his recommendations in the light of our own world. We hope that this new edition of *Storage and Stability* will be widely read so that different groups in government, academia, and the marketplace will review Graham's plans, and then explore how they can modify and use its advantages for our own and other nations' future well-being.

Irving Kahn
New York, NY
November 1997

Foreword

THIS study of the problem of surplus and unstable prices leads to the proposal that an excess supply of primary commodities be impounded on a composite basis, and that currency be issued backed by and convertible into the stored commodity units. The plan for basing money upon a store of staple commodities is frankly an invention. This would have been sufficient to condemn it in the prewar sound-money epoch. Most economists and solid citizens of that epoch were firmly convinced that no improvements could be made upon the Golden Rule or the Gold Standard. The most daring practical innovation of that time was the gold exchange standard, prescribed in desperate cases by good Doctor Kemmerer; the boldest theoretical venture was Irving Fisher's compensated or stabilized dollar.

Today we are living in the midst of monetary inventions. The pound sterling, the franc, the mark are pure inventions. The mark, indeed, is a whole nest full of inventions: blocked marks, tourist marks, export marks, propaganda marks, and whatever else conscripted financial ingenuity may devise. Our American dollar is an invention: paper backed ultimately by gold, which no one can get at except by consent of a government which has no intention of consenting.

All these inventions have one feature in common to distinguish them from the standard money of an earlier time. Their value and their stability depend upon the wills of men, mortal men, more certainly consistent than the rest of us. The dollar, the pound, the mark, the franc could be given a higher or lower purchasing power by administrative fiat.

The financial authorities who bear this responsibility mean honestly to hold the value of money to a fairly definite level, but muscles tire and nerves falter. One may compare their case to that of a Los Angeles crank, picked up as an anarchist because he had constructed a bomb. He declared indignantly that he was not an anarchist but an inventor, inventor of a wholly new type of bomb. Every other kind of bomb, he said, depended on a trigger device which would have to be pulled or otherwise disturbed to set the bomb off. His bomb had three triggers, and you had to hold them all back with all your strength, if they were not to go off on their own account. Schacht has just such an invention on his hands.

We are all fairly agreed as to the qualities we wish to see realized in our standard money. We want it to be as nearly as possible stable in value. A dollar should buy about as much of the necessities of life in 1977 as in 1937. We want this stability to be maintained by impersonal forces, not by the will of any official or group of officials. The gold standard currency was strong in the latter quality but weak in the former. Our various managed currencies may exhibit for a time greater stability in purchasing power than gold, but they depend on the personal will of legislators or administrators. Mr. Graham's invention is designed to meet both requirements.

The invention is of such startling simplicity that everyone who examines it must feel that he once had the idea himself. Base the money on the commodities themselves, safely stored away in warehouses. You put in commodities and take out money, or put in money and take out commodities just as formerly you exchanged gold for gold certificates, or gold certificates for gold. Gold and the paper based on it fluctuated in their value as measured by power to purchase staple commodities. Mr. Graham's standard cannot fluctuate in purchasing power because it consists of the commodities themselves.

Of course it is not possible to attain the desired result with absolute accuracy, because you cannot store all commodities, and if you could, some of them would become obsolete. But there are enough staple commodities to ensure an approximation to justice in the relations of creditor and debtor, and in other transactions involving time. Adam Smith pointed out that long-term contracts written in terms of corn were more likely to prove fair than those written in terms of money. A fixed amount of wheat would under any circumstances bear a positive relation to human life, while the value of a fixed amount of gold might conceivably dwindle to nothing. Mr. Graham's group of staples, being basal to the production of the chief necessities of life, must always carry a substantial weight in the standard of living.

One particularly attractive feature of Mr. Graham's invention is its modesty. Mr. Graham does not ask us to abandon our gold certificates, silver certificates, greenbacks, Federal Reserve notes, etc., and go straight over to his commodity reserve notes. If the plan were authorized by law today, the reserves could begin to accumulate in existing warehouses tomorrow, and little by little commodity reserve notes would be circulating among us. They would command the same value as other money unless inflation sapped the value out of government paper. The commodity reserve notes would then command a premium, having real values behind them. Gradually they would reverse Gresham's law and drive out the bad money.

In economics no stone ever kills a single bird. Mr. Graham, like all economic inventors who know their job, kills several birds with one stone. He not only gives us a money of stable value but he finds a highly desirable use for the surplus production which in present circumstances breaks our backs. Whenever there is overproduction, wheat and cotton, copper and tin and rubber and the other commodities making up his monetary units will flow into the reservoir and corresponding amounts of money will be turned loose in the community. If the reservoir gets too full, the amount of purchasing power set loose in the community will stimulate consumption and set in motion forces that will syphon the surpluses out again. Here we have a new kind of elasticity, the expansion or shrinkage of currency as production expands or shrinks.

One who reads Mr. Graham's book with a critical attention to detail will note that there are minor problems which the author has deliberately skimmed over for the sake of concentrating attention on the major issue. How would such a form of money work in international trade? What would happen if a great war drew out all the commodity reserves, after a nation had become habituated to this form of money? Mr. Graham has reflected much on most of these problems, but he has wisely and considerately left it to the reader to do some thinking for himself.

ALVIN JOHNSON.

NEW YORK,
October, 1937.

PART I

The Challenge of Surplus

"It cannot be beyond the power of man so to use the vast resources of the world as to ensure the material progress of civilization. No diminution in these resources has taken place. On the contrary, discovery, invention, and organization have multiplied their possibilities to such an extent that abundance of production has itself created new problems."

—King George V
Opening speech at the
World Economic Conference
June 12, 1933

Chapter I

THE CHANGING ROLE OF SURPLUS STOCKS

"If there is not a saving of grain sufficient for three years, the State cannot continue."
—Royal Regulations of Confucius
Sixth century B.C.[1]*

"The world may now look forward to a temporary respite from burdensome wheat surpluses."
—Chairman of the Canadian Wheat Pool, 1935.[2]

THAT surplus stocks of goods have played an overshadowing part in the depression of the 1930's can scarcely be gainsaid. The point was brought home in a spectacular manner by the government-sponsored plowing under of cotton and slaughter of pigs in 1933.[3] Even more striking, perhaps, in its relation to a national economy, has been the willful burning of millions of bags of coffee in Brazil over a period of several years.[4] Along with international conferences for the limitation of armament we have seen other and more successful intergovernmental gatherings to deal with the "menace" of too much wheat, sugar, rubber, timber, tin, coffee and silver; in addition to numerous similar international meetings and agreements among private producers of petroleum, copper, zinc, aluminum, nitrates, potash and tea.[5] (With beautiful irony the changed conditions of 1937 have produced a suggestion from the Bank for International Settlements that a world conference be called to restrict the production of *gold*.[6]) From such events, and from countless similar incidents of lesser magnitude, the popular consciousness has been imbued with the

* Notes to the chapter grouped at the end of the book, p. 237.

3

thought that the recent depression differs radically from those preceding, in that it was a phenomenon of surplus rather than of shortage.

If this is true the significance of the fact would almost defy overstatement. It would mean that a dividing line had been crossed in our economic development and that the principles and habits of thought suitable to the past are no longer valuable or relevant. At first sight it would imply that a marvelous improvement in the national living standard is well within our grasp, and that all we need is a little intelligence and a little enterprise in order to attain it. Second thought might suggest that the apparently simple problem of enjoying our ample productive capacity is in reality fraught with the greatest difficulties and dangers. It might require a political and economic organization at utmost variance with our traditions and personal inclinations. To attempt to realize it might raise at every step the bitterest and perhaps the most violent controversy as to whether the gain is worth the cost. Instead of passing blithely over into that Promised Land, flowing almost literally with milk and honey, it may be our destiny to wander a full 40 years or more in a wilderness of doubt and divided sentiments.

These are varying conclusions drawn from the assumption that we have emerged from an economy of shortage into an economy of abundance. But how valid is that assumption? Is it true that the whole character of our economic world was transformed before our unseeing eyes in the short decade between the depression of 1921–1922 and the crash of 1929? To the sober, sceptical mind this sounds most improbable. The financial literature of 1921–1922 is also replete with references to surplus.[7] Much was said about excessive plant capacity resulting from wartime expansion. Equal emphasis was laid upon the top-heavy inventories of our business corporations, with their accompanying burden of enormous bank loans. A concrete sign of the surplus problem at that time is found in the use of the Copper Export Corporation to finance and take off the market a part of the copper surplus.[8]

Along with these references to oversupply we find much reasoning of just the opposite import. In the orthodox view the postwar depression was the direct result of the *destruction* caused by the war.[9] If this means anything it must mean that—on balance, at least—the slump of 1921–1922 was a phenomenon of shortage and not of surplus. (There has since been some tendency to modify this position and to claim that both of the depressions since 1920 arose from *dislocations* rather than the destruction caused by the war.[10]) On the whole we must conclude that expert thinking as regards 1921–1922 has been seriously confused, leaning rather illogically in the direction of both shortage and surplus.

If we study earlier depressions we find that the element of surplus capacity or excessive stocks is present in these as well. In most cases collapse followed a period of overspeculation and overbuilding.[11] Yet a valid distinction may be drawn between the type of oversupply accompanying these depressions and the problem of surplus that we have recently been facing. The overbuilding of railroads prior to 1873 meant the creation of capital facilities of a certain kind disproportionate to the state of the country as a whole.[12] Similarly there has frequently been unreasoning speculation in individual commodities, giving rise to relative overproduction and to clearly excessive stocks. It would seem, however, that such overproduction in the past represented errors of judgment in individual fields. "Hard times" in certain localities may have been definitely related to a temporary oversupply; but the national concept of hard times was solidly grounded in the experience of *shortage*, especially through poor crops.

It is fair to conclude that, while surplus is not a brand-new characteristic of depression, the relationship between surpluses and depression has been undergoing a significant development. From a minor and localized factor the phenomenon of surplus has become a major and pervasive attribute of depression. Perhaps it is only the emphasis that has changed, but change of emphasis may well mean change of essence. It is not exact to say, as many do, that the problem of production has been solved and has given way to the problem of distribution.[13] Both problems have long existed and both still exist. But one might well assert that a critical change has occurred in the *relative importance* of these two problems in our economic life. Insensibly the balance has tilted from one side to the other. The signs and portents of a changed world that we see all around us are thus likely to be more than the mirages that accompany our recurrent journeys through the economic deserts. New factors are to be taken into account; new viewpoints are called for. But these viewpoints are not to be adopted lightly. Both the novelty and the supreme importance of the problem enjoin the utmost circumspection upon those who seek solutions for it.

It seems logical to believe that a fruitful field of study would be found in those surplus stocks of goods whose existence has been so vitally bound up with the course of the depression. Rather interesting observations may be drawn from the available statistics of inventories in various lines, particularly in the contrasting behavior of the curves denoting finished goods and raw materials respectively (see the Chart opposite). But in this chapter we shall deal with the subject from a more fundamental approach, and inquire how it has come about that large inventories are regarded as

INDEX OF COMMODITY STOCKS 1923–1936
(1923–1925 = 100)

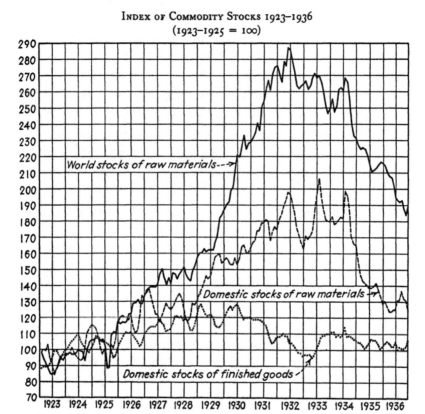

Source: *Survey of Current Business.* (The domestic raw materials index has been adjusted for seasonal variations by the author.)

a sign of weakness rather than of strength in the structure of business.

Surplus stocks—or stores, or inventories—may be defined as accumulations of consumable goods in excess of the amount normally required to carry on the processes of distribution. Until quite recently it would never have occurred to anyone to doubt that such surpluses are beneficial. Their economic function is twofold: as a tangible form of wealth and as a reservoir to protect against serious interruptions of normal supplies. This reservoir mechanism should obviously exert a stabilizing influence over market prices. Without it, prices would skyrocket whenever output failed and collapse whenever an excess appeared.

Simple and unquestionable as these benefits appear, their existence seems directly contradicted by our current experience and attitude. Though theoretically surplus stocks may rank as a form of wealth, in practice they have worked out as more of a liability than an asset. And far from acting as a stabilizing factor in the price level or in business conditions generally, they seem to have been the very focal point of instability and collapse. A contradiction confronts us here that may be found to lie at the heart of that mass of paradoxes which have made the depression at once so irritating to our common sense and so baffling to our intelligence. To understand its import we must trace briefly the varying role of merchandise inventories in the development of our capitalistic economy.

In the earliest stages practically all wealth consisted of land and consumable goods. The patriarchs' riches were measured almost exclusively by the size of their flocks.[14] Some centuries later the possessions of the affluent Hamilcar Barca of Carthage, as described in great detail by Flaubert,[15] covered a great variety of articles of necessity and of luxury, but all of them might be designated as merchandise. Money, too, was essentially merchandise which had taken on a certain added utility. Under these conditions wealth and surplus stocks were well-nigh synonymous terms. A nation and the individuals that composed it were alike considered fortunate in proportion to their ownership of bursting granaries and warehouses crammed with all manner of goods.

The industrial revolution introduced a new category of wealth, *viz.*, machinery and the plants that housed it, to which were soon added other important types of capital assets such as railroads. Coincidentally the development of investment banking and commercial banking resulted in that combination of phenomena now known as "finance capitalism," which involved important changes in the individual's concept of wealth. Wealth became more and more identified with money; money in turn lost all its original character as a special form of merchandise and became for the most part an entry on the books of a bank or documents equivalent thereto. Wealth, in short, became not so much the actual ownership of things as the ability to purchase them.

The growth of commercial banking meant, on the one hand, the expansion of money, in the form of deposits, and, on the other hand, the expansion of debt, in the form of business borrowings. This introduced in turn a new desideratum—that of *liquidity*, which means the ownership of cash or of assets readily convertible into cash.[16] Liquidity became increasingly desirable, partly because the growth of debts, which must be paid in cash, directed more and more emphasis upon the advisability of owning assets which could be turned into cash; partly because cash was coming to be prized more and more for its own sake, in preference to other forms of wealth. We seem to have reached the further stage where, instead of money being valued because it can purchase things, most things are valued only because they can be turned into money.

But these liquid assets, now so greatly sought after, themselves developed in such a way as to involve the whole concept in contradictions verging on absurdity. Liquid assets are supposedly distinguished from fixed assets. They correspond to Adam Smith's category of "circulating capital" as opposed to a "fixed capital."[17] This circulating capital consists of gold and silver money needed to carry on business transactions, together with stocks of merchandise which are constantly being turned into money because they pass into consumption and which are being constantly renewed by manufacture or importation. This classical definition is quite intelligible and useful. But liquid assets in a present-day balance sheet consist of the following items, ranged in order of liquidity:

1. Cash.
2. Government securities.
3. Other marketable securities.
4. Receivables.
5. Inventories—to the extent that they are readily salable.

(There is a growing tendency among credit men to exclude inventories entirely from the category of "liquid assets,"[18] including them in a separate designation of "current assets.")

If we scrutinize the first four items, we find that their liquidity is an artificial product of our financial system and has little basis in economic reality. Cash means currency and bank deposits. These are backed in part by gold which is inaccessible; in part by silver which is grossly overvalued; in good part by government bonds which are at bottom no asset at all; in part also by other bonds and stocks which chiefly represent fixed assets; and in rather small part now by commercial loans, which are other people's debts. The next three items in our list of "liquid assets" are those we have just discussed as banking assets behind deposits. Government and other securities are not liquid in the sense that they are or represent assets which in the normal course of business will turn themselves into cash. They are liquid because our highly developed stock exchanges provide a ready market for debts and interests in businesses, which otherwise would bear no relationship to the underlying concept of liquidity. It can readily be shown that the most "liquid" securities are those which, like government bonds, are completely divorced from "circulating capital," as Adam Smith defined it; or railroad and public-utility bonds which are backed almost entirely by fixed capital; or the common stocks of successful industrial corporations which derive the major portion of their value from an "earning power" that is supposed to be largely independent of tangible assets of any kind.

Receivables are truly liquid, of course, only to the extent that the debtor himself has liquid assets. If merchandise inventories are to be excluded from this category, we find that we have eliminated practically the only type of asset that has a true and inherent convertibility. The liquid assets which people prize so much are in good part meaningless in the national balance sheet, canceling out against individual or national liabilities. Thus we have formed individual concepts of what constitutes wealth, and what forms of wealth are preferable to others, which have no support in concrete realities and which depend for their validity on the persistence of a fundamentally irrational mass psychology.

The relegation of merchandise inventories to their present inferior and even dubious state as regards liquidity has been a gradual process of long duration. Nevertheless the speed of this transition was enormously increased during the years following 1921–1922. That depression, it will be remembered, was the aftermath of a brief but intense speculation in inventories, which itself was both a result and a cause of rising commodity prices. The ensuing collapse brought about huge losses in inventory account, accompanied by a critical banking situation due to the overextension of credit to finance this speculation in merchandise.

Business emerged from the 1921–1922 slump with an almost morbid fear of inventory expansion. A whole technique was developed for the sole purpose of holding inventories to a minimum. The "hand-to-mouth" buying policy formerly associated only with periods of hesitation now became firmly entrenched throughout the field of distribution. This was facilitated by the advent of quicker transportation and more dependable service from manufacturers. In fact the carrying of stocks of merchandise to meet any special demand has been made more and more the function and the burden of the producer. But the manufacturer, in turn, has accepted this burden with the utmost unwillingness, and has sought to mitigate it by introducing advanced methods of inventory control.[19]

A further development in the same direction, and one of extreme importance, is found in the changed status of the American farmer. From time immemorial the typical farmer has produced by far the greater part of what he consumed. His sales for money and his purchases for money have alike played a minor role in his economy. The storage of agricultural produce was the very heart of his method of living. Most of what he ate during the winter he had himself garnered and stored away in the late summer and fall. To the extent that he raised a "cash crop" he was familiar with the paradox that an output well above normal might bring him a smaller money income. But this was a phenomenon quite apart from his general experience and outlook. His underlying concept of wealth and well-being was tied up, not with money, but with land, buildings and implements, livestock and stored provisions. Broadly speaking, the more he owned under each of these headings the better off he was.

That the relative importance of cash in the farm economy has been steadily increasing is hardly open to question. A continuously larger percentage of the total farm output has been sold for cash, and a correspondingly greater percentage of the farmer's consumption has been purchased off the farm. More and more money has been needed for buildings and farm machinery. And the burden of farm debt, interest payments, installment payments, and farm taxes, has grown increasingly serious. The farmer has become steadily less self-sufficient; to an ever greater extent he finds himself governed by wants and obligations that can be satisfied only through a substantial cash income.

The effect of these changes has been to transform the farmer into a business man. He has been gradually adopting the business man's habit of regarding all aspects of his economic life in terms of money.[20] In particular, his view of stocks of agricultural commodities—whether on his own farm or elsewhere—has been tending insensibly to approximate that of the business man towards merchandise inventories. These stocks have been losing their attribute of useful wealth for their own sake and have come to be looked upon either as a means of making money or as an obstacle to making money, depending upon market conditions.

There has been a "farm problem" recurrently throughout the life of this republic. Certain elements of the problem seem to have remained fairly constant. Long standing are the complaints about the burden of debt and high interest rates, low prices for what the farmer sells against high prices for what he buys, excessive freight rates, political favors shown the industrial East, etc., etc. If it were claimed that the farm problem with which the Hoover and Roosevelt administrations have been struggling is entirely new, facts and authorities could easily be marshaled to disprove it. But the statement made above with respect to the phenomenon of surplus generally applies with especial force to the agrarian situation. The *emphasis* has shifted more and more upon this single point. Inability to sell at a fair price, inability to hold output in suitable relationship to effective demand appear to have become the chronic and central weakness of agriculture rather than the cause of merely sporadic and temporary maladjustment.

This difficulty seems identical with that of business generally during the protracted depression. It affected the farmer more severely than the manufacturer, because it is notoriously difficult to accommodate farm production to changes in demand.[21] It is claimed also that the individual farmer has only one way to meet the financial crisis caused by price collapse and that is by planting *still larger* crops.[22] In any event we find both the business man and the farmer bedeviled by surplus merchandise and convinced that surplus is the primary cause of their woes.

Let us now relate this experience and attitude to the functioning of the storage mechanism in our business economy. That mechanism will be found to have a reversible feature which may be highly disconcerting. Its normal function is to take up the slack between output and demand and to pay out that slack when needed. But if the wrong buttons are pressed, the storage or inventory machinery may operate in the contrary direction. Speculation may persist in building up stocks of goods in such a way as to create an artificial shortage in the face of ample production. Conversely, and more to our argument, the liquidation of inventories may prevent normal consumption from making itself felt on the demand side at the point of output.

Price is the factor that is relied upon to make the inventory mechanism function in the right direction. The low prices that accompany excess production are an inducement to build up inventories, and the converse is true when output fails or demand increases sharply. But this classical law of supply and demand does not operate automatically and impersonally; it acts through the sound common sense of business men. When this common sense is supplanted by speculative enthusiasm on the one hand or by fear or financial necessity on the other, we have exactly the opposite sequence of events—a phenomenon with which we are only too familiar in the stock market, where advancing prices usually tend to attract buying and declining prices to induce selling.

Economists are accustomed to view such contradictions of the law of supply and demand as temporary aberrations which do not affect the underlying structure of business. It may be true, however, that the almost pathological fear of increasing inventories, which business men have developed in the last 15 years, now interposes a really formidable obstacle to the normal functioning of the inventory mechanism as a stabilizing factor in upswings and downswings of the business cycle. Under less severe conditions this obstacle manifests itself in a deep-seated disinclination on the part of everyone in business to accumulate merchandise, even at relatively attractive cost. In serious depression we find the urge to liquidate is cumulative rather than self-correcting.

Many students have observed that the progress of finance capitalism has introduced increasing complexities and rigidities into our economic machine. It has subjected employer and employee alike to devastating forces beyond their control and largely outside of their knowledge; it has made it ever harder for the so-called natural forces of recovery and adjustment to assert themselves promptly and effectively when the business fabric gives way. Not the smallest part of these unsatisfactory attributes of modern economic life may be traced to the anomalous role that merchandise inventories have come to play within it. For on this point we now find a basic contradiction between the policy of our individual business men (and farmers) and our traditional and common-sense understanding of what lies in our national interest. Clearly it is a good thing for our nation to produce in abundance; is it not equally desirable, and perhaps essential, that we *should have on hand an ample store of consumable goods?* But our business habits and psychology are now running precisely counter to that obvious principle.

This distinction between national interest and individual interest may draw the challenge of many. If individual citizens in overwhelming numbers are seriously injured through the existence of surplus stocks, must it not follow that the aggregate of citizens, constituting the State, is correspondingly harmed? Is not recognition of this fact the moving cause behind the many government-sponsored programs of curtailment (and even of destruction), which have been by no means confined to the United States? In truth this concept of surplus as an evil has spread not only from the individual to the State, but from the several nations to the entire world conceived as an economic entity. A striking reflection of this wider attitude is found in the statement quoted at the head of this chapter, made by the chief of the Canadian grain administration apropos of the drought of 1935—that "the world may now look forward to a temporary respite from burdensome wheat surpluses."

Pondering these questions we are compelled to conclude that if surplus stocks do operate as a national liability, rather than an asset, the fault must lie in the functioning of the business machine and not in any inherent viciousness of the surplus itself. A world excess of wheat cannot be injurious in the sense that excessive rainfall, or excessive armament, or even excessive population is injurious. Everyone will still admit that a plenitude of natural resources is the very fountainhead of national—and world—prosperity. It is paradoxical in the extreme to believe that resources which possess immeasurable economic value when existing underground can be transformed into things of evil by the very processes of extraction and preparation which are essential to giving them any economic utility.*

Even the most conservative must realize that the recent transformation of surplus from an individual to a national disaster implies a scathing indictment of our capitalistic system as it has now developed. The phrase "poverty amid plenty" has already grown into a cliché, but the loss of its novelty does not signify that it has lost its bitter truth. Some means must be found to restore the Goddess of Plenty to the role of benefactress-in-chief that was hers without question under a simpler economy. A business machine that is disabled by its own productivity will not long endure in this restless and dissatisfied world.

* This paradox is matched only by the contrary anomaly in the case of gold. Apparently the only means now feasible of dealing with this enormously valuable and desirable metal is to withdraw it altogether from the sight and use of man, by reconsigning it to artificial mines, burrowed deep beneath earth's surface.

Chapter II

GOVERNMENT AND SURPLUS STOCKS

"And let them gather up all the food of the good years that come and lay up corn under the seal of Pharaoh and let them keep food in the cities."

—Genesis, XLI, 35.

IN the previous chapter we traced various stages of the relationship between surplus and business. In the earliest stage abundance was an unmixed blessing, alike for the individual and the state. In the second stage a surplus of goods has frequently proved detrimental to interested groups, but the welfare of the nation as a whole was clearly identified with surplus as opposed to scarcity. Viewing the distinctive characteristics of the recent depression, a third stage seems to have arrived, wherein the damaging effects of surplus have spread from the individual or group to the entire national or even world economy.

Surplus has thus become a challenge to the State. How can this challenge be met? Is it feasible to develop governmental policies which can counteract the modern tendency of surplus to disorganize the business machine? Does the choice lie between doing nothing on this score or embracing the collectivist formula of government control of all instruments of production? Some aid in the understanding of this problem may be afforded by a brief review of what has been done to solve it in the past.

The State may deal with actual or threatened surplus in one of four ways: (*a*) by preventing it; (*b*) by destroying it; (*c*) by "dumping" it; or (*d*) by conserving it. All four of these approaches are being used today by governments in various parts of the world. But in studying the historical record in this field we find that two major distinctions must be drawn at the outset. The first segregation is between raw materials and manufactures. State action dealing with surplus has been applied chiefly to raw products. Certain types of governmental encouragement have, it is true, been extended to European cartels controlling fabricated goods.[1] A more significant exception was provided by our NRA—a measure legislatively unique in that it gave governmental sanction and assistance (for an emergency period only[2]) to various devices for limiting *industrial* production. It need hardly be pointed out, however, that the characteristic attitude of the State has been precisely the opposite, forbidding and prosecuting all concerted efforts by manufacturers to restrict output or hold their stocks off the market.

By way of contrast we shall see that limitation of agricultural surplus has been the sporadic concern of governments even prior to 1930. The first Brazilian coffee-valorization scheme started in 1905.[3] In succeeding years State action was taken on behalf of hemp, cotton (in Egypt), currants, sugar and rubber. And, returning to the United States, we note that the governors of Alabama and Mississippi proclaimed a "Cotton Reduction Week" in October 1926,[4] and that President Coolidge in a message to Congress that same year recommended a reduction of one-third in the cotton acreage.[5] These were suggestions, of course, and not ordinances; but they reveal a governmental philosophy of agricultural restriction only a few years after federal attorneys had prosecuted and convicted the manufacturers of hardwoods for applying a similar theory to their production.[6]

The distinction between cotton and processed hardwood must have something fundamental about it, since the government's diverse attitude toward the two commodities provoked no widespread charge of inconsistency. This

placing of raw materials in a separate category from manufactured goods may be justified by two plausible arguments.
The first is that raw materials are more *important* in the
sense that they are basic and anterior, as it were, to manufactures. Stable agricultural conditions may be considered a
peculiar concern of government, because they in turn will
create satisfactory conditions in business generally. Of
equal weight is the argument that the manufacturer can
adjust his production to demand much more readily than
the farmer. Hence the latter needs to be helped at times in
the direction of desirable restriction, while the fabricator
must rather be prevented from a too ready resort to purely
self-seeking and undesirable measures of curtailment.
Whether this reasoning is altogether sound it is not our
purpose at this moment to inquire, being content to point out
the distinction itself and the thought behind it.

The second division must be made between the governmental measures taken prior to 1930 and those that have
characterized the depression. In fact it might be better to
divide the record into three parts of which the first runs from
the dawn of history to about 1900, the second comprises the
next three decades, and the third the short but momentous
period from 1930 to date. We shall show that throughout
the ages prior to the twentieth century the primary concern
of the State with agricultural surplus was first to promote it,
and secondly to *conserve* it for later needs by storage. With
the advent of the current century we find for the first time
that the agricultural surplus is becoming a persistent and
widespread *problem*, requiring State intervention to obtain
an adequate price for the producer. The war created universal scarcity; but hardly had peace returned when problems
of surplus returned with it, and the years between 1919 and
1929 were marked by a rapid growth of governmental
measures to support prices and control production. In the

current period we find an elaboration of these various techniques of control, reinforced by many new and extraordinary measures.

It is our intention to lay major stress upon the *conservation* of surplus, which is the form of State activity that has the longest historical background. For convenience we shall delay our treatment of this topic until we have completed a briefer discussion of governmental action of the three other types enumerated, *viz.*, prevention, destruction and "dumping" of surpluses.

Prior to the present century State-imposed restrictions on production were mainly of the predatory kind. They were intended to benefit others than those whose output was controlled. For example, it was standard colonial policy to prevent the growing or manufacture in the colonies of products that might compete with the parent country. Thus we find the cultivation of hemp and flax prohibited by the French masters of Louisiana between 1669 and 1763, while similar interdictions were laid by Spain against the raising of grapes in many of her possessions. Other kinds of restrictions frequently grew out of monopolies operated directly by the government or farmed out to agents. The most widespread monopoly has been that of tobacco. As early as 1619 a deal between the English Crown and the Virginia Company resulted in the complete prohibition of tobacco growing in England, in order to create an import monopoly. In France the direct governmental monopoly gave rise to drastic restrictions on domestic production of tobacco, beginning about 1680. An example of another sort is supplied by the Dutch East India Company which obtained a monopoly of the spice trade in its area at the beginning of the same century and imposed forcible restrictions upon the output of cloves and nutmegs in order to maintain high prices.

Other restrictions are recorded, however, more benevolent in their purpose. In 1533 the amount of sheep that any one person could own in England was limited to 2000 head, as a measure to combat the conversion of farms into pasture lands. During the Civil War a number of the southern states limited the plantings of cotton and tobacco, in order that more attention might be given to food crops.

Tobacco supplies also the only instance that the writer knows, taking place before 1900, of State restriction of surplus for the benefit of the producers themselves.[7] The American Colonies of the South—notably Maryland, North Carolina and Virginia—made use of many devices to obtain an adequate price for their tobacco crops, frequently invoking the aid of their legislatures for this purpose. The colonial records therefore reveal a number of measures with a modern flavor, including price fixing, limiting of production and even the compulsory destruction of growing or stored tobacco.[8]

But it was not until just after the close of the nineteenth century that a well-defined tendency appeared for State-sponsored curtailment programs in the interests of the producer. The first product receiving this aid appears to have been beet sugar. In 1902 an assembly of Spanish sugar manufacturers limited and divided up their production, presumably with the sanction of the government. About the same time the beet-sugar acreage was reduced in France. (Similar curtailment took place in Russia, but this partook more of action on behalf of a government monopoly.)

The coffee-valorization schemes began in 1905 and resulted in the cessation of all plantings throughout three Brazilian states. At about the same time the Greek government intervened on behalf of the currant trade and created a "privileged society" as its special agent in an attempt to "stabilize production and prices in the interest of the producers and the public." In 1912 we find the Mexican State of

Yucatan setting up an official regulatory commission to control the output and price of hemp. In 1914 Egyptian cotton was subjected to severe restrictive ordinances, which prohibited its production in Upper Egypt and limited planting elsewhere to one-third of each man's acreage. The announced policy of the government was to limit production of the staple to the needs of the market in order to obtain a reasonable price.

Between 1914 and 1930 the State control of agriculture went through some kaleidoscopic changes. The universal shortage caused by the World War impelled governments all over the world to encourage the production and control the distribution of many basic commodities. We find the State guaranteeing minimum prices to producers, setting maximum prices, buying abroad, selling at home and rationing supplies to consumers. In some cases, *e.g.*, hops in England and tobacco in Switzerland, we note a compulsory curtailment of output to release acreage for more essential products.

But the postwar depression of 1921–1922 created serious problems of the opposite tenor, and we now find governments again intervening to raise and maintain prices. In Brazil, where the State of São Paulo had closed out its second valorization venture at a large profit in 1919, the federal government was soon after (1921) persuaded to acquire the coffee surplus. In New Zealand the State, having hardly completed elaborate measures to deal with a wheat shortage, plunged actively into the task of protecting the farmer against a demoralizing grain *surplus*.[9] As the postwar crisis ran its course, government action to support prices tapered off. Yet during the new era of prosperity between 1924 and 1929 it was still true that many parts of the agricultural area were depressed, and so we find State activities continuing or instituted on behalf of a surprisingly large variety of products. Most notable of these later developments were the control of surplus wool in Australia by BAWRA between 1921 and 1924,[10] and the much criticized and defended Stevenson scheme for rubber restriction, sponsored by the British government in 1924–1927.[11]

The violent economic crosscurrents that were to create later havoc for the world manifested themselves by strange phenomena during these predepression years. We read of an international economic conference to deal with a general European famine in 1919;[12] two years later a more catastrophic and protracted famine in Russia enlisted concerted aid from all over the world.[13] Yet about this very time a world-wide problem of farm surplus made its appearance, and a few years later loud complaints were heard that Russian sales of wheat in large volume were demoralizing the export markets.[14] Simultaneously, also, one set of countries was paying bonuses for the production of high-cost wheat, cotton and sugar (to create national self-sufficiency in these commodities),[15] while another group of low-cost countries was being forced to curtailment measures which would culminate in the payment of bonuses for the *non*-production of those same products.[16]

The new collapse of farm prices that began in 1930 found governments already familiar with and sympathetic to many different kinds of protective measures. This latest period is distinctive therefore, not because such devices have been used, but because they have been employed so universally, so persistently and with such variety. Countries previously committed to complete *laissez-faire* were finally constrained to intervene on behalf of their farmers, *e.g.*, Holland, which took complete control of the wheat trade. Other governments extended their previous relatively mild intervention into a thoroughgoing State monopoly. (*Example:* Jugoslavia.) Finally we do find a large element of novelty in the individual measures resorted to throughout the world.

Most striking, of course, was the State-promoted destruction of produce. In addition to the instances already alluded to—slaughter of pigs and plowing under of cotton in the United States, burning of Brazilian coffee—we may mention also the acquisition and destruction of (damaged and refuse) tobacco stocks by the government of Greece.[17] While restriction of production by State order had developed quite widely prior to 1930, as we have shown, the provision of our AAA for payment of cash bonuses for nonproduction had aspects at once novel and deeply disconcerting. Quite extraordinary also was the action of the Government of South Africa compelling the export of a certain portion of each farmer's output of corn and tobacco. By this means the surplus is "dumped" abroad, *i.e.*, sold abroad at lower than the domestic price, which is thus maintained at a satisfactory figure.[18] The sum total of measures in aid of farmers runs a bewildering gamut, beginning with the familiar protective tariff, passing over into quota and mixing regulations and terminating with elaborate schemes of governmental control involving various kinds of benefits, inducements and compulsions.

It is time now to cast a critical glance over the history of restrictive control of surplus, briefly sketched in the foregoing pages. Two basic facts seem to emerge from this record. The first is that control of some kind is necessary; the second is that *restrictive* controls are unsatisfactory. It would be easy to assert, as the orthodox economists have done until recently, that all State interference with supply and demand is fatally unsound in theory, and therefore inevitably disappointing in practice. Yet if one pays due heed to the logic of events he must be rudely aware of the presence of an overwhelming economic tendency that confounds the principles of *laissez-faire*. A new economic theory will no doubt be perfected in time, which will give complete and classical expression to the necessities of the twentieth century. But in the meantime, while controversies rage over the exact form of this newer economics, the history of the last 30 years itself tells us that the balancing of production and consumption is a concern of government—not in war only but also under the stresses of peace; not in the exceptional and temporary case only, but more and more extensively and more and more continuously.

Whether we like it or not, government intervention in the face of surplus is here to stay. But control on the side of restriction can be defended neither by theory, by practical result, nor by the law of necessity. Surely no coherent economics has been developed, and surely none ever will, that will persuade our minds to believe that curtailment is the key to prosperity. From 30 years of restriction schemes, countless in their number and variety, not one has emerged which intelligent people everywhere are willing to accept as a permanent mechanism for stability. The law of necessity seems indeed to have dictated resort to some form of control, yet the restrictive measures adopted in response to this compulsion do not bear upon themselves any earmarks of inevitability. We feel instinctively that what has been done so far is not the correct, not the ultimate solution.

We come now in due course to consider the type of State activity mentioned but not yet discussed—that directed to the conservation of surplus by storing it for future use. It may be fairly said at the outset that this form of control recommends itself to the intelligence and the intuition of the average man. But it must also be true that it faces serious difficulties of a practical sort, since otherwise a solution so simple and logical on its surface would long since have been universally adopted. It is our purpose to examine into this question in detail, to determine what are these practical difficulties and how, if at all, they may be overcome. On this point the records of the past are especially interesting and instructive. Let us therefore retrace our steps through the halls of history, this time in quest of data on the conservation of surplus by the State.

We are all aware that until comparatively recently the storage of surplus commodities by the individual was basic to his economy, being viewed by him as equally necessary and desirable. Surplus was a boon, not a problem. Where the king was identified with the State, as was frequently the case in ages past, his personal wealth and the State treasure were one and the same—and both consisted in good part of huge stores of consumable goods. Thus we find in ancient Egypt the superintendent of the granaries was a high government official who collected rich supplies from the king's estates and from tributary countries.[19] In Rome, on the other hand, the management of the grain reserves was a public function, carried on with a special view to protection against scarcity. Since the Imperial City was fed by imported grain, and since for centuries the poorer people received free rations of bread or flour, the maintenance of governmental stores of wheat was an undertaking of immense scope and importance. The records show that in the fourth century A.D. there existed no less than 291 public granaries which were said to contain a supply sufficient to support the people of the capital for *seven years*.[20]

Similar activities were carried on by many governments in more recent times. In France, for example, we find (a) that Louis XIV set up a Royal Grain Administration to make public purchases for reserves and for the army; (b) that during the Revolution "granaries of abundance" were established in each district of France, and were continued until 1829; and (c) that Napoleon constructed "reserve granaries" to contain grain for three months' consumption by the city of Paris.[21] The early history of Virginia reveals legislation in 1619 requiring each householder to store one barrel of corn, and in 1623 a further law compelled each planter over eighteen years of age to contribute to a public granary.[22]

While the concern of the State to maintain a grain surplus is manifest from these and other instances (including some of compulsory planting), we find some ordinances that at first sight appear to aim in the contrary direction. Centuries ago the French farmers were forbidden to hold grain in granaries for more than two years. In England, too, a proclamation of Henry VIII ordered the justices of the peace to discover "any abundance or surplus of corn" and compel its owners to bring it into open market.[23] But edicts of this sort were directed against speculative accumulations or hoardings which advanced the price unnecessarily. It is a fact worth pondering that four centuries ago the evil of "an abundance or surplus" arose from its being kept off the market, while today the evil of surplus lies in its being thrown upon the market.

There are three especially important examples of State conservation of surplus to which somewhat more detailed attention might well be given. These are, first, the famous Biblical narrative of Joseph and the famine in Egypt; secondly, the comprehensive policy of storage practiced by the Peruvian Incas prior to the Spanish conquest; and lastly, the Ever-normal Granary system maintained in China for 20 centuries.

The tale of Joseph and his granaries is familiar to every child. For the Western World it is the original and standard example of foresight and common sense in dealing with the alternations of plenty and scarcity. We are likely to idealize the story somewhat, imagining it as an early illustration of wise and benevolent State planning for the economic welfare of the populace. The details, however, as recounted in Genesis[24] and supplemented by the historian Josephus,[25] lend a different color to the operation, and turn it rather into a tremendously successful speculative coup engineered for the profit of Pharaoh at bitter cost to his subjects. For it seems that Joseph's long-range weather forecast was kept secret from the Egyptian people.[26] Hence during the "seven fat years" it was possible to buy up the surplus grain at a nominal price. That, at least, is the accepted interpretation of the phrases "took the corn of the husbandmen" and "gathered up all the food" used in the Bible and in Josephus. When the "seven lean years" ran their catastrophic course, Pharaoh was able to resell his subjects their own grain at an exorbitant price; and thus he became the owner in turn of their money, their cattle, their lands and finally of their very persons. The narrative further states that the land was later leased back to the farmers at a rental equal to 20 per cent of the produce, thus explaining the tax in kind collected at that rate by the rulers for centuries thereafter.

The civilization of Peru under the Incas was replete with extraordinary features. Politically it was a depotism; economically it had many aspects of socialism. We are chiefly interested here in the system of storage magazines, constructed of stone, in which were deposited the surplus products and manufactures of the country. These magazines contained not only food products, but woolen and cotton stuffs, utensils of gold, silver and copper—in short, in the words of Prescott, they were stored with "every article of luxury or use within the compass of Peruvian skill."[27] These stores were held in part for the benefit of the ruling class and the priests; but a large portion was administered to supply the people in seasons of scarcity, "and to furnish relief to individuals reduced to poverty by sickness and misfortune."[28] Needless to say, these stores were established also for military purposes. The Spanish writers assert that the magazines of grain would frequently hold supplies sufficient for the consumption of the adjoining district for several years—sometimes, in fact, for a full 10 years.[29]

The storage system of the Chinese[30] was based on the economic precepts of Confucius and appears to have operated for many centuries as a mixture of benevolence and business sense. Its purpose was twofold: first, to maintain an adequate reserve of grain (chiefly wheat and rice) to protect the country against famine; secondly, to prevent excessive variations in the price of this dominant commodity. At the time of Confucius (sixth century B.C.) grain in storage was considered a most important category of national wealth, and it functioned as the equivalent of capital goods in the modern era. Hence the great teacher prescribed that the State should maintain an accumulated store equal to at least *nine years' consumption*. (Less than nine years' supply he termed a condition of "insufficiency"; less than six years', one of "urgency"; without a saving "sufficient for three years, the State cannot continue."[31])

The leveling of price fluctuations was achieved as part of their Reservoir system. In times of abundance the provincial governors filled up their granaries at a moderate discount from the standard price; when need arose they sold back these supplies at an equally moderate advance. This twofold mechanism of storage and price control was formally set up some five centuries after Confucius under the name of the "Constantly Normal Granary."[32] With considerable variations as to price policy, and with more or less serious interruptions due to political conditions, the system of the Ever-normal Granary has existed in China "in nearly all the ages from 54 B.C. to the present time."[33] There have also been other storage arrangements of a local character, known as the "free granary" and the "village granary," and involving both gifts and loans of grain to the people.

Let us move forward now to a consideration of more recent State activity involving the conservation of surplus production. The coffee-valorization schemes conducted in Brazil involved in each instance the purchase of surplus stocks by the State or national governments.[34] Of the four separate operations the first, which began in 1905, comprised also a restriction on planting, and the last, which followed a price collapse in 1929, included both restriction of planting and large-scale burning of surplus coffee. The two middle operations, however, running between 1917 and 1924, seem to have been confined to governmental purchases at low prices and their subsequent resale at a substantial profit. Contrary to general belief, the records indicate that each of the first three operations resulted in a large profit for the State,[35] although the earliest one ran into temporary difficulties before its successful conclusion in 1918.

The international tin agreement, which became operative in 1931, had the active participation of the Dutch government as a direct party in interest, and at least the tacit support of the other governments involved.[36] As extended in 1934 it provided not only for restrictions on production, but also for establishing a so-called "buffer stock" of tin. This reserve was intended both to take an excess supply off the market, and to provide a means, similar to the Ever-normal Granary, of checking extreme fluctuations in the price of the metal. This arrangement appears to have been successful in restoring a satisfactory degree of stability in the market for tin.[37]

But in modern times, as in the remote past, the major attention of governments has centered upon wheat. From the standpoint of permanent national policy the most interesting recent example is provided by the Swiss Confederation. Early in 1929, while world economic conditions were still normal, the people of this little country voted to establish a national reserve of grain. This new policy is actually embodied in their federal constitution itself, in the form of an article reading as follows:

"The Confederation will maintain such reserves of grain as are necessary for the provisioning of the country. It can oblige millers to store grain and to acquire grain held in reserve in order to maintain its condition through replacement."[38]

Since 1929 the Swiss government has proceeded with this undertaking and now holds a fair quantity of wheat in the "federal reserve."[39]

During this same period the governments of Canada and the United States have also been active in the acquisition and storage of wheat. The purpose of their activity has, of course, been entirely different from that of Switzerland. These large exporters of wheat were confronted with a heavy oversupply and a collapse in the world price. In both instances the government intervened on behalf of the producers by acquiring surplus stocks and holding them off the market.

The Canadian government fell heir to a large quantity of wheat which had accumulated in the hands of a central wheat pool representing the farmers' cooperative agencies. It first became involved in the situation (in 1930) by guaranteeing the large obligations of the wheat pool to the Canadian banks. Soon it took charge of the pool's activities. As the depression intensified, its holdings of wheat increased. By the end of 1935 it was committed, in one way or another, to the extent of 340,000,000 bushels. By that time the drought situation had grown serious, the world price had advanced substantially and it was possible to liquidate the government's entire position at little or no actual cash loss.[40]

We may insert a reference here to the somewhat different policy pursued by Argentina. Intervening as late as 1934, the government set up a grain board which guaranteed a fixed price to the farmer. About 4,000,000 tons were purchased and promptly resold abroad. The loss on the operation (9,000,000 pesos) proved much smaller than expected because of the effect of the drought in the United States, and was far exceeded by the profit on exchange resulting from grain exports. A guaranteed price was continued in 1935–1936 but proved unnecessary as the market price remained consistently higher.[41]

The wheat acquisition policy of the United States did not turn out so well as in the case of Canada and Argentina. We started to aid our farmers too early in the depression, and the desire of the Democratic Administration to try a new agricultural policy led to the sale of the government's wheat holdings at a low point in the market.

To summarize the story very briefly: In 1930 the Federal Farm Board was established under President Hoover for the purpose of stabilizing agricultural prices. It operated chiefly by purchasing and making loans upon wheat and cotton. It extended some assistance also to wool producers. The price-maintenance program of the Farm Board could not be carried through in the face of the world-wide collapse of commodity values. A portion of the supply of wheat and cotton was donated to the Red Cross for relief, but the larger amount of the wheat was liquidated in the open market at a heavy sacrifice. The Federal Farm Board was abolished in May 1933 and the total loss sustained through its operations was estimated at over $300,000,000.[42]

The Roosevelt Administration wound up the Farm Board experiment because it was committed to a new type of agricultural aid. It considered that a simple policy of purchasing or lending on farm products to bolster the price would inevitably encourage continued overproduction and aggravate the problem of oversupply. Hence it determined to lend money on farm products only to those producers who would participate in a crop-reduction program, which was embodied in the famous AAA. The Commodity Credit Corporation was set up to make such loans. It advanced 45 cents per bushel against corn in 1933–1934 and 55 cents per bushel in 1935; also 12 cents per pound on cotton in 1934 and 10 cents in 1935.

The Roosevelt loans naturally turned out better than the Hoover loans. They were made at lower prices, and at a time when economic conditions were about to turn upward instead of getting continually worse. The price situation for the stored products was also helped by the curtailment program and by the drought that followed. Hence the corn loans have been completely repaid—or virtually so—and it would have been possible to clean up the cotton loans with only a moderate loss.[43]

Our descriptive survey of State conservation of surplus has necessarily been rather sketchy, since an exhaustive study would require far too many pages. It is our belief, nevertheless, that certain general conclusions may fairly be drawn from the preceding material.

The first conclusion is that wherever surplus has been conserved primarily for future *use* the plan has been sensible and successful, unless marred by glaring errors of administration. The second conclusion is that when the surplus has been acquired and held primarily for future *sale* the plan has been vulnerable to adverse developments and it has required a combination of luck and good management to bring it success.

The distinction between conservation for use and conservation for sale should be evident from our examples. In the former case the reserve is established to meet a future need which experience has taught us is likely to develop—generally through war or drought. Such a reservoir system may operate through purchase and sale—as in the Chinese example—yet the sale is not the end in itself but only the means of bringing the stored surplus into use. On the other hand, the type of operation illustrated by our Federal Farm Board or the Brazilian coffee-valorization schemes is directed essentially at finding a better market for the product within a reasonably short period after acquisition. Characteristically these better prices are to be realized through sales *abroad*, so that the operation is obviously carried on for the financial benefit of the producer or the government, rather than to assure an adequate supply to the *consumer*.

In cases such as these we have merely commodity speculation on a large scale carried on by the State. If purchases are made when prices are relatively low, and particularly if short crops should then ensue, the operation may prove a financial success. It is more typical, however, for the government to intervene to support prices in the early part of their decline; and this support is itself a stimulus to increased production of that commodity when the economic picture calls rather for retrenchment. The claim frequently made that government intervention in the market invariably results disastrously is without doubt an overstatement.[44] But it may not be denied that State purchases of commodities *merely to maintain the price* are likely to be ill timed and unsuccessful.

Reviewing now our entire discussion of the problem of commodity surpluses, we reiterate our former conclusions: first, that State activity of some kind in the face of such surpluses is inevitable; and, second, that activity in the direction of *restriction* will not be accepted as a settled policy. A third conclusion may now be added: that the proper aim of the government must be the *conservation of surplus for future use*, as distinguished from mere market operations addressed solely to the maintenance of price.

We must now consider whether any feasible mechanism may be established to mobilize this surplus when it appears, to bring it out again into consumption at the proper time, and to make these operations self-financing and self-liquidating.

Chapter III

THE PROBLEM OF CONSERVING SURPLUS

"One clear lesson of history is: Grain should be considered a matter
of commerce and not a matter of administration."
—Prof. J. E. Boyle[1]

THE idea that the State should accumulate commodities
when they are in oversupply, and send them out into
consumption when they are needed, sounds reasonable
enough in principle. The difficulties are those of application,
and upon examination they seem to bulk very large indeed.
Several questions immediately suggest themselves, such as
the following:

a. What commodities should be accumulated?

b. Exactly when—or at what price and in what quantities
—should they be acquired?

c. What policies should be followed in disposing of them?

d. How can such a procedure be established without
incurring the fundamental economic weakness of valorization, viz., that it stimulates the production of favored
articles in relatively excessive quantities?

e. How long can these commodities be preserved, and at
what expense?

f. How may the acquisition and maintenance of these
stocks be financed?

It may be well to examine these difficulties in some detail
in order to appreciate their full import.

If we ask what commodities should be conserved by the
State, we find that history suggests two as particularly
eligible, viz., wheat and gold. As we have seen in the previous

37

chapter, the storing of surplus grain for future use has been practiced by governments in widely different times and places. At the present time, on the other hand, we have a storage mechanism applied to gold which bears a surprising resemblance to the old granary idea. With our paper money no longer exchangeable for gold, we may properly say that the practical "uses" of gold are now twofold: for consumption in the arts and to maintain the foreign-exchange value of the dollar. Our government is now acquiring and storing all the gold in the market that is not needed for the two uses described; and presumably it will return to the market whatever portion of these stores may later be called for by the arts or by foreign-exchange requirements.[2]

It is evident, however, that neither the acquisition of the wheat surplus, as formerly practiced, nor of the gold surplus as is now carried on, will suffice to meet the general problem of surplus. We are all aware that bread has lost its ancient standing as the primary article of consumption. The dollar value of our petroleum production exceeds that of our wheat.[3] Hence if government conservation of surplus were confined to wheat, it would constitute at best a very partial solution, and it might well be criticized as unduly favoring one group of producers out of many equally entitled to support. On the other hand, the valorization and storage of gold by various governments is a matter of monetary policy only, and has little relationship to the general surplus situation.

If it is concluded, then, that the field of State conservation must be extended to commodities other than wheat and gold, the choice of these commodities would seem a vexing problem. It might be asserted that in fairness every one of the countless articles of production is equally entitled to participate. Considerations both of theory and of practice will serve to simplify the question, by indicating that the acquisition of surplus may be confined to the *important durable raw materials.* These have been the subject of legislative policy in the past. The general problem of oversupply has proved most acute in this category. There is ground for believing that a reasonable equilibrium of market supply and market demand for this group will contribute largely to maintaining a fair degree of equilibrium in the business structure generally. It will be found that there are some 20 to 30 basic durable raw materials that would suggest themselves as suitable for conservation. We must consider later whether a group of this size can be handled without undue practical difficulty.

Assuming that the surplus production of basic raw materials should be conserved by the State, what principles should govern the acquisition of such surpluses? Looking back at history, we find that two widely different methods of approach are possible as illustrated (*a*) by Joseph's procedure in Egypt and (*b*) by the Chinese Ever-normal Granary system. In the Egyptian example, advantage was taken of the glut to acquire grain at an abnormally low cost, and the ensuing shortage was again exploited to obtain an unconscionably high price upon resale.

Could such a policy be successfully followed by governments under modern conditions? On the whole the answer is likely to be in the affirmative. It is true that the concept of a low price is necessarily indefinite, and in individual cases may prove to have been erroneous. But if we were to assume a policy based on some arbitrary but conservative formula, such as buying whenever the price fell to 50 per cent of the 10-year average and selling, say, at 25 per cent above this average, the net financial result of these operations could scarcely help but be favorable.

Such an arrangement would amount simply to putting the State in the role of a shrewd long-term operator in basic commodities, blessed with an unlimited bank roll. The objection to a system of this kind would arise from its mercenary character. It would be claimed that the State is profiting from the extremities of its citizens. Furthermore, if relief is delayed until prices have fallen so far below previous normal, the greater part of the damage due to the price collapse will already have been done, and the benefits from State support will be proportionately meager. The political pressure on the government is always to buttress prices before they collapse completely—as illustrated by the operations of the Federal Farm Board in 1930-1932.

The Chinese Ever-normal Granary system aimed both at conserving surplus and stabilizing prices. The State bought up excess supplies at a price slightly below "normal" and sold them out when needed at only a slight advance above "normal." This sounds both sensible and philanthropic. However, it presupposes a well-defined normal price for the basic commodity, which norm should not be subject to important change over a considerable period of time. It is quite possible to maintain such an arrangement in the case of a single commodity of overshadowing importance, such as wheat or rice when they represented the most important item of consumption, or such as gold because of its special monetary status.[4]

Under present-day conditions, however, there are a fairly large number of basic commodities of the same general importance. Their relative prices tend to fluctuate rather widely not only during brief periods but also in accordance with secular changes in relative production costs. Any endeavor to establish and maintain normal prices for each such commodity would involve the State in a valorization program especially objectionable because of its complex character.

A more definite idea of the problem involved may be obtained from Table IV in the Appendix, which sets forth salient data regarding 16 basic raw commodities. The diversity in price movements over a 25-year period is striking. Assume that, say, in 1920 the State had defined as a normal price for each commodity a figure about midway between the 1913 and 1918 quotations—this would correspond roughly to the 1921–1930 average for all commodities—and had stood ready to acquire surplus stocks whenever available at some slight percentage below this normal. It would soon have found itself purchasing much larger relative quantities of some commodities than of others. In effect, it would have loaded itself up with a number of products which had been artificially priced above the level that subsequent developments in supply and demand should have established for them. It would have offered a special inducement, *i.e.*, a relatively high price, to produce certain commodities in disproportionately large quantities. Instead of merely absorbing temporary excesses of supply over demand—to be sent out later into consuming channels—such a system would subsidize and perpetuate a state of unbalance between the individual commodities comprised within it. That arrangement could not properly be regarded as conservation for future use, but rather as an artificial and ill-advised stimulating of the production of one group of commodities out of their due relationship to the whole field of raw materials.

We see that a dilemma confronts the State in its effort to determine a suitable price policy to facilitate the conservation of surplus. If individual prices are definitely fixed for a number of commodities, at a level slightly under some supposed normal, the result is a disastrous inflexibility in the face of changed relative conditions. On the other hand, any endeavor to avoid this inflexibility by permitting suitable changes in the various buying prices introduces an exceedingly difficult problem of management. It would be almost impossible, even in the absence of political pressure, for any directing head to determine by either judgment or mathematical formula how the past relationships among commodity prices should be modified to reflect new conditions ·of demand and supply. This is preeminently the function of the open market. But the open market cannot decide this problem for the State, if at the same time the operations of the State dominate the market.

The difficulty that here confronts us is a serious one, but it is not insuperable. Our solution will be developed in the following chapter. Let us merely indicate it at this point by suggesting that the State acquire surplus commodities on a *composite basis*. Its fixed buying price would apply then to the group of commodities taken as a whole. Within the group the relative prices of the individual products would be free to fluctuate in accordance with economic developments.

The matter of *sales* policy does not present particular difficulties. If surplus basic commodities can be acquired in accordance with sound procedure and if they can be held until needed for consumption, it may be assumed that an aggregate price will be obtained for the stored products that bears a suitable relationship to the price paid for them. The primary requirement, of course, is that the surplus should not be pressed for sale until an effective demand develops for it. This condition brings us to the question of the possible period of storage and the method of financing governmental operations of this kind.

The durability of basic raw commodities in storage varies rather considerably with the individual items. Some, such as the metals, are virtually indestructible. Others, such as foodstuffs, are subject to more or less rapid deterioration. It is clear that only those commodities can be comprised in a storage scheme which may be held in warehouse for a period of some years. The danger of ultimate deterioration may be adequately disposed of by the well-established device of rotation. Under this arrangement, commodities which have been stored for some time are replaced by fresh commodities, the older product passing into consumption while it is still in good condition. Viewing the country as a whole, we find that there are at all times fair-sized private stocks of practically all the important commodities.[5] There are no major practical difficulties, therefore, in maintaining for as long a period as required nationally controlled reserve supplies of these same basic products. (As we pointed out in Chap. II, the Swiss have recently set up a mechanism for storing and rotating the federal wheat reserve; and the British are preparing a national storage scheme on a larger scale.)

Finally we must ask how serious is the problem of financing the storage of surplus basic commodities. The valorization of coffee imposed a serious fiscal burden on Brazil and resulted in difficulties affecting its foreign loans. The Federal Farm Board's operations in wheat and cotton involved huge sums, culminating in a loss of over $300,000,000. But, as we have hitherto pointed out, these and other schemes suffered from the fundamental weakness that they depended for their success upon advancing market prices. They represented speculative operations for future *sale*, not a conservation program for future *use*. A price-maintenance venture which is inherently unsound must in all probability—barring unusual good fortune—result in serious financial loss. But a rational plan for conserving surplus, which recognizes the relative importance of the products to which it applies, should not involve the State in financial difficulties. *The State can always afford to finance what its citizens can soundly produce.*

The acquisition of surplus basic commodities by the State might presumably be financed in the same way as other governmental activities—by taxation or by borrowing.

If it be conceded that these surplus holdings would constitute a valuable asset in their own right and that their acquisition by the State is a prime factor in preventing economic dislocation, it would be easier to justify borrowing for this purpose than for many others which have absorbed billions of Treasury funds.

Yet at this point a new and vitally important consideration obtrudes: Would not these basic commodities constitute a sound backing for the issuance of currency? We have a well-established process under which gold is acquired and held in storage by the State and currency issued thereagainst. The same operation has recently been carried out here on a large scale with respect to silver. In England at the present time gold is legally a mere commodity but it is arbitrarily held as a backing for bank notes. In that country gold has no definite standing as a monetary medium. It does not circulate as currency; bank notes are not redeemable in gold; the English pound has no fixed relation to gold, and the value of an ounce of gold may theoretically fluctuate in the market in the same way as the value of an ounce of platinum. Yet the Bank of England is continuously acquiring and storing gold and issuing its currency to pay for it.[6] By this device the purchase of the commodity gold offers no financial problem to the Bank of England, *i.e.*, the British government.

Why cannot the same procedure be soundly applied to other commodities as well as gold? The answer, of course, is that gold has a peculiar merit or acceptance as a monetary base and that other commodities, however useful, are not similarly eligible as a backing for money. This answer is impressive, but it may not dispose of the question. Some attention must be given to the present monetary status of gold, on the one hand, and on the other to the possibilities of a really sound marshaling of commodities as a currency base.

We have outlined in general terms the kind of problems that must be faced in any effort to conserve surplus, and the direction along which the solution of these various problems may lie. Our inquiry has reached the stage where a concrete proposal may now be advanced for the storage of surplus basic commodities. After setting forth this proposal in detail, it will be in order to consider whether it adequately accomplishes the purposes and adequately surmounts the difficulties attendant upon a comprehensive plan for the conservation of surplus production.

PART II

The Commodity Reservoir

"Boulder Dam is a splendid symbol. The mighty waters of the Colorado were running unused to the sea. Today we translate them into a great national possession."

—President FRANKLIN D. ROOSEVELT
Speech dedicating Boulder Dam
Sept. 30, 1935

"What we need is some financial engineers."
—Henry Ford
Saturday Evening Post, Feb. 11, 1936

Chapter IV

A PLAN FOR CONSERVING SURPLUS

"There should be built a new extensive up-to-date warehouse system into which should be taken the surplus products of the soil which, as experience over the ages has shown us, have always been consumed."

—BERNARD M. BARUCH[1]

IN summarized form the proposal is as follows:

The State is to acquire and store *composite units* of basic raw materials when there is a surplus of these commodities in the aggregate. The unit shall consist of as many important commodities (dealt in on recognized commodity exchanges) as may practically be included therein, their relative quantities to be proportionate to production or consumption over a suitable base period. The money value of the unit, *i.e.*, the quantity of the combined commodities equivalent to a dollar, shall be fixed at some appropriate level, such as the 1921–1930 average.

Commodity units shall be acquired whenever obtainable at a small discount below their established value. They shall be paid for in currency issued in exchange therefor, which currency shall be backed by and redeemable in the stored commodity units. If the composite price of the commodities advances above the established standard, currency will be automatically redeemed for commodity units, which will then flow into consumption. The producers of the component commodities, together with the exchanges dealing therein, shall to the extent necessary assume the burden of storing their share of the units and maintaining same in good condition. If and as the quantity of commodity units in storage shall grow beyond the amount deemed advisable to hold against future contingencies, suitable social measures shall be adopted designed to bring the excess into consumption, thus raising the national standard of living.

The effects of this plan will be:

First: To establish a Reservoir system under which a general surplus of basic commodities will flow into storage, without demoralizing the markets or the business structure, and remain so mobilized until a consumptive demand develops for them.

Second: The Reservoir system will function not only as an equalizer of business conditions, but also as a national store to meet future emergencies, such as war and drought, and—most important of all—as the concrete means of developing a steadily higher living standard for all. In addition, it may be utilized as the most rational investment of our national Social Security reserve funds, and also as the medium through which foreign balances due us may be settled most advantageously for debtor and creditor.

Third: The price level for the component commodities *as a whole* will be fixed in the same way as the dollar value of gold was formerly fixed. This will go far toward establishing a "dollar of constant purchasing power"; and, specifically, it will eliminate the wide fluctuations in the general price level of basic commodities which have proved so demoralizing to business in the past. The price of *individual* products will not be fixed, however, and will be free to fluctuate within the framework of the stabilized commodity unit in accordance with changes in relative demand and supply.

Fourth: A currency will be created essentially sounder than any we now have, because it will be backed by and convertible into tangible, basic goods that we use and need, in their proper relative amounts. The quantity of this currency will increase when an excess of goods produced calls for an increase in purchasing power; and conversely, its quantity will decrease when an excess of consumption or speculative buying indicates a need for contraction.

Let us now describe in some detail how the commodity unit will be established and how the Reservoir system will expand and contract automatically as the open-market quotations for the commodities as a whole tend to fall below or rise above the standard level. We shall then consider the interrelations of this proposed mechanism with various parts of the general economic structure, in order to develop and explore its widest implications. This will include a detailed study of the monetary and credit aspects of the plan. In a separate section we shall discuss the relationship of our proposal to the agricultural problem and in particular to the Ever-normal Granary-Farm Relief legislation now before Congress. Finally we shall examine the precedents and analogous proposals with a view to demonstrating the peculiar character of the instant plan as a synthesis of several ideas, each valuable but incomplete by itself.

THE COMMODITY UNIT

A proposal that embraces a number of commodities must meet two conflicting requirements. It must be comprehensive and nondiscriminating; but at the same time it must not be overwhelmed by the sheer number of the items with which it deals. We are fortunate in having two criteria which enable us to resolve this problem without difficulty. The commodities included in the unit must be dealt in on recognized commodity exchanges. Secondly, the exchanges (or others interested) must be prepared to assume part of the burden of storage, including the task of maintaining the stored product in merchantable condition by appropriate rotation.

The fact that a product is dealt in on an established commodity exchange immensely simplifies the practical execution of our proposal. As will be seen later, the commodity units will be accumulated in the form of ordinary purchases on the commodity exchanges, and they will be liquidated, or pass into consumption, by regular sales through the same channels. Deliveries against contracts made on these exchanges are effected by means of warehouse receipts. These represent the physical commodity held in storage in a licensed warehouse, duly inspected and certified as to grade and condition. All the minor problems of tenderable grades and other terms of delivery are taken care of automatically by this procedure.

At the present time trading in futures is carried on in the following products, on various commodity exchanges[2] in the United States:

Group *A*: Wheat, barley, corn, oats, rye, cocoa, coffee, sugar, cotton, silk, wool, copper, lead, tin, zinc, cottonseed meal, cottonseed oil, flaxseed, gasoline, hides, petroleum, rubber, tallow, tobacco.
Group *B*: Lard, bellies, ribs, mess pork, butter, eggs, potatoes.
Group *C*: Soybeans, pepper, linseed oil, mill feeds, field seeds, live hogs, canned goods.

The commodities in Group *C* must be excluded from consideration for various technical reasons.[3] Those in Group *B* are foodstuffs which must be held in cold storage, and therefore offer special problems both of storage expense and of frequency of rotation that are not met with in the larger list.[4] To simplify our study we shall exclude these cold-storage products from our commodity unit; although it may be true that the advantages of inclusion will so far outweigh the cost of storage that the producers and dealers, acting through the exchanges, will be more than willing to assume whatever burden is involved. To the extent that this is so, it would be a development favorable to our plan, since the commodity unit could stand a fairly substantial increase in the number of component items without reaching the stage of unwieldiness. (It should be pointed out, however, that the huge production of corn in this country is chiefly applied to fattening hogs, so that the heavy weighting to be given to corn in our unit will in large part constitute a recognition of the meat factor.)

Attention must be given also to the possible extension of futures dealings to other important commodities not now subject to such trading. The last decade has witnessed a rather considerable expansion of the number of commodities admitted to futures trading.[5] The possibility of inclusion in our reservoir proposal may stimulate the organizing of futures markets for some of the eligible commodities not now so traded. It should not be thought, however, that operations in the commodity units will in any sense monopolize or even dominate the markets in the component commodities. (This is an important point to which we shall return later.) Hence whether or not some addition product will achieve listing on a commodities exchange, and thereby become eligible for inclusion in our commodity unit, will depend primarily on whether the needs of the trade would be well served by the creation of an organized market therein.[6]

In setting up a provisional commodity unit for the purpose of this study we shall confine ourselves to items now subject to futures trading in the United States. As stated above, we shall eliminate the food products that require cold-storage servicing, and the ineligible commodities in Group C. We shall also exclude gasoline because statistically it would duplicate petroleum. This will leave us 23 products, which may be grouped as follows:

Foods: Corn, wheat, sugar, oats, coffee, barley, rye, cocoa, cottonseed oil
Textiles: Cotton, wool, silk
Metals: Copper, lead, tin, zinc

Miscellaneous: Petroleum, hides, rubber, cottonseed meal, flaxseed, tobacco, tallow

It will be noted that five of these items are not produced here at all, *viz.*, coffee, cocoa, tin, silk and rubber, while sugar is predominantly an imported commodity.[7] The inclusion of imported goods in the unit is highly desirable for at least two reasons: First, because a commodity-backed dollar should have behind it a representative group of the important materials that our dollars buy, regardless of their origin; secondly, because a reservoir of commodities for future use should lay at least as much emphasis upon essential materials not produced here as upon our own products, of which we cannot so easily be deprived. From the viewpoint of protection against future emergencies, the imported items constitute especially valuable components of the unit.

RELATIVE QUANTITIES IN THE UNIT

The proper weighting of the different commodities in our unit presents no great difficulty, since the technique has already been worked out and applied in the formulation of many familiar index numbers. The most prominent of these is the Index of Wholesale Prices computed monthly by the Bureau of Labor Statistics. This index comprises no less than 784 separate commodities (most of which are manufactured goods), each assigned an appropriate weight reflecting its quantitative importance.[8] An established index more similar to our commodity unit is Moody's Price Index of Basic Commodities. This is made up of actively traded commodities, which are weighted in proportion to their relative production or consumption in the United States, whichever is the larger.[9]

In making up our proposed commodity unit we shall follow the technique of Moody's Index. By taking the larger of the production or the consumption figures due recognition is given to the importance of the commodity in our economic fabric. The choice of the base period over which the relative quantities should be taken must necessarily be an arbitrary one. We shall use the decade 1921–1930 as being both comprehensive and representative. A shorter period, say, 1923–1929, would yield closely similar results. As we shall point out later, it is by no means vitally important that the weight or relative quantities be meticulously correct. Minor variations from exactitude will be of slight moment, either to the particular commodities affected or to the working of the scheme as a whole. A reasonable approximate reflection of the relative significance of the component products is all that is needed for a satisfactory result.

In Table V in the Appendix we present the statistics from which the weightings of the component items are derived. These are expressed finally in terms of the amount of each commodity that corresponds to a bushel of wheat. It should be noted that the matter of price does not enter in any way into these proportions. The weighting is solely a matter of the relative quantities produced or consumed over the base period. Hence price fluctuations during this period have no effect whatever upon the weightings; they make themselves felt only in the ultimate determination of how large a composite unit shall be made equivalent to a dollar.

SELECTION OF THE PRICE LEVEL

This is, of course, a matter of the highest importance, for it means establishing the purchasing power of the dollar in terms of basic raw materials. We propose that this standard value be fixed in the same way as the relative quantities, *i.e.*, that it be based on the average of the decade 1921–1930. An average so taken would be about 6 per cent lower than the 1926 figure, which is now frequently used as a statistical base. On the other hand, it would be about 4 per cent higher than the level prevailing in June 1937.[10]

In our opinion the arguments in favor of choosing this price level are quite persuasive. The 10-year period as a whole showed relatively small fluctuations, as compared with the war boom and collapse that preceded it and the slump and partial recovery that followed it. The inclusion of the two terminal years—1921 and 1930—tend to offset whatever exaggerations may have been due to the prosperity years, which incidentally exerted only a slightly stimulating influence on basic commodity prices. Against the contention that the 1921–1930 average is too high there stands the *de facto* devaluation of the dollar by 41 per cent. This means that a return to those prices in terms of our present paper dollar means the establishment of only 59 per cent of that price level in former gold dollars. In fact, this would result in a lower price level in terms of gold than existed before the war.[11]

It is not necessary for us to press overstrongly for the acceptance of our proposed 1921–1930 price level, since the mechanism of the Reservoir system is in no way dependent upon the particular level selected. This choice should in fact be made by the exercise of expert judgment at the time the plan is placed in operation.

It would be helpful in the inauguration of our proposal if a standard price level is chosen sufficiently above the then ruling figure to permit the acquisition of a fair amount of commodity units at the outset. The inflationary rise of early 1937 made it appear for a while that the 1921–1930 average might prove too low to be immediately practicable, but the subsequent severe recession has removed this objection.

In the light of present conditions the 1921–1930 average once more appears a "normal level," satisfactory for most

TABLE I.—THE COMMODITY UNIT

Commodity	Unit of quantity	Average production or consumption 1921–1930, millions	Weighted average price, 1921–1930	Average value of production or consumption 1921–1930, millions of dollars	Amount of commodity in 1000 one-dollar units	Value of commodity in 1000 commodity units, 1921–1930 average	Price, June 1937, cents	Value of commodity in 1000 commodity units, June 1937
Wheat.............	Bushel	824	$1.240	$1,022	84.4	$ 104.9	123	$103.8
Barley.............	Bushel	212	0.666	141	21.7	14.4	81	17.6
Cocoa.............	Pound	394	0.102	40	40.4	4.2	7.4	3.0
Coffee.............	Pound	1,421	0.172	244	145.5	25.1	10.9	15.8
Corn..............	Bushel	2,618	0.816	2,139	268.0	218.9	120	322.0
Cottonseed oil......	Pound	1,258	0.100	125	128.8	12.8	10	12.9
Oats..............	Bushel	1,220	0.443	540	125.0	55.6	48	60.0
Rye...............	Bushel	52	0.908	47	5.3	4.8	99	5.3
Sugar.............	Pound	12,670	0.061	771	1,297.2	78.9	4.6	59.7
Cotton............	Pound	6,588	0.205	1,349	674.8	138.2	12.7	85.6
Silk...............	Pound	74	5.890	437	7.6	44.8	183	13.9
Wool..............	Pound	263	1.156	304	26.9	31.2	100	26.9
Copper............	Pound	1,485	0.143	211	152.2	21.6	13.8	21.0
Lead..............	Pound	1,370	0.070	96	140.4	9.8	6.0	8.4
Tin...............	Pound	154	0.484	75	15.8	7.7	55.8	8.7
Zinc...............	Pound	1,003	0.063	63	102.7	6.5	6.8	7.0
Cottonseed meal.....	Pound	4,064	0.018	71	416.0	7.3	1.6	6.7
Flaxseed...........	Bushel	37	2.460	91	3.8	9.3	192	7.3
Hides.............	Pound	949	0.168	160	97.2	16.4	16.8	16.3
Petroleum.........	Barrel	772	1.640	1,265	79.1	129.5	136	107.5
Rubber............	Pound	824	0.308	253	84.4	25.9	19.3	16.3
Tallow............	Pound	510	0.078	40	52.2	4.2	8.0	4.2
Tobacco...........	Pound	1,346	0.210	283	137.9	29.0	25 (est.)	34.5
Total.............				$9,767		$1,000		$964.4

practical purposes. We have accordingly adopted this level in Table I, by setting as equivalent to a dollar that quantity of the various commodities which had an aggregate average value of a dollar during 1921–1930. To arrive at this figure it was only necessary to divide each average quantity by 9767 million, which was the aggregate dollar value of these quantities. Another way of arriving at the size of the dollar unit is as follows: A unit consisting of one bushel of wheat together with a proportionate amount of the 22 other commodities had an average value of $11.65 during the base period. Hence the one-dollar unit would consist of 1/11.65 or 8.58 per cent of a one-bushel-of-wheat unit.

GENERAL MECHANICS OF THE PLAN

A monetary agency—presumably in the Treasury Department—would be prepared to issue currency upon delivery to it of warehouse receipts calling for any quantity of *complete* commodity units. Conversely it would be prepared to deliver warehouse receipts for the correct amount of complete commodity units in exchange for, *i.e.*, in redemption of, any amount of currency that might be tendered for this purpose. (Presumably a fairly large minimum unit of coinage and redemption should be adopted as a matter of convenience, but this would in no wise interfere with the mechanical operation of the measure.) The warehouse receipts would represent actual ownership of the stored commodities. They would be similar to the receipts used in the regular dealings on the commodity exchanges. In other words, exactly the same warehouse receipts might represent either commodities which are part of the monetary storage system or those which are in private ownership.

It will be seen that the general method of "coining" and redeeming commodity units would correspond in all respects to the former issuance of gold certificates against deposit of gold, and the delivery of the gold itself upon tender of the gold certificates. The gold held against gold certificates was formerly actually coined or stamped into ten- or twenty-dollar gold pieces. These have now been melted down into bars of gold, and thus they now exist in the form of a commodity rather than pieces of money. The analogy between the gold now held against gold certificates and the commodities to be held against "commodity-unit certificates" is now very close, indeed, except that the gold certificates are not permitted in circulation and they are no longer freely exchangeable for the gold which they are supposed to represent. In the case of the commodity units and the related "unit certificates" it would be possible to reestablish the free coinage and free convertibility which was formerly the cornerstone of the gold standard.

The actual terms of our Commodity-reservoir plan can be summarized in a single sentence:

It proposes to accord to a composite group of basic commodities exactly the same monetary status as was formerly given to gold.

The former 23 gr. of gold in the dollar are to be replaced by 23 small quantities of different basic raw materials.

The actual accumulation of the commodity units could either be done by the Treasury Department itself or be made open to everyone. On the latter basis, which appears preferable—at least after the initial period—the operations would be carried on by specialists or "arbitragers," who would keep track of the current quotations on all the different exchanges. Whenever the combined prices were such as to permit the purchase of the various units at a cost slightly under their standard or "coinage value," these specialists would buy appropriate amounts of all the component commodities and tender them, *i.e.*, deliver the warehouse receipts, to the Treasury, receiving currency therefor.[12] While the work of accumulating units would be fairly technical, there is plenty of skill in this field available, and the competition among the different arbitragers would keep their profits to a minimum. This means that at no time would the price level, as measured by the sum of the individual quotations, fall more than a nominal percentage below the coinage level.

This percentage would be increased by any "seigniorage" fee that might be imposed to defray expenses, in accordance with the usual practice in coining money. We shall discuss the matter of seigniorage when we come to consider the cost of operating the Reservoir plan.

The mechanism of redeeming or liquidating commodity units would be the exact reverse of that just described. Such redemption would take place automatically whenever the aggregate value of the component items, as quoted on the exchanges, advances slightly above the standard level. For at such times it would be profitable for the arbitragers first to sell on the exchanges the commodities corresponding to a number of units; then to present currency to the Treasury, receiving warehouse receipts for commodity units in redemption therefor; and finally to deliver these warehouse receipts in settlement of their sales contracts. In this way commodity units would be broken up and brought into the various open markets.

A brief study of the process outlined above will make it clear that the general price level for basic raw materials in the open market would be held close to the standard level by the most direct method possible, viz., the purchase of these commodities in the open market whenever the price level tended to decline, and their sale in the open market whenever it tended to advance above the standard level. It will be noted also that a declining price tendency would result in the emission of more currency as commodity units were acquired; while, conversely, an advancing tendency would be counteracted by a reduction in the volume of currency outstanding, as the result of its redemption in commodity units.

The stabilizing mechanism would therefore operate on two fronts at the same time. It would increase or decrease the money supply, and it would decrease or increase the (open-market) supply of commodities, to countervail any general tendency of raw materials prices to decline or advance.

This entire machinery of stabilization bears a close analogy to the orthodox method of stabilizing the foreign exchanges under the gold standard. When the gold values of the pound and the dollar were in the fixed proportion of 4.8665 to 1, the foreign-exchange quotation of the pound on this side and the dollar in England was automatically kept within the limits of about $4.85 and $4.89—known as the "gold shipment points." Whenever all the miscellaneous operations in foreign exchange resulted in quotations a trifle above or below these critical points, it became profitable for specialists or arbitragers to redeem currency for gold in the cheaper market and to ship the gold to the other market for exchange back into the dearer currency. For example, it was worth while to buy paper pounds at $4.85 each, and redeem them for gold which was worth $4.8665 when shipped to New York and exchanged for "yellowbacks" (gold certificates). The difference of 1.65 cents per pound covered the freight and insurance on the gold, loss of interest and a reasonable profit.

For an even closer resemblance to the actual details of the commodity-unit mechanism, we may point to an important type of trading operation which was carried on in Standard Oil securities in the years 1912–1919. After the dissolution of the parent Standard Oil of New Jersey into 39 constituent enterprises, a market was established for each of the individual companies. But at the same time trading continued in the "old shares," meaning thereby the package of securities which the holder of one old share received. These "old shares," known also as "Standard Oil, all on," were, in effect, composite units made up of diverse amounts of 39 different securities.

The Standard Oil specialists kept track of the market in all these new issues, and they maintained a close parity between the quotation for the unit "Standard Oil, all on" and the fluctuating prices of the constituent stocks. This they did by buying units and breaking them up into the individual issues, or by reversing the process, whenever a small profit was obtainable by one means or the other.[13]

The commodity-unit mechanism now proposed will be somewhat simpler than the Standard Oil arrangement, because the value of the unit as a whole will be fixed even though the constituent items will be free to fluctuate. In the Standard Oil transactions both the individual issues and the composite unit were subject to changing market values; but even under this more complicated set of facts specialists were able to maintain a proper relationship between the individual prices and the composite price.

INAUGURATION OF THE PLAN

The immediate result of the adoption of the Reservoir plan would depend to a considerable extent upon the attendant conditions. The variety of possibilities might best be studied by assuming inauguration of the plan at different periods during the past quarter century.

If the plan had been made effective in 1914, on the eve of the World War, the then current price level would no doubt have been chosen. A small amount of commodity units might have been accumulated, but all these would soon have been drawn out as the war demand developed. The subsequent rise in prices would have made the reservoir entirely inoperative and it would have been necessary to reestablish it later at a higher price level. We shall point out below, however, that if the Reservoir system can be *fairly started* before a war supervenes, the stored commodity units would prove immensely valuable.

If the mechanism had been set up just after the close of the war, the choice of a price level would have presented difficulties, since conditions were in a state of flux. We might assume selection of the mid-point between 1913 and 1918, which would have been close to our proposed 1921–1930 average. This would not have afforded a brake on the 1919–1920 commodity speculation (since there would have been no reservoir supply available)[17]; but it would have been highly useful in checking the price collapse and consequent deep depression of 1921–1922.

Assuming the plan had been operative from that time on, or had been introduced in any year prior to 1929, it would not have prevented the overspeculation that led to the crash, since this was directed to securities and real estate rather than to commodities. (As we point out later, the abuses of the 1920's must be guarded against through credit control.) But while the stock market collapse would still have been inevitable, the reservoir mechanism would have completely insulated the basic commodity price structure from the effects of the Wall Street cataclysm, and thus prevented also the complete paralysis of the business world which grew out of the ruinously low commodity price level. Certainly both the length and depth of the depression of the 1930's would have been far smaller had the commodity reservoir been in operation.

Our plan was first made public in early 1933,[15] at the very bottom of the depression. Were it to have been introduced under such conditions, with the primary price level at some 40% of the 1921–1930 average, it might have seemed more conservative to select a somewhat lower standard than now proposed[16] and to allow for a gradual advance to the new base. Incidentally it would have been possible to acquire a large quantity of commodity units at a substantial discount from the standard level, thus establishing a "coinage profit" available to pay the costs of storage for many years to come. We submit that the adoption of the plan in early 1933 would have been directly instrumental in turning the tide of depression by raising the price level and increasing purchasing power, and that it might well have induced substantial recovery without requiring the enormous expenditures of the past four years.

The stock market collapse of the fall of 1937, and the widespread fears of another deep depression, make our proposal especially appropriate at this time. Its timeliness is increased by the new problem of agricultural surpluses which has led to the call of a special session of Congress to enact farm relief legislation.[18] In Part IV we shall compare in detail the functioning of our plan, both as farm relief and as an Ever-normal Granary device, with the provisions of the farm bills introduced last spring.

In these later chapters we shall endeavor to show that the Reservoir system would afford a much more advantageous method of comprehensive farm relief than the measures about to be considered by Congress. But from a still wider viewpoint, the stabilization of basic prices and the additions to purchasing power which would follow the introduction of the reservoir mechanism should make it tremendously valuable in staving off another catastrophic depression.

Accumulation of Commodity Units

Under some conditions prevailing in the past twenty years the Reservoir plan might have proved temporarily ineffective upon adoption, owing to the inability to acquire a substantial quantity of commodity units before the price level advanced. But let us suppose that instead of there being an insufficient amount of commodity units available at our standard level, the effect of our plan were to stimulate production to an extent resulting in the accumulation of an enormous stock of commodity units. This assumption raises a central question in relation to the entire plan. Is it best that a very small, or a moderate, or a very large amount of commodity units should come into existence? Our natural attitude would be to fear the creation of large stocks of commodity units, because we have been taught by experience to regard the existence of such stocks as a menace to business equilibrium. It is difficult to dispel an apprehension of this kind, grounded as it is in our everyday observation.

But it is vital to the understanding of our proposal that we grasp the distinction between surplus stocks of goods that are let loose in the market places of the world, like Victor Hugo's carronade on shipboard, and goods of the same sort that are mobilized and impounded for future need and use. Our citizens would view with equanimity the possession by our government of a virtually unlimited quantity of copper and cotton in the form of ammunition, because there would be no danger of these supplies coming into the commercial markets and "hurting business." Our plan envisages a similar mobilization of the munitions of peace, in such wise that they will come into the market only when a consumptive demand develops or is developed for them.

If this point is grasped, the accumulation of any quantity of commodity units, however large, ceases to be in any sense a cause of apprehension, and presents merely a challenge to our social ingenuity in finding suitable means of bridging the gap between the commodities ready to be consumed and the millions only too anxious to consume them. That problem is reserved for a later chapter.

But as far as this last assumption is concerned, *viz.*, that commodity units will prove available in unlimited quantities, we might dismiss that as a consummation devoutly to be wished, but impossible of fulfillment. Commodity units cannot possibly be accumulated in unlimited quantities under our proposal because the process of accumulation involved a continuous increase in the *currency supply*. The influence of such increased currency must be in the direction of higher prices all around, including higher costs of production of the component commodities. It is not asserted here that prices must advance coincidentally with, or in proportion to, any given emission of currency. But that continuous additions to the currency, at a greater rate than the expansion of business, must ultimately give rise to higher prices is an economic axiom. Insofar as the plan results in the accumulation of commodity units its influence cannot fail to be inflationary. This would be a serious defect were it not for the additional fact that the stored commodity units themselves constitute a check and protection against that very inflation. For any rise in price above the standard level immediately reverses the mechanism, causing redemption and contraction of the currency and throwing the weight of the dispersed commodity units upon the open market.

Chapter V

THE RESERVOIR SYSTEM AND THE
INDIVIDUAL COMMODITIES

"If we are to restore stability of prices and confidence in the future of the market for the great primary commodities, we must look for some means of regulating supplies in such a way that they shall not be from time to time completely out of relation to the absorbing capacity of their markets."

—NEVILLE CHAMBERLAIN
August 1932[1]

WE have already described in general terms the purely mechanical process by which commodities will flow into storage, in the form of units, whenever there is a surplus which expresses itself in a tendency for prices to decline;[2] and, conversely, how the commodities will flow out of storage into the open market when there is a shortage, or undue speculative activity, expressing itself in a tendency for prices to advance. Let us now consider in somewhat greater detail the effect of the Reservoir system upon the component commodities. We shall reserve for later chapters a discussion of the price-stabilization element of the plan, its monetary aspects, and its effect upon general business.

The point should be made here (and probably repeated later) that the primary object of the proposal is to deal intelligently and constructively with the problem of surplus. Hence the storage aspect constitutes the heart of our plan. The fact that, in addition, our plan will result in stabilizing the general price level for basic commodites and will supply a sound form of currency secured by these necessary commodities is of secondary and collateral importance. Basically the plan could be operated without the price-stabilization feature—for it might permit the price level to fluctuate within wide limits before commodities were acquired and later liquidated. Also, in theory the plan could operate without its monetary aspect—for acquisition of commodity units could be financed by borrowing, as are other governmental activities and purchases. We are convinced, however, that both of these subsidiary aspects of the plan are highly advantageous and that their inclusion makes the proposal far more attractive than it would otherwise be. Nevertheless, to clarify the issues, we are emphasizing the distinction that must be drawn between the primary character of the plan as a reservoir mechanism and its secondary advantages.

INTERRELATION OF THE COMPONENT COMMODITIES

It is obvious that all the component commodities, *i.e.,* their producers, will be benefited by inclusion in the plan. It must be recognized, however, that the mechanics of the proposal create a certain degree of interdependence between the market prices of the component items. Since the *general* price level will remain unchanged, an advance in the quotation for some of these commodities must be offset by a decline in the price of others. This point may be made clearer by considering various possible developments.

Let us assume that all commodities are selling at their 1921–1930 averages as given in Table I. Now let us suppose that a shortage of wheat develops, as a result of which the price tends to advance as much as 50 per cent, say, from $1.24 to $1.86. If no other price changes took place, this rise in wheat would increase the value of a $1 commodity unit in the open market to $1.05. It would then be profitable, of course, to redeem commodity certificates and sell the related commodities in the open market. The effect of these operations would be to put down the price of all the component commodities. If it is assumed that they all decline by the same percentage as the result of these sales, we would end up with wheat selling at $1.77 per bushel, and all the other commodities selling 5 per cent lower than previously.[3]

To complete the illustration, let us make an opposite assumption, *viz.*, that an oversupply of cotton would tend to cut its price in half, from 20 to 10 cents. If other commodities did not change in price the value of a $1 unit would then be only 93 cents; consequently it would be profitable to assemble units on the exchanges and present them for "coinage." The effect of these purchases would be to advance the price of all the commodities. Assuming the advances are spread evenly, the price of cotton would then recover from 10 to 10.7 cents and all the other commodities would advance by 7 per cent.

These two illustrations should make it clear, first that a change in the price of any one commodity must ordinarily affect all the others; but also that a very large change in one commodity will affect the others only slightly, because the one large change is absorbed by twenty or more small changes.

The question may well be asked: What if there develop a shortage in some one commodity—whether through natural or artificial causes—which forces its price up to a terrific height? Would not this enormous rise have to be offset by a decline in all the other commodities in the unit, thus demoralizing their markets and hurting their producers?

To this objection three answers may be advanced. The first is that no such completely disproportionate advance has actually occurred in any one of the components, certainly during this century and probably throughout the last.[4] The reason is, of course, that these are basic commodities, produced in many parts of the world, and a five- or tenfold advance in price within a short period is (barring war) a commercial impossibility. The more restricted the source of supply, *e.g.*, tin, the less the importance of the item in the unit as a whole. A fivefold advance in the price of tin, highly improbable as that is, would affect the other commodities in the unit by as little as 3 per cent.

The second answer is that our proposal admits readily of the replacement of "spot" commodities by futures. Ordinary contracts for future delivery command a higher price than the spot or cash product, sold for immediate delivery. The speculative or hedging owner of futures does not have to pay storage or interest charges on his commitment until the delivery date, and therefore prefers futures to spot holdings. The premium of futures over spot prices therefore tends to approximate the carrying charges for the period involved. But when there is a shortage or "squeeze" of some kind this normal relationship is reversed and the spot commodity sells higher than the futures contract.

Under our proposal futures contracts (accompanied by cash to pay for them) may always be accepted in lieu of a physical commodity comprised in the unit. Furthermore a physical or spot commodity held in monetary storage may always be sold in the market and replaced by futures contracts, whenever this can be done at a cash saving. To the extent that the units include contracts for future delivery, instead of the physical commodity in storage, there must be reserved an amount of currency equal to the dollar value of the futures contracts. (Obviously no one would be entitled to receive this currency unless the physical commodity were delivered against it.) When this delivery takes place under the futures contracts, the currency is issued in payment therefor and the physical commodity unit is completed.

It follows that the commodity units will consist at all times of either actual commodities or commodity exchange futures contracts, maturing not later than one year, against which the proper amount of currency will be reserved.

This arrangement will have a threefold advantage. In the first place it will prevent any extraordinary run-up in the price of a component commodity. Such run-ups almost invariably reflect a temporary shortage, and hardly ever carry over into a second crop year. For by that time there have been large plantings to take advantage of the higher price, or corresponding increases in production in the case of other commodities. The second advantage is that a more stable and orderly market than heretofore will be constantly maintained in the individual products. The fact that the commodity-unit holdings will be available to equalize or properly adjust the price for spot and futures will go far to prevent speculative excesses, temporary squeezes, and other abuses of the open market.

Finally this provision can be employed as a source of profit which may be applied against the cost of the Reservoir system. If desired, the replacement of spot commodities by futures contracts may be made only at some small cash differential, which will then operate in the same way as a "seigniorage" charge.

In recent months there has been an extraordinary tendency for spot commodities to sell higher instead of lower than future deliveries. Fully half the commodities in our unit have shown this unusual price relationship, which reflects a technical shortage aggravated by speculative operations. The premium of spot corn over distant futures has actually exceeded 50 per cent and in the case of other products the premium has exceeded 30 per cent.[5] Were our Reservoir plan in operation, these unsound discrepancies could never come into existence, but instead the reservoir would supply the needed spot commodity in exchange for futures at a moderate differential in its favor.

It should be clear from the preceding discussion that there is little reason to fear any great disturbance from an unruly advance in some individual commodity. There remains a sovereignly effective method of dealing with such a contingency, *viz.*, the temporary suspension of the offending commodity from the unit. From the standpoint of the unit itself, or the Reservoir system as a whole, such a step would have no great importance, for it cannot be of vital moment whether the unit comprise 22 rather than 23 commodities. As a corrective against a runaway market in any one commodity this provision should be most salutary; for it may mean not only that the item is excluded from new commodity units, but even that the previous holdings will be sold out at the high price then prevailing.

The rule for suspending a commodity from the unit must necessarily be more or less arbitrary. It is suggested that discretion be given to the monetary agency to suspend or exclude a commodity whenever its price had advanced to a figure 100 per cent above both the previous calendar year's and the previous 10-year average.[6] An appropriate rule may be made for the reinstatement of the commodity in the unit.

A possible objection may still be raised against the principle of offsetting a rise in one commodity by declines in all the other components. Why should the cotton growers suffer if there is a shortage of wheat?[7] In reply it should be pointed out, first, that these adjustments will be made impartially among all the products, so that any disadvantage suffered in one year may well be offset by an advantage gained in some other year. Secondly, as already pointed out, the effect of a rise in one commodity when spread over the other 22 is likely to be unimportant. And, finally, these realignments within the unit cannot possibly bear as hard upon any of the components as do the recurrent collapses in commodity prices which our reservoir mechanism is designed to prevent.

A question that deserves attention is whether the normal operation of the commodity exchanges will be disturbed or unduly dominated by transactions related to the accumulation or liquidation of commodity units. The government's acquisition of silver, pursuant to the Silver Purchase Act of 1934, undoubtedly exerted a powerful influence upon the price of silver; and the suspension of these purchases in 1935 was an equally potent depressing force. Is there reason to fear similar disruptive effects upon the various commodity markets from the operations therein by or on behalf of the monetary agency?

There is in truth no similarity between the government's silver policies and the Reservoir plan herein proposed. The Silver Act envisaged the acquisition by the Treasury of a quantity of silver exceeding twenty times our annual production of the metal. It was necessary to give the Treasury large discretion as to the rate of purchase and the price to be paid; but even so any serious effort to carry out the policy laid down by Congress was bound to introduce a completely abnormal element into the silver market. Similarly, the endeavors of the Treasury to prevent speculators from reaping a harvest by anticipating its operations were equally certain to play havoc with what had become an entirely artificial price situation.[8]

The relation between the reservoir mechanism and the commodity markets is of quite a different character. The reservoir will acquire only the *composite surplus* of current production above consumption. The presence of such a surplus manifests itself by a tendency of the composite price level to fall below the standard figure. At such a time the reservoir functions as a supporting buyer ready to take whatever quantity would not otherwise be absorbed at the established price level. But it must be borne in mind, first, that such support is accorded only to the commodity group taken as a whole and, secondly, that on such a group basis the surplus can represent only a minor fraction of the current production.

It would be quite extraordinary if within a year's time the reservoir could acquire as much as one-fifth of the year's production of *each* of the component commodities. Except in an extreme economic collapse—which the Reservoir system itself should adequately safeguard against—the disproportion between production and effective demand for basic commodities *as a whole* is quite unlikely to reach any large percentage of the total output.[9]

If we were to assume, therefore, that the normal trading on a commodity exchange during a year should be measured by a year's production, we could assert with confidence that the buying "on reservoir account" would rarely be a major element in the total transactions—though it might well exert a major influence in maintaining the price. However, this assumption is contrary to fact for two reasons. On the one hand, a large proportion of the commodity's output is sold off the exchange, and never enters into an exchange transaction. On the other hand, there is a great deal of speculative buying and selling that bears no relation either in its origin or in its quantity to the actual production and consumption.

The result is we have a wide variation among the different commodities in the relative amounts of annual production (or imports) and annual trading in futures. Data on this point are supplied in Table IX in the Appendix. These figures show that while some commodities, *e.g.*, wheat and cotton, are subject to extremely active trading in enormous aggregate volume, many of the others in our list have only nominal markets, with transactions of only negligible proportions.

If this condition were to continue while our Reservoir plan was in operation, the effects of "reservoir buying" and "reservoir selling" would be entirely different in one group of commodities than in another. These transactions would be important but by no means overshadowing in the markets where trading is now conducted in large volume; but they might completely dominate the trading in the less active markets.

Fortunately there is little danger either that the latter situation will continue for a long time, or that during its continuance it will result in nonrepresentative prices for the commodities affected. It is not at all likely, for example, that reservoir buying of petroleum on the Commodity Exchange (where trading is now dormant) will result in an artificially high price due to an absence of offerings. The offerings will come in quickly enough from producers and those holding oil in storage as soon as a price just slightly higher than the "outside market" is established on the exchange. The same will be true if the petroleum is to be sold, along with the other commodities, out of the reservoir.[10]

What should happen, in sum, is that the operations on reservoir account will materially assist the newer commodity markets in establishing their proper place in the economic scheme. If the commodity is really basic and if it has a large number of both producers and consumers, there is presumably sound justification for an active futures market.[11] If there is no need for a futures market, it is doubtful whether the sporadic and limited activity created by the reservoir operations will make it worthwhile for those interested to meet the expense of maintaining a highly organized and carefully regulated market of that sort.

Two technical elements that deserve attention relate, first, to the method of adding further commodities to the unit after the system is in operation and, secondly, to changes in the relative quantities to reflect changes in the consuming habits of the country. It is contemplated that, just as the admission of commodities to exchange dealings in recent years has made items eligible which would not previously have been so, in all probability other products will be admitted to exchanges and thus become eligible for inclusion in the unit in future years. It is also desirable—in theory, at least—that the relative amount of each commodity in the unit be kept in fairly close agreement with its economic importance. We must emphasize once more that a high degree of accuracy in computing these relative quantities and frequent changes to bring them constantly up to date are by no means essential to the proper working of the Reservoir system. It is quite feasible, however, to institute periodic revisions—say every 10 years—which will serve to prevent the creation of any anachronisms in the unit. To keep this chapter more readable we have relegated our discussion of the technique of these revisions to the Appendix (p. 279).

In order to protect the Reservoir system from becoming too cumbersome through a possible multiplication of futures markets in lesser commodities, the number of commodities in the unit might well be limited, say, to forty. If more than 40 products were otherwise eligible, the criterion of acceptance would become the total dollar value of production or consumption during the base period. The unit would be composed of the top 40 commodities. The periodic revisions would then not only change the relative quantities of the items in the unit, but also possibly result in the dropping of one or more commodities at the bottom of the list and their replacement by other eligible products which had grown to be more important in terms of dollar value.

Chapter VI

THE QUESTION OF PRICE STABILITY

"We shall seek to establish and maintain a dollar which will not change its purchasing and debt paying power in the succeeding generations."

—President Franklin D. Roosevelt[1]

OUR Reservoir system is not dependent upon a fixed value for the commodity unit, and hence it would be possible to discuss its effect upon the general business structure without reference to price stabilization. But since our specific proposal does involve the stabilization of basic commodity prices as a whole, it seems more realistic to examine first into the stable-price aspects of our plan, and then pass on to the effect of the combined reservoir and stabilization attributes upon the economic fabric.

The question of a stable price level has aroused considerable controversy. The havoc caused by the tremendous fluctuations in prices during the last generation has generated a widespread desire for greater stability. Many economists have espoused the cause of the stable dollar and suggested various ways of bringing it about. As our chapter heading indicates, the maintenance of "a dollar of stable purchasing power" has been an announced objective of the Roosevelt Administration.[2]

On the other hand, numerous eminent economists have opposed the idea of a stable dollar, first, as impracticable and, secondly, as undesirable. These two reasons are, of course, entirely unrelated. The attacks on the stable dollar as impracticable are based on technical weaknesses in those plans that have received most attention to date. Such plans propose to keep the "general price level" stable, either by varying the gold content of the dollar or by following various methods of credit control. We believe that the criticisms advanced against these plans by authorities such as Dr. B. F. Anderson are for the most part well founded,[3] and that the schemes would not prove workable under stress, because they seek to affect prices in an indirect manner. Our Reservoir proposal is of quite a different type. Its mechanism concerns itself not with all prices, or the general price level, but only with the aggregate value of the specific commodities in the unit. This value is kept stable, not by maneuvers of a management character, but by establishing a direct interchange between money and commodity units. To repeat the point, we follow exactly the same procedure that kept the value of gold stable at $20 per ounce before we left the gold standard.

It should be evident, therefore, that our proposal will actually stabilize the value of the commodity unit *as long as any units remain in monetary storage*. If it is assumed that all the units are withdrawn through redemption of the currency, we would have the same situation as if all the gold reserves had been withdrawn through redemption of gold certificates (or other currency payable in gold). Under either supposition the price of gold or of the commodity unit could then advance above the fixed or coinage level.

Were such complete withdrawal to take place after our Reservoir system had been in operation, we should be back to where we were before we started. We should have had the benefit of both the reservoir and the price stabilization as long as they lasted. Equally important, perhaps, the existence of the commodity units later drawn out would have been most beneficial in meeting the demand that manifested itself in their withdrawal, and in acting as a brake on what otherwise might prove a skyrocketing price level. The reservoir mechanism would be ready to absorb commodity units again when the inevitable decline of prices took place, and by this renewed functioning it would prevent a complete price collapse of the kind with which we have been distressingly familiar.

This assumption that all the commodity units are later withdrawn becomes more improbable as the quantity of units in the reservoir increases. It must be remembered that these units are not, like gold, easily hoarded and transported. Commodities coming out of the units into the market will have to be absorbed by consumers or by speculators willing to pay rather heavy carrying charges. Hence a relatively small redemption of currency for commodities is likely to prove quite effective in checking any price advance based largely on speculative factors. The reader is more likely to be apprehensive of an unwieldy accumulation of commodity units than he is of the plan's becoming inoperative through the complete withdrawal of the units. It is indeed probable that the normal functioning of the Reservoir system will be marked by a tendency for the stored units to increase. We have already argued, and shall emphasize again later on, that such an accumulation will prove a boon rather than a menace. But, in any event, to the extent that a steady increase in the stored units is probable, the prospects of their complete withdrawal through redemption become more remote.

Assuming we participate in a major war, it then becomes quite possible that the commodity-unit supply will be absorbed during the conflict. *Silent inter arma leges.* It is not to be expected that any stabilization or Reservoir system can continue to function normally throughout a great war which is the negation of all things normal. A moment's thought will suggest that, regardless of how long the price stabilization can stand up under war conditions, the existence of a substantial quantity of these commodity units at the outbreak of the war will prove of incalculable advantage to our country.

There remains a final observation about the maintenance of the standard price level in peace times. If the system is ever fairly started the only remotely possible condition that might draw out all the commodity units would be a wild speculation in commodities, more intense even than was seen in 1919, prior to the postwar collapse. Such speculation is inevitably financed by bank credit. It can be held in check by rational credit policies, of a kind we have been working out since the depression started. As a last resort—and one that it is hard to conceive as necessary—we might suggest that bank loans be made repayable at the option of the banks in commodity units. By such a provision speculators would be prevented from reaping any advantage from an advance in the value of the commodity unit above its standard level, for they would have to acquire units at their enhanced value and deliver them in payment of their bank loans.[4]

So much for the question whether the price level of basic raw materials will actually be stabilized under our Reservoir proposal. Let us now address ourselves to the criticisms that have been directed against a stable price level itself as an undesirable thing. The gist of this criticism is that the price of goods should fall as improved methods of production make them cheaper to produce. This argument has the very respectable support of the Brookings Institute,[5] which concluded from its excellent series of economic studies that the best way to cope with depression is by steadily cheapening the price of goods so that the masses may buy them in ever larger amounts.

In dealing with this contention let us consider first the extent to which it is relevant to our proposal. The plea for steadily lower prices gets its chief support from the field of manufactured goods. It is possible to point to many articles which are now produced at a small fraction of their former cost. Mass production at low cost has made possible mass consumption at low prices, to the great economic benefit of all. Examples such as automobiles, electric lamps, radios, etc., come readily to mind.

But it is not possible to point to similar developments in the group of basic raw materials comprehended in our unit. It is true that laborsaving devices have greatly reduced the man-hours required per bushel or hundred pounds produced. But on the whole this saving has been offset in dollars by the higher wage scale and by higher costs of items other than labor. The evidence would indicate that there has been no net decrease in the dollar cost of producing our commodity unit over several generations past.

This observation is supported by a study of the price charts prepared by Dr. Carl Snyder and others. Snyder states specifically that "commodities at wholesale have shown no secular trend in a century (or two centuries), while almost all other types of prices have generally risen."[6] Warren and Pearson divide all commodities into "industrial products," which have fallen somewhat, and "biological products except textiles," which have risen somewhat in some 130 years. "The chief characteristics of the prices of all commodities are extreme fluctuations and long periods of rise and decline."[7]

The last century has been marked by an extraordinarily rapid advance in living standards, or the per capita consumption of goods of all kinds. Obviously it was not necessary in bringing about that advance to have a downward tendency in the price of raw materials. Our proposal would therefore not involve any change in the underlying price conditions upon which our great material progress has been based. There will indeed be an important change in that the recurrent wide but temporary fluctuations in the price level of basic commodities will be suppressed. But it will not be seriously argued that such devastating variations were inherently necessary to our economic progress. On the contrary, it seems more plausible to contend that the elimination of these disturbing fluctuations will serve both to quicken the pace of national progress and protect it against major setbacks.

It is worth while to penetrate a little farther into this question of a stable versus a declining price level. The argument that prices generally should decline with improved productive efficiency has two serious theoretical weaknesses. The first involves defining just what is meant by "prices generally." The general price level includes a number of rather disparate components, such as commodities at wholesale and retail, rents, wages, fees for professional services.[8] Critics of a "stable dollar" contend that it is difficult to determine just what combination of prices is to be kept stable. It is equally difficult to determine just what combination of prices should show a declining trend in order to reflect lower costs of production. The common-sense view would suggest that the declining-price idea should be applied only to those individual products, whatever their number, which have received the benefit of important specific improvements in their technique of production.

The second difficulty with the doctrine of declining prices relates to the question of what should properly be meant by a dollar. To have some sort of rational meaning a dollar should be defined as representing either a fixed quantity of gold, or some fixed combination of other goods or services, or possibly so many hours of (unskilled) labor. A dollar consisting of a fixed quantity of gold is subject to wide fluctuations in its purchasing power, which usually have very little to do with changes in productive efficiency. For increased efficiency may itself be properly reflected either in lower prices with the same wage scale, or in a higher wage scale with the same prices or a combination of both.

As far as current business and the wage-earner's status is concerned, it makes little practical difference which path is followed. The people really affected by the choice are the parties to long-term contracts to pay money. What is at stake, at bottom, is the allocation of the benefit of greater productive efficiency as between the long-term debtor and the long-term creditor. To the extent that prices decline the creditor receives the advantage, for the dollar he lent will buy more when he gets it back than when he parted with it. To the extent that wages advance and the price level is maintained, the advantage goes to the debtor, for he can pay off his debt with less labor than was required when the money was borrowed.

It seems to the writer that as good an argument on grounds of abstract justice can be advanced in favor of the second arrangement as of the first. From a more practical angle it is distinctly better that wages rise rather than prices fall. For the debt structure is inherently a dangerous element in the economic system. On the whole it is advantageous to the creditor as well as the debtor that the repayments of debts be facilitated insofar as reasonably possible. This would be done by giving the debtor the benefit of increased productive efficiency, in the shape of a higher wage level rather than a lower price level.

The rather considerable space given to the question of stable versus declining prices has been due to the writer's respect for the economists who espouse the latter cause.[9] It is not necessary that our arguments on the other side be accepted in order to justify our proposal that a dollar be made equivalent to a fixed composite of basic commodities. For certainly there is at least as much sense in defining a dollar in this way as in defining it as either 23 or 16 gr. of gold. If the fixed commodity content, in place of the fixed gold content, will facilitate the operation of a Reservoir system designed to deal rationally with the problem of surplus, then this redefinition of the dollar vindicates itself by its practical results.

Let us pass on to the relationship between our stabilized price level for basic commodities and the price level for other commodities and for services. It should not be thought that prices outside of the commodity unit will be stabilized to the same degree as the unit itself. It may well be that in the case of fabricated goods the declining trend recommended by the Brookings Institute will manifest itself alongside the unchanging level for the basic raw materials. Very likely this would be the optimum combination.

Is it possible, however, that the situation may be reversed and that a stable price level for basic materials will be accompanied by an *advancing* trend in all other price groups? There is a specific reason for suggesting this hypothesis. The growth of the commodity-unit reservoir will give rise to a corresponding expansion in the currency total. The normal result of having more money in circulation would be an advance in the general price level. If the level for basic commodities is fixed by the mechanics of our proposal, then the advance might well take place in all the other non-stabilized groups.

A development of this kind may materialize to a minor extent; but there are conclusive reasons for believing that, regardless of the volume of money, it will not be possible for prices of fabricated goods to advance far above the corresponding level of raw materials. The forces of competition must necessarily keep finished-goods prices fairly closely in line with production costs. These in turn depend primarily upon raw-materials prices and wage rates. Should the wage scale be advanced too spectacularly the cost of production of the stabilized raw-materials group will rise to a point which will check the total output and set in motion definite forces of contraction. The *natural* relationships between the price levels of the various groups of goods and services may be relied upon to prevent the creation of any serious long-term disparities growing solely out of the money supply.[10]

But whatever the long-term trend may be, there is little doubt that the stabilization of basic commodities will go far to reduce the harmful *short-term* fluctuations in other price groups. Price statistics show clearly that instability in raw-material prices is a prime cause of instability of other prices. It is the basic commodities that decline fastest and farthest, carrying other prices down with them. They also advance soonest and farthest in boom times, and again influence other prices in the same direction.[11] The reason for this causal connection is obvious. Most fabricated goods are made of these very raw materials, so that the cost of the former directly affects the price of the latter. Once a protracted move in commodity prices gets under way, the level of wages tends to change in the same direction. Even rents ultimately move in a similar sense, partly because they are bound up with construction costs, which in turn consist of material and labor expense.

We need have little hesitation in asserting, therefore, that our machinery of stabilization of the basic-commodity price level will operate very powerfully in the direction of restricting cyclical variations in prices generally.

Chapter VII

THE RESERVOIR SYSTEM AND THE GENERAL
BUSINESS CYCLE

ITS RELATION TO THE PROBLEM OF UNEMPLOYMENT

> "Perhaps the gravest problem that our modern economic and industrial structure has now to deal with . . . is the maintenance of some fair degree of stability of values and the prevention of such a catastrophic fall in prices, and values, as has been witnessed in the last four years."
>
> —CARL SNYDER[1]

GENERAL business is just as indefinite a concept as the general price level. Nevertheless we know sufficiently well what we mean by the term to be able to talk intelligently about it. There are, in fact, accepted composite indices of general business, and if we wish to appear quite specific and arithmetical we can use the percentage figures compiled by the *New York Times* or by *Business Week.*

Individual businesses suffer from a variety of ills, including the wrong kind of long-term trend and frequently also the mistakes of their managers. But business as a whole is definitely subject to cyclical variations of prosperity and depression. Exactly what causes business cycles is still under investigation and in controversy. It is by no means certain that business cycles are bad things, in the sense that we would be better off if all such fluctuations could be eliminated.

We *are* certain, however, that a downward business cycle of the intensity experienced between 1930 and 1933 is a very bad thing indeed. We are also certain that the extreme severity of that downswing was caused, or in any event measurably aggravated, by the world-wide excess stocks of basic commodities which overhung the markets, broke the price level and demoralized the entire business fabric.

A Reservoir system that will draw off the surplus supply of important commodities and immobilize them as far as the open market is concerned cannot fail to be of enormous help in checking a collapse such as we recently experienced. Viewing the picture from another angle, we may point out that by stabilizing the position of the raw-materials producers our proposal will help mightily to keep general business on an even keel. As studies of the Department of Agriculture indicate, the course of business change tends to run much more from the farm to the city than *vice versa*.[2] Depression does not spread from the city to the farm so often as the other way around. The reason is that the farmer's consumption of manufactured goods is more variable than the nation's consumption of farm products.

Our Reservoir system will be of chief direct advantage to the farmer. About 70 per cent in dollar value of the commodity units is produced on American farms. The presence of a constant market for these important farm products, at a fairly stable price in the aggregate, will go far to improve the stability of the American farmer and in that way will make for relative stability in business generally.

It is not contended that our proposal will eliminate the business cycle. Fairly wide variations may take place in general business conditions, even while the price level of basic commodities remains stable. The great boom of 1926-1929 took place in the face of a relatively motionless level for the commodities in our unit.[3] One might well ask, therefore, whether the same boom and the same collapse might not have taken place even if our Reservoir system had been in operation, and whether they cannot take place again even if our proposal is adopted.

The boom of the late 1920's was mainly a stock-market and real-estate boom, financed by an unduly liberal extension of credit. Production and distribution of commodities expanded substantially but by no means spectacularly.[4] Prices of commodities advanced not at all. Consumption was kept on a par with production by the loaning of huge sums to foreign nations to enable them to pay for our goods, and also by a substantial development of consumer credit here (installment buying). Our "prosperity" was clearly based on a credit structure over-extended and therefore vulnerable in several directions.

To prevent the repetition of the unsound situation of the 1920's a more effective credit policy is imperatively called for. The new machinery of control set up in recent banking legislation will prove very useful to that end, and there is abundant evidence that those in charge are keenly alive to the desirability of exercising these powers at the proper time. Whether or not the control devices will prove adequate to deal with the possibilities of explosive credit expansion implicit in our present banking situation—and aggravated by the inflationary effects of government deficits—remains, however, a doubtful question.

In a broader sense it may well be true that undue credit expansion accompanies prosperity because there is a tendency for effective cash purchasing power to fall short of the dollar value of production. Credit extension is necessary to make up the difference. The equilibrium thus created is a precarious one, because it depends upon a continuous expansion of credit. To what extent this contention is correct is a very controversial point in current economic theory. The idea was expounded long ago in plausible form by J. A. Hobson,[5] and it has been developed into an elaborate— but highly questionable—doctrine and program by Major Douglas, under the name of "social credit."[6]

The defense of our reservoir proposal does not require that we set up a "purchasing-power theory" that will convince economists of every school. We may venture the opinion that there is at least a modicum of truth in the assertion that ordinary consumption tends to fall short of production during a period of business expansion. If this is so, our Reservoir system takes on a new stature as an essential regulatory mechanism for the normal systole and diastole of the breath of business. In other words, we set up not merely an emergency apparatus to deal with a sudden onrush of commodity surpluses, but rather a balance-wheel arrangement which can function as an integral and indispensable part of a smoothly operating business machine.

From this point of view we may conceive of the commodity reservoir as taking the place of speculative credit expansion (or of government deficits) as the marginal or effective factor in maintaining prosperity. That this newer mechanism is preferable to the old would seem to go without saying; for it does not involve the ever-increasing financial weakness and tension, because of which each period of prosperity has been said to bear within itself the seeds of its own collapse.

It may appear that far too much is claimed for our reservoir mechanism in view of the limited group of commodities comprised therein. If there is overproduction or underconsumption in good times, or if equilibrium is maintained only by undue extension of credit, such effects are distributed throughout the range of raw and fabricated goods. But analysis of the economic process will show that the maladjustments of supply and demand created in the field of manufactured goods are of a different character and a lesser order of magnitude than those existing in raw materials. Control over production is well established in finished lines. (Too well established, indeed, in the opinion of some economists, who feel that the chief adjustments of supply to demand should take place by reducing price rather than curtailing output.[7])

If the business picture were confined to manufactured goods, we should probably see relatively moderate "overproduction" in an upswing and a relatively rapid readjustment after the downturn. The business cycle, while real enough, would still be confined within sufficiently narrow upper and lower limits to prevent its developing into a challenge to the economic order. The severer dislocations arise within the area of raw commodities. The *composite* collapse in general business may be viewed in two ways. We may say either that the supply-demand demoralization in raw materials communicates itself to the finished-goods markets (which otherwise would make a fairly rapid adjustment), or else that the failure of finished goods and raw materials to follow a similar pattern of change creates new disparities and stresses which accentuate the general disturbance.

These considerations lead us to affirm that a Reservoir system need include only the important raw materials to supply an effective offset to the really demoralizing factors in the business cycle. A corresponding reservoir of finished goods is not so necessary or so beneficial, because the crisis to be met is not so serious. Hence we conclude by remarking that if the raw-materials markets are reasonably well stabilized the finished-goods markets will take care of themselves—not, of course, to the extent of an undeviating progress, but within limits of easily tolerable variation.

THE RESERVOIR SYSTEM AND UNEMPLOYMENT

The problem of unemployment and the problem of surplus seem to be dual aspects of the same underlying paradox. In a practical sense, we cannot find room for idle workers because those at work already produce too much. Widespread unemployment operates as a crude mechanism for correcting the unbalance of demand and supply. An unemployed person produces nothing and consumes something. This obvious but relatively unnoticed fact is one of the important self-correcting elements in the business cycle. As unemployment increases during a depression, production declines faster than consumption. Surplus stocks are drawn upon, and the need for replenishing these depleted stocks finally pushes the pendulum back in the direction of increased business activity.[8]

If unemployment were a purely cyclical phenomenon the Reservoir system herein proposed would go quite far towards banishing it. In the field of basic raw materials our system would maintain aggregate output close to the maximum permitted by the stabilized average price level. It would not only maintain employment in this primary economic area, but it would also maintain the purchasing power of all those embraced within it—chiefly the farming population. This primary purchasing power is an essential element in the demand for manufactured goods.[9] Hence demand, production and employment in the industrial field as well would be upheld by a powerful stabilizing force.

Perhaps this is merely another way of stating that since the Reservoir system will go far to mitigate the fluctuations of the general business cycle it will correspondingly alleviate the calamity of unemployment that accompanies the cyclical downswing. Let us once more disclaim any contention that the business cycle will be abolished under our plan. Even if we had complete stability in the area of raw material production—and this would be only relatively true under our system—there might still be a high degree of instability at the other end of the economic spectrum, viz., the field of capital goods. Expansion and contraction in this sector are by no means completely governed by impersonal economic laws. The element of free choice, arbitrarily concentrated or postponed buying, enters very largely into the picture. Analysis will show that the capital-goods market is quite similar to the stock market in its domination by a mixture of psychological and business factors inherently antagonistic to long-continued stability.

It is not claimed for our plan, therefore, that it will solve the vexing problem of cyclical unemployment in the capital-goods industries. (We do not pretend, as did the darky preacher, to "unfathom the unfathomable and to unscrew the inscrutable.") But just as the direct stability we offer in the raw materials field will contribute indirectly but powerfully towards stability in fabrication and distribution, so the lessened variations in general business will undoubtedly *reduce* the swings in capital-goods production and employment.

It is now recognized that unemployment is more than a cyclical problem. Through some deficiency in the adjustive powers of the body economic, improvements in production methods tend to displace workers faster than we can absorb them through increased consumption, the development of new wants and through shorter hours of work. We are quite accustomed to the thought that the machine can take the place of labor in the sense that the owners of the machines may consider themselves relieved of the social obligation to work, having contributed their machines to society in lieu of their much less productive personal labor. What seems to have happened is that the machine insists upon supporting not only its owners but many other unemployed people as well. Thus in the middle of 1937, after four years of recovery, and with the index of business activity suggesting a return to the area of prosperity, we are still faced with an unemployment problem of the first magnitude.[10] There seem to have developed two classes of unemployed who are maintained by the abundant productivity of the machine—the unemployed who live on their dividends and the unemployed who live on their dole.

This is a statement of what is and not what should be. Since the voluntarily unemployed stockholder or bondholder is not a problem to himself, he need not worry the economist. But even though it may be economically feasible to maintain the unemployed worker on the dole, in the same way as the stockholder is maintained on dividends, this arrangement is so obviously defective in the personal sense as to clamor for correction. Some means must be found to put the unemployed worker to work, either producing additional goods or reducing the task of other workers.

The Reservoir system offers two contributions towards meeting the problem of technological unemployment[11]— sometimes referred to as the "hard core" of unemployment. On the one hand, it offers direct additional employment in producing commodity units for storage. In our next chapter we shall consider in detail the various uses to which these stored commodity units may be put. We may suggest the homely analogy of the woodpile which was always ready for the ministrations of the able-bodied man who knocked at the farmhouse door and asked for a meal and a night's lodging. From the employment angle, the production of basic commodities for storage may operate as a sort of "national woodpile," exacting useful labor in return for subsistence.

The Reservoir system should facilitate also the process of adjustments to greater technological efficiency. The absorption of workers through shortening hours runs foul of individual problems of production costs and profit margins. The process of building up the commodity-unit reserve, with its accompanying issuance of additional money, is likely to have a generally beneficial effect upon profit margins. A readjustment of hours and hourly wages, suited to the absorption of excess manpower, may best be carried on during a period of prosperous and relatively stable business conditions.[12] The Reservoir system, by providing a permanent stimulus to trade and production, and by interposing an effective buffer between business stresses and depression, should supply a sturdy foundation upon which to construct a sane and flexible employment policy.

Chapter VIII

ULTIMATE USES OF THE STORED COMMODITY UNITS

"I expect to see the day—and it won't take more than twenty years—when the Government sees to it that one-third of the population which is at present insufficiently clothed and fed will have a decent living standard."

—HARRY L. HOPKINS[1]
Federal Works Progress Administrator

IF we assume that our Reservoir system will function through a fairly long period of normal business conditions —meaning by "normal" conditions which are not clearly and incontrovertibly abnormal—will there be an underlying tendency for commodity units to accumulate? More accurately, will such accumulation tend to proceed at a more rapid rate than the secular growth in consumption? Conceivably this might not be the case, and the reservoir may grow larger in some years and smaller in others, without showing a definite trend upward.

There are a variety of reasons for believing, however, that the normal trend of the reservoir will be in the direction of expansion. It may be argued from analogy that since this is a scheme for valorizing commodity units, it will have the same consequence as other valorization schemes (including the valorization of gold and silver) and will result in a persistent accumulation of the things valorized. Or, putting the same thought differently, one might claim that since this is an attack on the problem of surplus by a process of impounding, it is to be expected that surpluses will be larger than they otherwise would have been and the impounding of surplus will proceed quite steadily. Or, by a third state-

ment of the case, the recurrent deficiency of effective purchasing power will no doubt create repeated additions to the
commodity store, in very much the same way as the somewhat related process of saving adds continuously to the
country's capital investment.

Let us look forward, therefore, to an expanding commodity-unit reservoir and consider what uses may be made
of these assets. In theory nothing at all needs to be done with
them, except to permit them to continue as a larger and
larger balance wheel of our economic machine. This would be
similar to the function of our gold holdings, which seem to
have no other purpose to serve than the stabilization of our
currency and credit system.

But these commodities are too useful in consumption to
allow us to accept their being immobilized permanently in
ever-increasing quantities, in the same way as our gold hoard
has just been buried at Fort Knox, Ky. A certain quantity
of commodity units must be viewed as needed for the repeated ebb and flow, out of the reservoir and into it again,
that will characterize the operation of the system under the
ordinary fluctuations of business. A large additional quantity
would be highly desirable as an emergency store. The two
chief emergencies, of course, are war and the failure of the
food supply through drought.

Unfortunately no apology is necessary for stressing the
supreme value of an ample commodity-unit reservoir as a
measure of military preparedness. Today war is at once a
terrible memory, a grim reality and a sickening threat.
Enjoying the blessings of peace, this nation is spending some
900 millions this fiscal year for national defense—a sum
far larger than the *entire* expenditures of the government in
1916. In the 160 years of its existence the United States has
fought six wars. From 1776 on most of our people who
attained the age of sixty have sustained the hardships of

two wartime periods. Recalling the experience of 1917–1918, we realize that modern warfare brings with it a universal shortage of important commodities. The last war inflicted heatless Mondays and meatless Tuesdays, a severe rationing of flour and sugar, the diversion of steel, copper and other metals from less essential to more essential industries.[2] Nearly every one of the basic commodities comprised in our unit was subject to an especially heavy demand during the World War.

No matter how large a supply of commodity units we may accumulate during peacetimes, it seems unlikely that they will exceed the amount necessary to carry us without deprivation through a war of the first magnitude. We should be justified, therefore, in viewing our commodity-unit stock, however large, merely as a war chest which is far more dependable than a huge hoard of gold.[3] The existence of such a war chest might go far to strengthen our prestige and frighten off any would-be assailant. It would differ from an array of armies and armaments, because we know the latter serve the cause of war and not of peace. Our commodity units will constitute a protection and not a threat.

The second type of emergency is that through which we have just been passing, *viz.*, actual or threatened shortage of food by reason of widespread drought. This type of difficulty differs from the challenge of war because it relates to only some of the commodity group rather than to virtually all of them. Our plan must be sufficiently flexible to permit the temporary use of some of the commodities held in "monetary storage" when there is specific need for them. This can readily be done by permitting the withdrawal of any commodity from the stored units and its replacement by an equivalent volume of futures contracts (together with currency equal to the dollar amount to be paid on delivery), as already explained in Chap. V.

Such an arrangement will be financially advantageous in times of shortage, for such occasions are marked by a "premium" for spot delivery, *i.e.*, the futures can be bought at a lower price than the cash product can be sold for. The appearance of such a "premium" can be used as the automatic signal for replacing a commodity in the reservoir by contracts for future delivery. In this way our Reservoir system can be profitably drawn upon to make up temporary deficiencies in the supply of individual commodities.

Certainly the presence of a large surplus stock of a group of individual commodities *must* in one way or another supply a safeguard against the adverse effects of a shortage in any one of them. Even if the simple mechanism we propose—that of replacing the physical commodity by futures contracts—should prove inadequate, other methods undoubtedly will suggest themselves to permit soundly the use of whatever commodity may be badly needed.

The beneficial possibilities of the commodity-unit reservoir are by no means exhausted by considering their use in times of emergency. Assuming once again a persistent tendency for the reservoir to expand, we may put forward two broad lines of development which may be followed in deriving practical utility from these accumulating assets.

The first concept relates to the social security scheme which we have already initiated by legislation. The chief object of the Social Security Act is to supply protection against old age and unemployment by means of the insurance principle. The idea of the old-age-insurance plan is to set aside sums year by year to permit our people to sustain themselves without working after they have reached the age of retirement. This means, as is well understood, that a huge reserve fund must be accumulated over the next 30 years or more. The reserve fund will represent the amount due those already drawing benefits, together with part of the amount eventually due those who will later be entitled to benefits.

The question of the proper composition or utilization of these old-age-insurance funds is one that is causing great perplexity. Hitherto it has been possible to think of insurance in purely financial terms and to consider the problem of insurance reserves in the same way as that of individual savings. More thoughtful students may indeed have given some consideration to the implications of a rapid growth of our insurance and savings structure to the economic fabric, particularly from the angle of the ever-increasing debt burden of which the insurance assets are the counterpart. That problem, until recently very little thought about, has been brought sharply to the fore by the projected reserves of huge dimensions that are implicit in the Social Security Act.

The new legislation provides that the reserve funds are to be held in the form of obligations of the United States. It is pretty well taken for granted that such restrictions are necessary because investment of these enormous funds in other securities would create apparently insurmountable problems. However, the creation of a 47-billion-dollar reserve fund consisting of United States government securities has challenging aspects.[4] Are these securities really assets from the national standpoint? Can these assets be considered as earning interest from the national standpoint? Is it not true that a national fund consisting of evidences of a national debt really cancels itself out, and is at bottom nothing at all? Is it not also true that interest paid on such a national fund consists at bottom of amounts paid out of one pocket of the national government into another, and may in no true sense be considered as earnings?

This is undoubtedly an overstatement of the case. While national debt, nationally owned, does cancel itself out, this does not mean that the specific fund which contains a national debt is worse off than if it contained some other asset. If one could assume that the same amount of national debt would exist anyway, then the presence of government bonds in the social security fund would mean that a corresponding amount of private funds would have to be placed in other, and presumably more productive or more real, kinds of investment. It is also conceivable that the national debt in the social security fund might be incurred to acquire valuable assets, and to that extent it would have the same amount of tangible backing as sound corporate or individual debt.

While these assumptions have a certain validity, they do not dispose entirely of the problems raised when we envisage the holding of huge national reserves in the form of evidences of national debt. On the one hand, this arrangement is likely to afford a continuing incentive to lax governmental financial policies. In addition, of course, there is always the question as to the status of the beneficiaries in the event that the purchasing power of the paper dollar be greatly reduced through inflationary developments.

If we reflect on this entire situation we are likely to reach the conclusion that commodity-unit certificates, representing the physical commodity units in storage, would constitute an ideal medium of investment for our social security fund. On the one hand, they would represent concrete usable things which it is the inherent purpose of the fund to place ultimately in the hands of the aged and unemployed for consumption. Secondly, a fund of this kind would not involve the problems of sound versus unsound investment, or sound finance versus unsound finance, which seem bound up with the administration of these huge sums along ordinary insurance-company lines.

This seems a desirable point at which to discuss the relationship between our basic commodities in the unit and the matter of consumption goods and capital goods in general. We have referred to the units as representing the things which the people of the country consume. This statement may be objected to as inaccurate on the ground that the actual articles of merchandise consumed in this country are in good measure different from the raw materials in our unit. To answer this contention properly we shall state a thesis which may be called "the principle of equivalence of useful goods." By this we mean that any fund of goods which are unquestionably valuable to the nation may be considered as economically equivalent, on a fair basis, to other valuable goods.

Speaking concretely, if we assume that the beneficiaries of the Social Security Act had a fund consisting of basic commodities, all of which were useful, this fund would have the same financial value to them and the same economic value to the nation, as if it consisted of the actual manufactured goods which they could be expected to consume. For in the ordinary economic process a free and desirable interchange could take place between the raw commodities which they held and the manufactured goods which they want. This idea does not imply that an unlimited supply of a *single* useful commodity would do as well as our commodity units. For the supply of the single commodity might be so disproportionate to that of other commodities entering into consumption that its economic value was thereby greatly diminished. Our diversified commodity unit avoids this serious pitfall.

Hence we assert that commodity units should fairly be regarded as the equivalent of a corresponding dollar value of other goods or services. Our argument is buttressed by the fact that the larger part of these other goods may be made up of our basic commodities in processed form; but it does not depend on this point. Furthermore, our reasoning with respect to goods entering into consumption applies also to various kinds of investment or capital goods, and to an interchange between useful capital goods and useful consumption goods.

The most serious objection to our proposal that commodity-unit certificates enter largely into the social security reserve fund would arise from the fact that these certificates, as currency, do not bear interest. Hence the actuarial calculations, which assume a certain rate of interest earned by the fund, would be vitiated. The writer is convinced that the proper answer to that argument must be that *the social security fund cannot properly be expected to earn interest.* The easiest way to support our statement is by assuming— as has invariably been done—that the fund will consist of government obligations. Then it is obvious that from a national standpoint it makes no difference at all whether government securities bear interest or not. This interest is certainly paid by the nation to itself and it does represent a transfer from one pocket to another—if the security fund may be considered, as undoubtedly it should be, as being held for the benefit of the nation as a whole, in the same way as government debt is a liability of the nation as a whole.

It follows that actuarial calculations might just as readily be made on the assumption that the social security fund is in the form of non-interest-bearing obligations, or of currency. If it is necessary to increase the total of the fund by amounts equivalent to annual interest, this can as logically be done by government contributions as by the payment of interest on government bonds in the fund. It may be said also that the amount of interest paid on these obligations is very largely a matter of arbitrary determination by the government itself.[5] If we assume that the greater part of future government financing will be between itself and government-controlled banks as at present, or between itself and the government-controlled social security reserve fund as seems to be projected in the new law, it would follow that the rate of interest will be pretty much what the government wishes to make it. Hence for practical purposes, one might just as well conceive that the fund is drawing no contractual interest, but rather is receiving, if necessary, increments from the government similar to the payments made under the British Unemployment Insurance Acts.[6] Such is, in effect, the significance of the provision in the Social Security Act itself whereby the government guarantees interest of not less than 3 per cent on the bonds held in the reserve fund.

From what may seem to be a theoretical angle—but which may actually be one of great practical significance—the elimination of interest on the social security fund will have the great advantage of avoiding the "fallacy of compound interest." By this we mean the fallacy of believing that sums, however large, can always be invested for an indefinite period of time so as to bring some more or less fixed rate of interest compounded annually. Both a priori reasoning and experience teach us that as these funds grow larger and larger the geometrical rate of growth by compound interest ultimately defeats itself. There is warrant for believing that depressions, with their accompanying debt readjustments, constitute in part an inevitable "liquidation of compound interest." A social security reserve fund of the magnitude envisaged, if set up in the ordinary insurance way, might develop into a harrowing illustration of the fallacy of compound interest.

It seems a fortunate coincidence that the proposal of a large reservoir of basic commodity units can be made at a

time when a correspondingly broad-gaged proposal for a
social security reserve fund has taken concrete shape. The
earmarking of a large proportion of the commodity-unit
certificates as assets of the social security reserve will serve
a double purpose: first, to create an obviously useful function for the commodity units (in addition to their function
as regulator of the supply-and-demand situation) and,
secondly, to find a medium of investment for the social
security funds which bears the closest tangible relationship
to the ultimate purposes of these funds. It is not suggested,
of course, that the entire 47-billion-dollar reserve to be
ultimately created under the Social Security Act of 1935
should be held in the form of commodity units. Sentiment
has developed very strongly against the huge-reserve-fund
device, and is favoring the meeting of deficiencies between
receipts and pensions by current taxation. A sensible com-
promise between the full-reserve and the no-reserve idea
might look to the ultimate accumulation of a "working
reserve" of several billions in the form of commodity units.

The question of the ultimate use of the stored commodity
units may be approached on an even broader ground than
that of tying them up with the social security reserve funds.
If it is assumed that the supply of commodity units grows
well beyond the amount deemed necessary (*a*) for a stabilizing reserve, (*b*) for national defense and other emergency
purposes, (*c*) as a social security reserve, we then face the
simple situation that both production and dollar purchasing
power have been growing faster than the actual utilization
of this purchasing power in consumption. It must be remembered that the creation of commodity units is accompanied
in every instance by the creation of *direct purchasing power
in the form of currency*. The fact that this currency is not
actually spent, in such a way as to bring the commodity
units themselves into consumption, would have to be due

to one of two reasons. The first would be that the nation as a whole is already consuming all the goods it wants and does not or cannot effectively use its more abundant production. No thoughtful person could accept such an hypothesis.

The other explanation is that the dollar purchasing power lies in the wrong hands—at least in the sense that if it were in the hands of people with lower incomes it would be spent, whereas under our assumption it is only hoarded. Let us point out that purchasing power which accrues to wealthy people *and is invested in capital goods* is equivalent from the standpoint of aggregate consumption to that which goes to poorer people and is spent for consumption goods. Hence our assumption that commodity units accumulate in very large quantities means not only that the corresponding purchasing power goes to wealthier rather than to poorer people, but also that the wealthier people are not in fact investing this purchasing power.

If we have the situation called for by these assumptions, it would then seem that we have a clear mandate for a further equalization of purchasing power, as between different levels of the population, so as to translate this purchasing power into actual purchasing—for either consumption or investment. It is not necessary to suggest specifically what steps in the direction of greater equalization should be taken. A great part of the government's activities are already of this kind—imposing taxation of various sorts on the wealthier and conferring benefits of various sorts on the poorer. All that would be needed under our assumptions would be further developments along the lines already well established.

Among its other advantages, our Reservoir system will be found to possess the signal merit of offering an index or barometer that may guide us in the application of measures for social progress and for greater economic equality.

Chapter IX

THE COST OF THE RESERVOIR PLAN

"A total of $17,359,000,000 had been appropriated and allocated for relief purposes up to Oct. 31, 1935."
—*New York Times*, Jan. 6, 1936

THE only expense connected with instituting and maintaining the Monetary Storage system is the cost of storing the various commodities in the unit. The actual acquisition of the commodities does not involve any expense *or entail any annual interest charges*, for they pay for themselves by qualifying as the backing for currency—in the same way as our gold and silver reserves have always done. The administrative expense is an entirely negligible factor. In this respect our proposal differs essentially from many of the important measures adopted during the depression, which involved personal contacts and dealings with millions of individuals and a correspondingly elaborate organization of officials and government employees. The Reservoir system is completely impersonal in its operation. Its administrative mechanism is as simple, basically, as that involved in the coinage of gold—the difference arising solely from the greater volume and variety of the commodities we handle.

The expense element in our plan may be approached from three angles: (*a*) the actual cost of storage, (*b*) the possibilities of collecting offsetting income and (*c*) the relation of the net cost to the benefits derived from the Reservoir system. The cost of storage will, of course, depend upon the size of the reservoir. As pointed out in an earlier chapter, it is not possible to make any definite predictions as to the quantity of commodity units that will accumulate. It may be feasible, however, to establish a policy governing effectively the average size of the reservoir over some fairly long period, say 10 years. This would be done by offsetting a natural tendency of the reservoir to expand, through the extension of present social legislation aiming at a more equitable division of national income. With this control possibility in mind, we feel justified in discussing storage costs on the basis of a hypothetical average of six months' supply in the reservoir.

The actual storage of the commodity units can be carried out in three ways: There are, first, the ordinary commercial warehouses and elevators. Secondly, we may utilize part of the storage facilities of the producers and consumers of certain of the commodities. Finally, we may supplement these facilities by government-owned warehouses. It should hardly be necessary to point out that the commodity units need not be held together and stored as a physical combination. The widest flexibility is possible as to the place and manner of storing the individual products. Methods must be found, however, for making each of these stored commodities deliverable under the terms of contracts made on the respective commodity exchanges.

The starting point in calculating storage expense should evidently be the regular commercial storage charges for the various commodities. In Table II we present a schedule of the ruling rates quoted by members of the commodity exchanges for carrying contract lots of each commodity, and these charges are also expressed as an approximate annual percentage of the 1921–1930 average price.

The figures show a startling variation in relative storage expense, ranging from less than 1 per cent of value per annum for tin and silk to as high as 40 per cent for oats. The average for the entire unit would work out at the very

TABLE II.—ESTIMATED ANNUAL COST OF STORING COMMODITY UNITS

Commodity	Unit of quantity	Annual storage rates— commodity-exchange basis, cents	Average price, 1921–1930, cents	Per cent of storage cost relative to average price	Commodity-exchange basis, cost of storing 1000 dollar units	Estimated cost of storage to Reservoir system	
						Rate, cents	For commodities in 1000 one-dollar units
Wheat	Bushel	18	124.0	14.5%	$ 15.19	6	$ 5.06
Barley	Bushel	18	66.6	27.0	3.90	6	1.30
Cocoa	Pound	0.46	10.2	4.5	0.19	0.3	0.12
Coffee	Pound	0.46	17.2	2.7	0.67	0.3	0.44
Corn	Bushel	18	81.6	22.1	48.24	2	5.36
Cottonseed oil	Pound	0.9	10.0	9.0	1.15	0.5	0.83
Oats	Bushel	18	44.3	40.6	22.50	6	7.50
Rye	Bushel	18	90.8	19.8	0.96	6	0.32
Sugar	Pound	0.4	6.1	6.6	5.18	0.2	2.59
Cotton	Pound	0.56	20.5	2.7	3.78	0.3	2.03
Silk	Pound	1.57	589.0	0.3	0.12	1	0.08
Wool	Pound	1.08	115.6	1.0	0.29	1	0.27
Copper	Pound	0.24	14.3	1.7	0.37	0.1	0.15
Lead	Pound	0.18	7.0	2.6	0.25	0.1	0.14
Tin	Pound	0.27	48.4	0.6	0.04	0.1	0.02
Zinc	Pound	0.18	6.3	2.9	0.18	0.1	0.10
Cottonseed meal	Pound	0.3 (est.)	1.8	16.7	1.25	0.2	0.83
Flaxseed	Bushel	18	246.0	7.3	0.68	6	0.23
Hides	Pound	0.9	16.8	5.4	0.88	0.6	0.58
Petroleum	Barrel	36	164.0	21.9	28.48	6	4.76
Rubber	Pound	0.32	30.8	1.1	0.27	0.2	0.17
Tallow	Pound	0.9	7.8	11.3	0.47	0.4	0.21
Tobacco	Pound	0.3	21.0	1.4	0.41	0.2	0.28
Total					$135.45		$33.37

burdensome figure of 13½ per cent. A little further consideration of the problem will indicate, however, that these commercial schedules are in no wise indicative of the costs of storage on a comprehensive scale—particularly for those items which make up the bulk of our unit.

The commodities entailing the largest commercial storage rates are the grains, sugar and petroleum. By far the most important single item is corn. The experience of the Commodity Credit Corporation with corn loans to farmers suggests that the corn component of the unit can be stored on the farm in sealed cribs, and that the individual farmer can safely be held responsible for the corn entrusted in his keeping.[1] The expense of this type of storage is practicably negligible. The technical method of establishing this type of storage would consist of a trade between the commodity-unit authority and the farmer, whereby the latter is given the regular warehouse receipts representing corn in elevators in exchange for his corn held on the farm. A suitable price differential would be charged the farmer, but the exchange could be effected on terms sufficiently attractive to make it well worth the farmer's while to assume the responsibilities of storage.

An arrangement of this kind would readily take care of any problem of maintaining the quality of the stored grain, for it would then be a very simple matter for the farmer to replace old corn by new corn every year or two. There is a peculiar fitness in the concept of having the largest component of the commodity unit maintained by the producers themselves at various points of production. While the Reservoir system is in essence completely impersonal, a wholesome exception may be made in the field of storage in order to establish some modicum of personal contact between the reservoir mechanism and the farmers who are its chief beneficiaries. There may also be some sentimental or symbolical value in reestablishing the old verity of the well-stocked granary on countless farms as a visible and trustworthy sign of national abundance. But in any event the saving in dollar cost of storage will be of major benefit.

Wheat storage is not fully practicable upon the farm and requires suitable structures of the elevator type.[2] While the standard charge to commodity-exchange customers appears to be 18 cents per bushel per annum, the regular commercial rates for the trade are stated as 12 cents per bushel.[3] The recently published report of the President's Committee on Crop Insurance deals briefly with the cost of storing wheat in substantial quantity—which is an integral part of the committee's concrete proposal. The opinion is expressed, based on conferences with warehousemen, that in a large-scale storage project the regular commercial charges can be cut in half.[4]

To minimize the cost of storing products such as petroleum, tobacco and sugar the cooperation of the large processors could readily be enlisted, for these enterprises will be benefited by increased stability in the price of their raw material. Undoubtedly the sugar refiners have surplus storage facilities available at small cost, and with the added advantage of facilitating frequent rotation to preserve the quality. A like arrangement can undoubtedly be made with the large tobacco manufacturers, who store enormous quantities of leaf for periods of years.[5] The same holds true for the producers and refiners of petroleum who own a huge amount of tankage. That petroleum may be stored without undue deterioration for many years, if proper facilities are available, is shown by the experience of Stanolind Oil Company which held for over 13 years the major portion of some 20 million barrels of oil placed in storage in Wyoming between 1921 and 1923.[6]

Viewed from the practical angle it seems evident that storage on a comprehensive scale should not involve a high rate of expense. The physical requisites for storage are exceedingly simple. For most products all that is needed is a substantial building and watchmen. The country is replete with obsolete manufacturing plants and other unused structures which could be acquired at nominal cost and converted into warehouses. There is no dearth of unemployed available as watchmen; and even if unemployment were no longer a problem, this simple type of occupation would be socially useful for many who are unsuited to other work. Since the commodities will be stored at many separate points, the fire hazard and other risks will be widely spread, permitting the project to carry its own insurance. The average actual losses are certain to be very small, especially since there will be a minimum of human activity about the storage structures.

The writer has not had the opportunity to make an exhaustive study of the storage problems involved in the Reservoir plan. He feels justified, however, in venturing the statement that large-scale storage of commodity units can be effected, by one device or another, at a dollar cost not exceeding 3½ per cent per annum of the value of the stored units, as indicated by the estimates presented in Table II. In any event it would be entirely feasible to limit the cost to the government to 3 per cent, or a smaller figure, by requiring the producers of any commodity to bear that portion of its storage expense which exceeds, say, 3 per cent of its average value. Arrangements of this kind could be worked out with the producers, e.g., for corn; or the processors, e.g., for sugar; or with the commodity exchanges, which would have a vital interest in having their various products included in the unit.

Assuming a 3 per cent average storage expense and an average holding of five billion dollars of commodity units, the entire cost of the scheme would approximate 150 millions annually.

This cost may be offset by various types of income arising from the operation of the Reservoir plan. There is, first, the possibility of initial acquisition of commodity units at less than their standard dollar value. Secondly, a "seigniorage" may be collected in connection with the issuance and redemption of the commodity-backed currency. Finally, there will be opportunities to replace the physical or "spot" commodities in storage by futures contracts, when the latter are selling at a discount.

The first two of these features are a matter of discretionary choice in setting up our system. If our plan had been put into operation at the time it was first published, early in 1933, it would have been possible to acquire commodity units at a large discount from their 1921–1930 value.[7] Undoubtedly a sufficient "profit" would have been realized through that procedure to take care of the storage costs for an indefinite time in the future. If we choose to delay the inauguration of the Reservoir system until the next severe recession in commodity prices, we could undoubtedly establish a substantial initial profit to be used for subsequent expenditure.

Seigniorage charges are a time-honored method of defraying the cost of coining money. Upon delivery of the precious metal to the mint the owner is paid slightly less than its monetary value. (An extension, or rather abuse, of the seigniorage idea is found in our present practice as regards silver, under which the government coins silver at $1.29 per ounce, but pays the producers 77.6 cents and pockets the difference under the heading of "seigniorage."[8]) It is entirely practicable to establish a seigniorage charge in connection with the coinage of commodity units, to be applied toward the cost of storage. Such a charge would be equivalent to a differential between the "buying" and "selling" price of commodity units and would in turn establish upper and lower limits for the value of the commodity units in the markets. This would correspond to the former "gold-shipment points" in foreign exchange, which set bounds to the fluctuations of the pound in terms of the dollar.

A seigniorage charge as high as, say, 3 per cent, with a corresponding range of fluctuation in the price level, could be imposed without detracting seriously from the stabilizing features of the Reservoir plan. To what extent such income and such price variations should be provided for is entirely a matter of judgment. The writer is inclined to the view that it would be better to sacrifice the seigniorage profit to the principle of maintaining the dollar value of the commodity unit invariable.

In Chap. V we commented upon the unusual relationship recently existing between the spot and the futures prices for many of the commodities in our unit. From Table X in the Appendix it would appear that a very large profit could have been realized, were our Reservoir system in operation, by selling spot products out of the reservoir and replacing them by contracts for future delivery at a much lower price. It is not to be expected, of course, that an unlimited quantity of the stored commodities could have been replaced by futures at the wide differentials then existing. But the Reservoir system could undoubtedly realize a substantial cash profit from exchanges of this sort on occasion; besides saving storage expense on the products sold and also helping to relieve a tight situation in the commodity markets.

To summarize the foregoing discussion, we may think of the *gross* cost of the Reservoir plan as somewhere in the neighborhood of 150 millions per year, against which considerable offsets may be expected from various sources. If our conception of the advantages of the Reservoir system has any validity, the item of cost assumes very minor proportions. For we are proposing, through this outlay, to transform surplus production of raw materials from a source of national disaster into a bulwark of national strength and well-being; to prevent the recurrent disorganization of our economic structure and the paradox of want amidst plenty; to introduce a high degree of stability into the price level and into general business; and to create both an abundance of material resources and a means of administering them in such wise as to produce a steadily improving standard of living for all the people of this land.

The money cost of the Reservoir plan literally fades into insignificance when it is compared with the financial burden which the great depression imposed upon the nation. This toll is staggering enough if measured by the governmental outlays it necessitated, or by the ensuing increase in federal debt.[9] A still more stupendous figure is reached if we take as the cost of the depression the shrinkage it created in the national income since 1930.[10]

A more modest comparison may be made between the probable cost of the Reservoir plan and the expenditures to which the government is still committed by reason of the depression. Looking forward to the Treasury's fiscal year ending in June 1938—fully five years after beginning of the upswing—the President's budget message still indicates that recovery and relief expenditures will exceed two billion dollars.[11]

If the monetary storage of basic commodities is a sound attack upon the twin problems of excess production and a deficient purchasing power, the cost of such storage must surely be viewed as relatively inconsequential.

PART III

Monetary Aspects of the Reservoir Plan

"There must be provision for an adequate but sound currency."

—President Franklin D. Roosevelt
Inaugural Address, Mar. 4, 1933

"The ladies could not, for a long time, comprehend what the merchants did with the small pieces of gold and silver, or why things of so little use should be received as the equivalent of the necessities of life."

—Samuel Johnson
Rasselas, Chap. XVI

Chapter X

THE CURRENCY OF THE UNITED STATES

"All forms of money issued or coined by the United States shall be maintained at a parity."

—48 U.S. Statutes, 113

OUR study of the possibilities of conserving surplus has led us to advance a proposal which is first and foremost a Reservoir system for impounding and releasing basic commodities. Because of the special character of the mechanism proposed, we find that it can be made self-liquidating through a monetary feature. It is to this monetary aspect that our discussion will now be addressed. For thoroughgoing treatment we must consider the essential character of the commodity-backed currency, its relationship to other currency of the United States, its effect upon the country's credit structure and its bearing upon the foreign exchanges.

Before we treat of the proposed new currency, it may be well to consider briefly the rather heterogeneous present currency structure of our country in its relation to certain underlying characteristics of currency generally. We shall not attempt a comprehensive survey of a subject that has been investigated so often and at such length, but we shall confine ourselves to certain elements that are particularly relevant to our proposal.

On June 30, 1937 there was United States currency in circulation aggregating over $6,400,000,000. It consisted of 10 different varieties, not counting gold coins which still exist but are no longer in circulation. Following are the names and amounts of our different kinds of money:

KINDS OF MONEY IN CIRCULATION,[1] JUNE 30, 1937
Millions of dollars

Gold certificates	$ 88
Silver dollars	38
Silver certificates	1,078
Treasury notes of 1890	1
Subsidiary silver	341
Minor coin	144
United States notes	281
Federal Reserve notes	4,169
Federal Reserve bank notes	38
National bank notes	269
Total	$6,447

Let us briefly describe the nature of each of these various currencies, including a reference to the now invisible gold pieces.

1. Gold Coin

Gold pieces of various denominations contain 23.22 gr. of pure gold (25.8 gr. nine-tenths fine) for each dollar they represent. As the result of the devaluation of the dollar in 1933[2] the gold coins are now worth more than their face value in dollars. The various developments affecting gold coins may be summarized as follows:

a. The gold in these coins is now worth in the markets of the world about $1.70 for each dollar of face amount.

b. Ownership of gold coins by American citizens and residents is illegal. They must be surrendered to the Treasury in exchange for other currency at the old rate.[3]

c. Since the value of gold may be changed from time to time at the discretion of the President, there is now no basis on which the United States may issue gold coins. Hence all the old gold coins which have come into the possession of the government have been melted down into bullion (gold bars).[4]

A number of gold coins of the United States are undoubtedly still held here and abroad. But since their face value is no longer representative of their true value, they can no longer be regarded as currency. They are now in fact only small ingots of gold. For this reason the official statement of United States currency now outstanding does not give any figure for gold coin, even though the amount of such coins in existence might be susceptible of estimate.

2. *Gold Certificates*

This is paper currency which states that an equivalent amount of gold coin is held for the account of the owner of the certificate and is payable to him on demand. Gold certificates have been viewed as "warehouse receipts" or "trust receipts" for gold, and were intended to represent merely a convenient method of handling gold currency.[5]

Coincident with the devaluation and nationalization of gold in 1933, American holders of gold certificates were required by law to surrender them in exchange for other money, in the same manner as gold coins.[6] Gold certificates held abroad are not subject to confiscation, of course, but their owners now have no rights except to exchange them for dollars at the reduced gold value.

It is clear that gold certificates have not worked out as the exact equivalent of gold coin—which they were once thought to be—since foreign holders of United States gold coins are 70 per cent better off than foreign holders of gold certificates.

Some 8900 million dollars of gold certificates are held by the Federal Reserve banks, and constitute their chief asset.[7] These certificates have taken the place of the physical gold originally held by the banks, but delivered to the United States Treasury in 1933 in exchange for gold certificates. About half of the certificates are technically deposited with Federal Reserve agents as collateral for Federal Reserve notes outstanding.

3. *Silver Dollars*

These contain 412.5 grains of silver, nine-tenths fine, equivalent to a bullion value of $1.29 per ounce.

4. *Silver Certificates*

These are similar to gold certificates in that they are issued as receipts for physical silver held on deposit in the Treasury. They may still be freely exchanged for metallic silver dollars.

5. *Treasury Notes of* 1890

These are the small residue of a currency issued in connection with the government's silver purchase policy of some half-century ago. They have been in process of retirement, being replaced by silver certificates.

6. *Subsidiary Silver*

These are our dimes, quarters and half-dollars. They differ intrinsically from silver dollars because they have a lower metal content: 385.8 grains, nine-tenths fine, to the dollar, equivalent to a value of about $1.38 per ounce of silver.

7. *Minor Coin*

Our one-cent and five-cent pieces are made of copper, nickel, and other base metals, with an intrinsic value of but a small fraction of their nominal or face value.

8. *United States Notes*

These are the remainder of the "greenbacks," issued during the Civil War as fiat money without backing of any sort. They are now secured by a gold fund of some 156 million dollars held in the Treasury. Under the Thomas Amendment to the Farm Act of 1933, the President was authorized, if he deemed it necessary, to issue three billion dollars of additional United States notes, or greenbacks.[8] None has been issued to date under this authorization.

9. Federal Reserve Notes

These are obligations of the United States and also of the Federal Reserve banks. At the present time they are secured 100 per cent by deposit of gold certificates with the Federal Reserve agents as trustees. Originally they were intended to be secured in part (not less than 40 per cent) by deposit of gold and as to the remainder by deposit of "eligible," self-liquidating commercial paper.[9] By this means an elastic currency was to be provided, which would expand and contract with the growth and decline of commercial borrowings. The Glass-Steagall Act of 1932 permitted United States obligations to be used as part security for the notes in lieu of commercial paper.[10] Under present conditions it does not appear likely that commercial paper will enter to any controlling extent into the creation and retirement of Federal Reserve notes.

10. Federal Reserve Bank Notes

These were originally an intermediate form of currency, backed by United States government bonds and issued in connection with the early operations of the Federal Reserve system. By 1932 nearly all of them had been retired. Under the Emergency Banking Act of 1933 the Reserve banks were empowered to issue these notes against pledge of various kinds of banking assets. An appreciable amount of Federal Reserve bank notes were issued at that time.[11]

11. National Bank Notes

These were obligations of the National banks and of the United States. They were secured by deposit of certain kinds of government bonds and by a gold redemption fund of not less than 5 per cent of the issue.[12] In 1935 the bond issues securing this currency were retired;[13] other currency was deposited as security in lieu of the bonds; and the National bank notes, like the Treasury notes of 1890, are now being withdrawn from circulation as rapidly as they find their way into the banks or the Treasury.

Even from the above foreshortened account the reader can hardly fail to be impressed by the extreme variety of our present forms of currency, and by the frequent innovations and changes in our monetary structure. The last four years in particular have witnessed a complete metamorphosis of the status of gold, a radically different silver policy than heretofore,[14] the projected retirement of all the National bank notes, a new authorization of Federal Reserve bank notes— and finally the authorization (not yet availed of) of an enormous issue of unsecured or greenback currency.

For a better understanding of the numerous varieties of United States currency, we suggest that all currency may be classified into three kinds: physical or intrinsic currency, self-liquidating currency and fiduciary currency. Physical currency is supposed to obtain all its value from the material of which it consists or for which it is directly and unquestionably exchangeable. Self-liquidating currency is issued under such conditions that it may be depended upon to be retired in the normal course of business if such retirement is desired. Fiduciary currency obtains its value from the good faith and credit of the issuer, so that maintenance of this value depends upon the financial policies of the issuer. A given variety of currency may represent a mixture of more than one of these three basic types.

Gold and Gold Certificates

At the moment the United States has no true intrinsic or physical currency. When gold and gold certificates were in circulation they evidently met our definition of physical money. This definition says that physical money "is supposed to obtain all its value from the material, etc." The word "supposed" is used because there may now be some doubt whether the intrinsic value of gold is really equal to its monetary value. That question will be considered in more detail later.

Scepticism is justified also as to whether gold certificates may again qualify as intrinsic money. They once were considered as "directly and unquestionably" exchangeable for the deposited gold. But this "unquestionable" privilege has been suspended twice within 20 years—the first time, unavowedly but nonetheless emphatically, during the war;[15] the second time, without pretense or apology, during the depression. Strictly speaking it may be claimed that from now on the value of gold certificates will depend, just as does the value of greenbacks, upon the good faith and sound policies of the government.

Silver and Silver Certificates

These forms of currency would be similar to gold and gold certificates (on their old basis) if the intrinsic value of silver were considered to be $1.29 per ounce, which is the coinage value of the silver dollar (or a somewhat higher figure in the case of subsidiary silver coins). But since the world price of silver is only about a third of this coinage value, and since it has been well below $1.29 per ounce for the last 50 years (except in 1919–1920),[16] it is clear that the coinage value given to silver by the United States government is in large measure arbitrary and artificial.

Our various kinds of silver money must therefore be considered as physical money only to a minor degree, and as fiduciary money in respect to the major portion of their value.

Minor Coin

In view of the small intrinsic value of these 1-cent and 5-cent pieces, they must be regarded as fiduciary currency in essence.

United States Notes

These were originally fiduciary currency *par excellence.* There is now a gold "coverage" of about 40 per cent of the total issue,[17] which would seem to give them some partial characteristics of intrinsic currency.

Federal Reserve Notes

The original combination of a 40 per cent gold coverage with a 60 per cent coverage of high-grade commercial paper made this currency uniquely self-liquidating. A contraction of business borrowings would normally result in the retirement of part of this currency out of the proceeds of the repayment of the deposited commercial paper.

At the present time the Federal Reserve notes are secured almost exclusively by deposit of gold certificates, into which, however, they are not convertible. The gold certificates in turn are secured by deposit of metallic gold into which they, too, are not convertible (except at the pleasure of the Treasury). For a time between 1933 and 1936 it was the announced policy of the Treasury to permit the banks to exchange gold certificates for metallic gold if exports of the latter were needed to maintain the new gold value of the dollar in foreign exchange. Under the new "three-power agreement" accompanying the devaluation of the franc, it appears that necessary gold exports will be handled only by the Treasury.[18] At this writing, therefore, there seems to be no convertibility of any of our currency into gold, except in operations of the government itself.

The question may well be asked, what is the real nature of currency secured by assets into which it is not convertible?

If the assets will in due course of business be turned into cash, and if the proceeds will be adequate and actually used for the retirement of the currency, then the currency is *self-liquidating*, by our definition. Such currency, while not convertible in the proper sense, is nonetheless perfectly sound. But if the currency is neither convertible nor self-liquidating, it must be considered as *fiduciary* in character regardless of the value of the assets deposited or "pledged" to secure it. The French assignats belonged in this category.[19] When first issued in 1790, it was claimed that they were absolutely sound because they were "backed" by State-owned lands worth far more than the currency emitted. But the holder of the assignats could not exchange them for or convert them into the pledged land, nor was there adequate provision for the sale of the land to retire the issue. The value of this currency depended at bottom, therefore, on the *good faith* of the republic in refraining from an over-issue of assignats. By our definition, therefore, this was fiduciary currency from the very start. As it happened, France continued to emit assignats until the "backing" in land ceased to have any meaning, and the currency lost all its value.

Similar reasoning compels the conclusion that money backed by gold *into which it is not convertible* is essentially fiduciary in character. It would seem at first that if a currency issue were covered 100 per cent by a specific gold fund, —as our Federal Reserve notes at present—it would make no practical difference if the holder of the currency could not get his gold in exchange. The gold would still be there as a "guarantee" of the value of the currency. But the fallacy of this viewpoint lies in the fact that if the currency is inconvertible we cannot soundly assume that the gold coverage is irrevocably and inviolably set aside for the benefit of the currency holders. For if that were so there would be no point at all in making the currency inconvertible. The suspension of convertibility of a 100 per cent backed paper currency must mean one of two things: either a dilution or confiscation of the gold backing is in prospect or else the holders of this paper currency may be compelled to surrender it for some other currency without 100 per cent gold backing.

Our argument may seem more convincing when applied to inconvertible currency secured by less than 100 per cent in gold, but the principle is the same in either case. It should be recognized therefore *that all the currency of the United States is on a fiduciary basis,* and that it will remain on that basis until an unquestionable convertibility into some medium of tangible value is again established.

The currency envisaged by our plan, which will be convertible into pledged basic commodities, would certainly seem to have a strong theoretical superiority to our present 10 different varieties of currency, all of which are in great part, at least, of a fiduciary nature. It may be thought, however, that in a comparatively short time it will be possible to reestablish our old gold standard, involving unlimited convertibility of all paper money into gold. Such an arrangement would be considered by many as highly desirable; and it may be objected that our commodity-backed currency proposal would hinder its adoption and thus be objectionable. We must consider therefore the relationship between our currency proposal and the maintenance of a (now nonexistent) gold standard. As a preliminary thereto some thought should be given to the present status of gold and silver.

Chapter XI

THE STATUS OF GOLD AND SILVER

"Gold and silver in short seemed to be the only things in Cuzco
that were not wealth."
—Prescott[1]

MEASURED by its purchasing power, gold commands
a higher price today in the markets of the world than
it has for generations. It would seem a fair inference that
the position of gold—as a commodity, or a monetary medium,
or both—is stronger now than ever before. The facts, however, are quite otherwise. The utility, or intrinsic value, of
gold as a commodity is now considerably less than in the
past; its monetary status has become extraordinarily
ambiguous; and its future is highly uncertain.

There is thus a contradiction between the superficial and
underlying status of gold today. This anomaly has been
created in turn by the paradoxical economic policies pursued
by nations generally during the depression. Let us summarize
briefly the developments of recent years which, in our
opinion, have undermined the real position of gold at the
same time that its apparent value has been enhanced.

Gold was first merely a commodity, then a commodity
with special utility as money, then a monetary medium
with special value as a commodity and, finally, a monetary
"device" with negligible utility either as a commodity or as
actual money. The histories of money tell us that gold was
greatly prized for itself before it was used as money.[2] Its
adoption as a circulating medium recognized but did not at
first appreciably enhance its high intrinsic value, which

arose chiefly from its ornamental qualities combined with its scarcity. Gold was, and undoubtedly still is, well adapted to use as coin. Hence as the trade of the world increased the usefulness of gold as money must be regarded as having added not a little to the value it possessed for other reasons. Up to comparatively recently, economists were justified in holding that gold possessed a high intrinsic value for a composite reason, and that it was not possible to separate out the monetary and non-monetary components of this value.

During the past century the functions of gold underwent a gradual transformation, the significance of which was scarcely realized. Its utility increased in some directions and decreased in others. On the one hand, it became a sort of super-money, with power to lend validity to large amounts of secondary moneys which were tied to and dependent upon gold. These were paper moneys of various sorts—United States notes, Federal Reserve notes, etc.,—and also, far more important in this country, demand deposits in banks. (While there are technical distinctions between demand deposits and paper currency, the underlying monetary status of the two is substantially identical.) These moneys were popularly accepted at par, first, because they were backed by gold holdings in an amount considered adequate, and secondly because the holders of such money could exchange it freely for gold at any time.

The second added utility of gold came from its employment as stabilizer of foreign-exchange rates. By a combination of gold shipments between countries and a manipulation of the central bank rediscount rates, it was possible to keep the relative values of important currencies virtually constant; and this was of considerable benefit in promoting foreign trade.

Both of these added uses were ingenious devices for multiplying the utility of a given quantity of gold—devices necessitated, at bottom, by the fact that in the past century the volume of money and money equivalents (bank deposits) tended to expand at a greater rate than the gold supply.[3]

But while the technical utility of gold in the monetary field was increasing, its utility in other directions was definitely diminished. For one thing, its use as ordinary hand-to-hand money contracted steadily. Other forms of money proved just as reliable and more convenient. Their reliability was derived in principle from their relation to gold, but as far as the habits of the American people were concerned, paper money and the check book virtually supplanted the gold piece. (The same was true, but to a somewhat lesser extent, in other leading countries.) This tendency was accelerated by the World War, which drove gold out of circulation practically everywhere. With the return of "normalcy" in the postwar period, it was possible for gold to return to the pockets of the people—but there was then no desire for it.

The disappearance of gold from ordinary circulation was due not only to the acceptance of paper, but also to another vitally important development: the loss of interest by people generally in the ornamental qualities of gold. Gold plate, gold adornments, heavy gold watch chains have become less and less popular and fashionable among those "advanced" nations whose monetary policies are important.[4] The use of gold in industry has not expanded in any significant degree. The lure of gold for its appearance's sake, on which its original monetary value was securely founded, has ceased to be a controlling factor in its status. Gold is coveted for what it will buy, not for how it looks. Hence even the aesthetic or covetous pleasure that people used to find in handling gold coins seems largely to have disappeared.[5]

By 1929, therefore, gold had become an immensely important factor in an elaborate currency and banking mechanism, but it had lost a great part of its age-old double utility as a source of aesthetic satisfaction and as a physical medium for carrying on business transactions.

When the great depression broke over the world, gold proved unequal to the strains imposed upon it, and it could not continue to function either as the guarantor of paper-money values or as the stabilizer of the foreign exchanges. By the nature of the case, these functions could not stand up under violent stress. Permanent parity between paper and gold depends on convertibility in some form or another; convertibility can be maintained only when the desire to convert is limited. This was evidently true in 1929 since there were $14 of bank deposits, supposedly withdrawable in gold, for each dollar of actual gold in the country.[6]

Similarly the maintenance of foreign-exchange parities by means of free international gold movements presupposed that international debit balances could be kept within reasonable limits. The system could not operate in the face of huge and irresponsible movements of liquid capital, i.e., bank deposits, from one financial center to another, requiring offsetting shipments of enormous quantities of gold.[7]

We must recognize an important distinction, therefore, between the two early uses and the two later functions of gold. The value of gold as ornament, during the time of its ascendancy, was direct and unconditional. Similarly with the use of gold coin as ordinary money. But the usefulness of gold as backing for larger quantities of other money, or money equivalents, and as stabilizer of foreign exchanges was dependent upon certain conventions being observed within the financial system. Hence, while the newer utilities of gold may have been more important to the welfare of the world than the old ones which were disappearing, the transformation really meant the replacement of primary and unassailable qualities by derived and vulnerable ones.

During the World War conversions into gold were suspended here without official confession, but accepted as a matter of course.[8] It was not expected that an essentially artificial arrangement could be maintained under conditions of unprecedented stress. Nor was there much reason to question the future workability of the gold standard because of that failure; for at that time we were optimistic enough to view the war conditions as completely abnormal and outside the pale of recurrent human experience.

Many people may feel that the breakdown of the gold standard between 1931 and 1936 is a similarly abnormal, temporary and nonrecurrent phenomenon. Once the currency realignments are completed and suitable international agreements are reached, it will be possible, they say, to go back on a definite gold standard and stick to it permanently. Whether or not this is so must be a matter of opinion. But surely there are ominous reasons for regarding this view more as a pious hope than an inescapable conclusion. Neither the prospects for continued peace nor the probabilities of avoiding another cataclysmic depression are sufficiently encouraging to permit us to talk of "normal conditions" in the future with the same rather naïve confidence that characterized our postwar attitudes.

This realization is shared by the most influential friends of the gold standard. Eager as they are for a return to a fixed value of currency in terms of gold, the gold standard they now advocate is something quite different from the mechanism of predepression days. Free convertibility of currency—and therefore of bank deposits—into gold is recognized as a standing invitation to monetary disturbance. It is suggested therefore that gold continue to be completely retired from circulation and that it no longer be deliverable in exchange for paper currency. Except for the relatively small demands of the arts, the uses of gold are to be restricted to forming the metallic reserves of the central banks and to settling international balances.[9]

Just how would this modified type of gold standard function in practice? The price of gold to the mines, in terms of paper money, would be established, as before, by the willingness of the Treasury to issue a fixed amount of paper money for each ounce of gold tendered to it. But this exchangeability would be a one-way affair; it would not be similarly possible, as formerly it was, to tender a given amount of paper money in exchange for an ounce of gold. (Exceptions would be made, as at present, for the needs of dentists, goldsmiths, etc.) What, then, would assure the value of this inconvertible paper currency? The answer is, the maintenance of a minimum relationship, prescribed by law, between the quantity of gold held by the central banks or the Treasury and the total of currency and of bank deposits outstanding. Of the two former safeguards of the value of paper money, viz., free convertibility and the maintenance of a minimum gold reserve, the first would be suspended but the second would be retained.

In the international field, the old machinery of free gold shipments would be substantially restored, except that the transfers would take place only from one central bank to another. It would not be expected, however, that all the annual merchandise-and-service balances would be defrayed by gold shipments, since they might readily be offset by international-security transactions or by short-term credits. Presumably there would not be so much reason as heretofore to fear irresponsible flights of liquid capital from one center to another, for in no center would it be possible to exchange these bank deposits for gold.

This proposed improvement in the gold standard would undoubtedly work better than the old model, and in our opinion there is a fair chance of its being adopted. It would be quite similar to the arrangements actually obtaining in the United States at the present time. The only important changes needed would be the withdrawal of the President's discretionary power[10] to vary the gold value of the dollar between 50 and 60 cents and a mandatory direction to the Treasury—instead of its present discretionary *right*—to ship gold to central banks abroad when necessary to maintain the foreign-exchange parities of the dollar.[11]

If we seek to appraise the true significance of such a modified gold standard we shall see that its superior powers of resistance will be gained by the sacrifice of most of its tangible contacts with the lives of the people. Gold becomes an invisible, almost legendary, hoard. Some minor driblets will find their way into the arts; but that vast national store, now valued at 12 billion dollars, will escape the touch, the sight and even the thought of those who possess it. Its very ownership, in fact, will be shrouded in ambiguity. No one can say with certainty who really owns the gold. Consigned to its underground repository at Fort Knox, Ky.,—far removed in distance and by law both from the bankers who were wont to hold it in substantial amounts and from the man in the street who once had a sentimental or aesthetic fondness for gold coins—that golden treasury becomes a concept to tease the thoughts of poets and philosophers. What a strange inversion of all the old legends! Midas amassed gold that he might feast his eyes and let his fingers play upon it; Fafnir became a dragon that he might center his whole existence upon guarding the Nibelung hoard that had come into his power. We now possess a miser's hoard more fabulous than that imagined in any tale; but it belongs at once to everyone and to no one. It excites no human emotions; it is as impersonal as a mathematical formula—into which, in fact, it appears to have been transformed.

The Martian observers, having noticed that small amounts of a yellow metal dug out of the bowels of the earth had been the cause of every possible crime and misfortune, will now conclude, no doubt, that mankind has repented of its fatal folly and has ordained that all the gold in the world must be returned to its former subterranean hiding places. Omar Khayyám spoke of "aureate earth . . . that buried once man wants dug up again." A modern poet would speak now of "aureate earth, that once dug up man buries yet again."

It is hard to avoid the conclusion that the status of gold is threatened with a *reductio ad absurdum*. We are witnessing before our eyes its transformation from physical into metaphysical money. One must not underestimate the importance of the metaphysical, even in economics. It may seem that gold has been promoted from mundane to higher uses. But like the ascension of Elijah, this translation may mean the end of its prophetic mission. Perhaps its mantle, like Elijah's also, will fall upon other shoulders.

The intriguing question remains, how is it that the market value of gold has been increasing precisely while its utility seems to have been diminishing? For the answer we must plunge once again into that wonderland of economic paradox created by the phenomenon of "depression through surplus." At the bottom of the depression the great need of the world seemed to be for higher prices for raw materials. Nonremunerative prices for primary products were recognized as the central element of the vicious spiral of deflation.[12] This involved lower prices for fabricated goods; lower employment, wages, purchasing power, production and consumption; increasing bankruptcies, foreclosures, bank failures and hoarding; and general industrial and financial demoralization. From the standpoint of an individual nation, the problem was how to sell more goods, at home and abroad, and at higher prices.

The "solution" was discovered, as if by accident, through England's being forced off gold in 1931. It is generally agreed that this step was taken reluctantly and by compulsion.

Yet it is generally agreed also that this same step proved highly beneficial to Britain, and gave it an important advantage over other nations. When the pound lost its fixed gold value, a new and variable open-market value was established, averaging some 30 per cent less than the old parity. The paper pound became substantially cheaper in terms of gold and in terms of the important foreign currencies still tied to gold. English manufacturers could sell goods abroad at lower foreign prices than previously and get a higher return in terms of pounds. Internal prices, as quoted in paper pounds, ceased their demoralizing decline—although on a gold basis they continued to fall in England as well as throughout the world generally. Britain's rather unexpected experience demonstrated that by reducing the value of paper money in terms of gold a nation could at the same time get higher prices for its goods at home and sell them at lower prices abroad—a double consummation devoutly to be wished.

The British devaluation was both involuntary and indefinite. No new and lower value for the pound was established by law; its relation to gold and other currencies was left at first to the tender mercies of the open market, later tempered by an ingenious new contrivance known as the Stabilization Fund. A year and a half later the United States improved upon the British example by devaluing the dollar both deliberately and definitely. The price of gold was officially raised from $20.6 to $35 per ounce, which meant that the gold content of the dollar was reduced by 41 per cent. The result was a rise in the internal price level in terms of these cheaper paper dollars,[13] and also a great benefit to our exporters who could now afford to sell at lower prices in terms of foreign currencies.

There seems little doubt that the countries which devalued obtained a foreign-trade advantage over those who clung to the old parities; also that they had more success in turning the tide of internal deflation. After a struggle of more than three years to preserve the integrity of their currencies, the three chief "gold-standard countries"—France, Holland and Switzerland—were compelled in 1936 to join the rest of the world in devaluation.[14]

Hence all over the world an ounce of gold will buy more paper money and more commodities than it did before. But no one will assert that this is true because people attach a greater sentimental value to gold than they did before, or that a substantially greater *monetary need* has developed for the same quantity of gold, thus raising its monetary value in accordance with the law of supply and demand. The fact is that the rise in the price of gold had nothing to do with value or demand in the ordinary sense. It was an artifice or expedient resorted to by nations in order to produce a certain effect upon the price structure—absolutely, at home; comparatively, abroad. The currencies of the world, like so many Alices in Wonderland, have drunk out of the bottle labeled "Devaluation" in order to reduce their statures to more convenient dimensions.

We may view the same picture from a somewhat more fundamental angle, if we think of nations with a surplus of goods which they feel compelled to turn into money. Logically considered, there is no earthly reason why the money should be any more useful to the nations than the goods; but the tangle of creditor-debtor relationships needs money to unravel it rather than goods. (Money now has a special utility, *viz.*, the power to *settle debts*—which is something quite different from its essential property, *viz.*, the power to *purchase goods*.) To a nation in such a predicament the hocus-pocus of calling an ounce of gold $35 instead of $20 turns out to be a very useful piece of self-deception. We can now trade a $600 automobile for 17 ounces of gold instead of 30 ounces, and we can tell ourselves contentedly that we are getting the same price as before. If the essence of a good business deal is mutual satisfaction, advancing the price of gold is a masterpiece of business wizardry. The buyer gets far more than before for his little nugget of gold, and the seller is just as happy to get a little nugget as he was to get a big one. With these delightful advantages offered to both sides, trade cannot help but improve.

Absurd as all this sounds, its practical efficacy arises, of course, from the fact that we have more goods than we can successfully distribute, and hence almost any means of disposing of the surplus for a financial *quid pro quo* is welcomed as a solution. There is a close analogy here with the pre-1929 policy of lending huge sums abroad to permit the purchase of our export surplus. The foreign debts—and the rather similar installment-purchase obligations at home—created a nasty problem of repayment. When we stopped lending, our debtors stopped paying, and much financial havoc ensued. If we must trade a surplus for money, it does seem a simpler arrangement to take a small amount of gold in exchange and agree among ourselves to *call it* a large amount of money. Of course this means *giving away* our "surplus" in good part, instead of using it and enjoying it; but this device, ridiculous as it seems at bottom, at least has the merit of ameliorating a still more ridiculous situation, *viz.*, the collapse of our business structure beneath an abundance of goods.

As an economic expedient, advancing the price of gold has obvious limitations. It is useful as an internal measure only when the process of deflation has reached a critical stage and the time is ripe for injecting a new psychological factor that will turn the mind of the people inflationward. The external advantages are entirely of a *competitive* sort. The benefit accrues to the nations that devalue at the expense of those who do not. It disappears when all have devalued equally. Attempts to regain the lost advantage through further devaluation are surcharged with possibilities of an international "currency warfare" as unsettling and ominous in its effects as it is absurd and fatuous in its essence.[15] Certainly nothing could be weirder from the standpoint of rational economics than the concept that nations can derive real and lasting benefits from a progressive deterioration of their currencies.

The rise in the price of gold is seen, therefore, to have grown out of the development of two new and quite anomalous functions for the yellow metal: as a *weapon* in international trade and as a *manipulative factor* in dealing with depression. With the return of currency stabilization—an event greatly desired by nearly all economists—these "uses" of gold will disappear. There would then remain two "normal" uses of gold: (*a*) as a sort of international banking ballast, to be shifted from one center to another when needed to keep the foreign exchanges on an even keel, and (*b*) as an invisible governor of the domestic-credit structure, operating by means of arbitrarily established and computed "reserve ratios." The latter function will be discussed concisely in our chapter on credit controls. Neither of these contemplated standard functions of gold bears any close resemblance to the historic sources of its value. There is a third possible use for a nation's hoard of gold, *viz.*, as a war chest. One cannot help but raise the question whether the possession of a few thousand tons of gold will carry with it any assurance to a belligerent nation of ability to meet the insatiable demands of modern warfare for food and munitions.[16]

During recent months widespread doubts and fears have developed with regard to the intrinsic value and position of gold. We have been experiencing a "gold scare" of an unprecedented kind. Instead of apprehending a shortage of gold and a loss of value of our paper money in terms of the precious metal, we are now afraid that the world is producing too much gold,[17] that the United States is taking in too large a part of it, that we are paying too high a price for it, and that our huge accumulated supply will turn out to be relatively useless and burdensome.

The ostensible reason for this recent uneasiness is that under our "sterilization policy"[18] the government must borrow to pay for gold imports, so that the more gold we receive the more it will cost the United States in interest charges. Actually this burden is not heavy enough to warrant *in itself* any great concern as regards our gold accretions. (The short-term money rate of about 1 per cent per annum means that the government can carry a full billion dollars of sterilized gold at a cost of some 10 million dollars per year.)

Undoubtedly the true cause of this popular apprehension is not the relatively minor interest burden (which we can avoid easily enough by other means if we wish),[19] but rather the fear that the gold we are buying in the markets of the world may prove to be of no real value to us. This underlying uneasiness is well illustrated in the following quotation from an editorial published on Apr. 19, 1937, in that citadel of financial orthodoxy, the *Wall Street Journal:* "For the first time since the discovery of gold by man, we have what looks like the beginning of a possible doubt concerning his attitude towards it as the one ultimate form of wealth. With the earth perspiring gold at an unprecedented rate, with gold coin disappearing from use as currency and piling up in government vaults, will man continue to treasure it as he has done from the dawn of human history?"

In similar vein we find the chairman of Rand Mines, the world's largest gold producer, voicing this serious doubt as to the situation of his own product: "How long will governments continue to absorb gold in excess of their requirements?"[20]

As far as the United States is concerned our gold policy seems to involve us in an awkward dilemma. If we are, in fact, taking in too much gold, and at too high a price, the obvious remedy is to reduce the buying price or to stop purchasing altogether. If we stop buying or reduce our buying price substantially, it seems certain that the price of gold will fall severely in the markets of the world. This decline would mean in turn a considerable loss in the dollar value of our gigantic holdings of gold. Furthermore, it would probably precipitate a severe recession in the price of commodities and securities, create an unwanted advance in the foreign-exchange value of the dollar and introduce new difficulties in carrying out the three-power agreement for so-called currency stabilization.

On the other hand, if we maintain the present gold price we may ultimately find ourselves owning so large a portion of the world's gold that other nations will learn to do without it.[21] This prospect is genuinely alarming, because it is now realized that the value of gold arises largely, if not chiefly, from international convention. If other nations should decide to ship us annually a billion dollars' worth of newly mined gold, for which they themselves profess to have no desire, we should soon be convinced that we were getting by far the worst of the bargain, and we may find ourselves viewing our mound of gold with the same misgivings as we displayed towards the foreign I.O.U.'s that we accumulated in such enormous volume prior to 1929. The determining feature of a valorization scheme is that the commodity is bought not because the buyer wants it but because he fears the consequences if he fails to buy. Judged by this test, the present gold purchasing policy of the United States appears to be a valorization operation in exactly the same sense as were the Brazilian Coffee schemes or the Federal Farm Board acquisitions.

THE STATUS OF SILVER

The confusion of motives and functions that has attended the gold policies of the nations is manifest to an even greater degree in the developments affecting silver. Rather ironically, the devoted advocates of the gold standard are quite contemptuous of the monetary value of silver. In fact they criticize silver in terms that are likely to be applied more and more insistently to the yellow metal which they espouse. It will suffice for our purpose if we summarize briefly some of the contradictory aspects of the status of silver.

Silver is somewhat more useful in the industrial arts than gold—at least, when relative cost is taken into account. Its ornamental appeal is certainly smaller; but this is now a minor factor in the case of both metals. From the monetary standpoint, silver has no definite status anywhere in the world. There is no important country on a silver standard, either by itself or in conjunction with gold. Nevertheless, silver has a long monetary history, dating from times when it outranked gold in importance (though never in value per ounce) as a medium of exchange.[22] The white metal is used everywhere as *subsidiary* coin—a function derived from its original acceptance as a primary store of wealth. It still has this underlying appeal for millions in the Orient; but as far as the Western World is concerned silver now carries very little personal interest of any kind. A silver coin has hardly any different significance for Americans than a coin of copper or nickel. It is the stamp, not the metal, that gives it its value.

Despite the almost complete disappearance here of the popular appeal of silver as a monetary metal, it is now more strongly entrenched than for generations past in the country's financial structure. The reasons for this contradiction are, first, that silver offers a convenient medium for a disguised inflation and, second, that the representatives of the silver-producing states have been particularly persistent and skillful in promoting its cause. Silver is in small part *intrinsic* currency and in greater part *fiduciary* currency; but most of all it is *political* currency.

The Silver Purchase Act of 1934 authorizes and directs the Treasury to purchase silver at home and abroad until the monetary value of our silver holdings and circulation equals one-third the value of our gold supply.[23] The Treasury has been carrying out this policy in three different ways. All private holdings of silver were taken over at 50.01 cents per ounce by Executive Order dated Aug. 9, 1934. All newly mined silver has been purchased at the price first of 64.6 cents per ounce, then at 71.1 cents, and now at 77.6 cents. Finally, large amounts of foreign silver have been acquired in the open market. The cost of this silver has averaged about 60 cents per ounce,[24] but during the period of acquisition the market price has ranged from 45 to 81 cents and back to 45 cents.

During the period from Dec. 31, 1933 to Jan. 31, 1937 the United States acquired a total of some 1188 million ounces.[25] Their average cost was about half of the arbitrarily assigned monetary value of $1.29 per ounce. These purchases may thus be made to yield the Treasury a neat "profit" of over 800 million dollars.[26] The program has been self-financing (though by no means self-liquidating). For from Dec. 31, 1933 to June 30, 1937 the government issued $671 millions in new silver certificates, which are just as acceptable as any other currency. Additional silver certificates of approximately the same amount could be issued at any time against free metallic silver now in the Treasury's possession.

One of the strong arguments of the silver advocates was the favorable effect of an advancing price of the metal upon the purchasing power of Oriental silver-using nations. Opponents of the policy claim that it has greatly injured instead of aiding the economies of these nations and has actually forced China off the silver standard and onto a managed paper-currency standard. It is scarcely necessary to go into the merits of this controversy. Few people are likely to believe that the soundness of our silver policy—involving the possible issuance of billions of dollars in currency—can depend in any serious degree upon financial developments in China and India.

The orthodox economists are undoubtedly right in their contention that our present silver policy is in both motive and effect primarily a disguised resort to greenbacks, *i.e.*, unsecured paper currency. When we issue $1.29 in paper or silver coin against an ounce of silver worth 45 cents in the markets of the world, we are in effect printing 84 cents of greenbacks together with 45 cents of silver-backed currency. The "unsecured component" of our silver money now far exceeds in volume the maximum amount of fiat currency emitted under the stress of the Civil War, which created the great greenback depreciation of the 1860's.[27]

Chapter XII

COMMODITY-BACKED VERSUS OTHER CURRENCY

"The admission of the principle that non-perishable staple commodities can be included in currency reserves to a limited extent would go a long way toward solving the world's monetary problems and also the present problem of surplus stocks."

—Dr. Paul Einzig[1]

THE discussion of the last two chapters should aid us in reaching a reasonable estimate of the intrinsic qualities and comparative status of the commodity-backed currency projected by our Reservoir plan. At the outset let us point out that ours is not a revolutionary proposal in the sense that it contemplates replacing our present currency structure by an entirely new kind of money. The currency resulting from the monetized commodity units will merely take its place besides the numerous other currencies now coexisting in our monetary system. Instead of ten different kinds of money, we shall have eleven—a change not in itself either striking or important.

There is a widespread opinion that a nation's currency is a highly sensitive mechanism, any tampering with which is likely to prove calamitous. The history of our money hardly confirms this view. On the contrary, it seems extraordinary how much tampering a monetary system can stand before loss of confidence creates an appreciable effect. For years Americans have carried around in their wallets a bewildering variety of paper currencies, with scarcely a realization and certainly no understanding of their differences. In the last three years the changes in our currency status have been kaleidoscopic and revolutionary. The abandonment of the orthodox gold standard; the cut in the gold content of the dollar; the authorization of an unlimited amount of currency secured by "banking assets," and the issuance of a sizable amount thereof; the further authorization, with no issuance so far, of three billion dollars in old-style fiat-money greenbacks; the actual greenbackery on a large scale involved in the silver-purchase program; the increase of money in circulation to unprecedented figures[2]—this well-nigh overwhelming combination of disturbing developments has had an incredibly slight effect upon the standing of our currency. The actual rise in the price level from March, 1933, to date is no greater than might have taken place in the ordinary process of recovery from deep depression.[3] Our paper dollar still buys considerably more than in 1929; on a gold basis, it buys far more than it did before the war.[4]

The powers of resistance shown by our paper money are little short of amazing. This may not prove altogether fortunate. There is more than a fanciful danger that the popular mind will become convinced that almost anything can be done to our currency with impunity. Advocates of fiat money—direct or disguised—will advance plausible theories to justify a progressive increase of our unsecured paper currency. Like the bull market of the late 1920's, such greenback-ism may be carried on successfully to an extreme where all the critics are confounded and the old natural laws seem to have been repealed. But the longer the inevitable is postponed the more inevitable it becomes—and the less expected. We often mistake the absence of warning signals for the absence of danger. We shall be lucky if, deceived by the strength of our currency, we do not stretch it to the breaking point.

This may seem like a strange warning to come from the proponent of a "new-fangled currency scheme." But it is the thesis of this chapter that the commodity-backed currency envisaged by our Reservoir plan will constitute "sound money" in the old-fashioned and conservative sense. In the conflict between "hard money" and "soft money," we are definitely on the side of hard money. In the conflict between a "managed currency" and an automatic currency, we are definitely on the side of an automatic, self-generating and self-liquidating currency, free of management and political pressure. Our currency belongs in the group represented by gold, the original Federal Reserve notes and (with serious reservations) silver. It is opposed to the group comprising unsecured currency, government-bond-secured currency and all "secured" currency where the intrinsic value of the security is definitely less than the money issued against it.

Whether currency secured by commodities is sound or not depends upon the details of its issuance. If the pledged security is worth less than the currency issued against it, the money is obviously deficient in soundness. (This is the patent weakness of the silver certificates with which the country has been flooded.) If the money is fully secured by a *single* commodity, however basic, there may still be some question as to its soundness; for a change in the status and the market price of that commodity may make inadequate a security which once was sufficient.

It is the virtue of our commodity unit that it may *soundly* create its own standard of value. We *define* the dollar as equivalent to the commodity unit, in the same way that it was formerly defined as equivalent to 23.22 grains of pure gold. The presence of this quantity of gold on deposit behind each gold certificate and the ability of the certificate owner to exchange it for the gold constituted the most definite assurance of the value of paper money with which we were familiar.

But while this gold-secured and convertible paper dollar was 100 per cent sound in the technical monetary sense, it suffered from a very serious practical weakness. This was, of course, its tendency to wide variations in purchasing power. The holder of paper money was not interested in gold *per se;* it was goods that he wanted, not gold. The gold backing was important as assurance that the paper money was more than mere paper—that its purchasing power could not vanish. But the extreme gyrations in its exchange value—the "dance of the dollar," as Irving Fisher called it—made the orthodox gold dollar a far from perfect medium of exchange or standard of value. Even had there arisen no problem of maintaining free convertibility of paper money into gold, the mercurial behavior of the gold dollar might eventually have compelled some reform of the currency base.[5]

Our commodity-backed currency has all the definiteness of the gold dollar, and in addition it will possess a considerable stability of purchasing power. Its convertibility into the composite group of basic commodities will mean *ipso facto* the stabilization of the price level for those commodities as a group—or, conversely, a fixed purchasing power for the dollar in terms of those commodities. As we pointed out above, price stability for this primary group is certain to carry with it a substantial measure of stability for other classes of commodities and services.

It does not seem an exaggeration to say of the commodity-backed dollar that it will be essentially sounder than the gold dollar. It will be more closely related to the things people want and use. Its value will not be based on convention or traditional acceptance, but on direct and everyday utilities. It will not run the risk of being manipulated into a magnificent desuetude. It will do the real job of money, *viz.,* to serve as a *stable* medium of exchange and of debt settlement.

This may be a suitable point to consider what will be the relationship between the commodity-unit currency and the gold standard. Does one exclude the other? Could we have a double standard for the dollar—in terms both of the commodity group and of gold?

The writer is firmly convinced that the *modernized* gold standard can easily be maintained in this country alongside of the commodity-unit currency system. In fact, even the old-fashioned, freely convertible gold standard could more readily be reestablished in the future with the Reservoir plan in operation than without it. The reason is, of course, that gold convertibility can be maintained only when economic conditions are fairly normal, *i.e.*, when little conversion is going on. The Reservoir system will be a powerful force making for normal business conditions; hence it will protect the gold standard from its own limitations.

The modernized gold standard is primarily a matter of maintaining fixed foreign-exchange ratios by means of international gold shipments. Hence a detailed discussion of this subject should be deferred to the chapter on the international aspects of the Reservoir plan. Similarly, the credit-control function of gold reserves will receive attention in the next chapter, on the Reservoir plan and control of credit.

If we assume the return of fairly normal general conditions, even the old-fashioned gold standard, involving free convertibility, could no doubt be reestablished, just as it was after the dislocations of the war had been patched up. (Whether it could be maintained indefinitely is another question.) The presence of the proposed commodity-backed currency should in no wise interfere with the operation of the unqualified gold standard. Prior to 1933 many different kinds of currency coexisted here, and all were maintained without difficulty on a par with each other and with gold. There is no reason to believe that any greater difficulties in this respect would follow from the advent of commodity-backed currency.[6]

The maintenance of the 1921–1930 price level is assuredly in no wise opposed to free convertibility into gold at $35 per ounce—70 per cent above its monetary value during the 1921–1930 period. Hence we are not faced with the old stumbling block of bimetallism, namely the excessive loss of gold that would flow from an unlimited offer to give gold for silver at a price for the latter far above its exchange value in the markets of the world.

Our present enormous holdings of gold suggest a possible variant of our plan, to give it a superficial resemblance to currency with which the country has already had considerable experience. It is quite feasible to provide that the commodity-unit currency shall be backed to the extent of 40 per cent by gold and the other 60 per cent by commodity units. This setup would be similar to that of the Federal Reserve notes, which are legally secured by (not less than) 40 per cent in gold and the remainder in commercial paper and government bonds. Among the eligible types of commercial paper are acceptances covering staple commodities stored in warehouses.[7] Our suggested currency backed by 40 per cent gold and 60 per cent commodity units would have quite the same sort of ultimate physical security as Federal Reserve notes of the kind just described.

It is true, of course, that those Federal Reserve notes had as intermediate security the obligation of the owner of the commodities, and that it was contemplated that the obligation would be paid and the Federal Reserve currency retired with the proceeds. But while this feature makes for a very deep technical distinction between the Federal

Reserve notes and the currency we propose, the basic security behind the two currencies is not so different and their psychological appeal is likely to be much the same.

The addition of a 40 per cent gold component to our commodity-unit currency will not involve any practical difficulties or any important variations in the mechanism of issuance or redemption. All it really means is that 66⅔ cents of gold certificates will go along with each dollar's worth of commodity units, and that $1.66⅔ of commodity-unit currency will be issued against the combination. Conversely, on presentation of $1.66⅔ of this currency for redemption, the holder will receive $1 in commodity units and 66⅔ cents in gold certificates. Since the commodity-unit currency and the gold certificates will be interchangeable in circulation—as are all our various kinds of currency—the exchange of one kind for another will simply be part of the technical mechanics of the arrangement, and will be taken care of without difficulty by the banks. (The same technique exists in the creation and redemption of Federal Reserve notes.)

Little argument is needed for the point that our commodity-unit currency will be intrinsically sounder than such of our currencies as are *not* based on gold. These comprise the United States notes (greenbacks), our various silver moneys, minor coin, Federal Reserve bank notes and—retrospectively—our government-bond-secured National bank notes, now in process of retirement. The problem, such as it is, will obviously be to keep these currencies on a par with commodity-unit currency, rather than the reverse.

The relation between the commodity-backed money and our Federal Reserve notes deserves a little more attention. At present the Federal Reserve notes are really gold certificates "once removed," being secured by gold certificates proper which in turn are "backed" by gold. But the original conception embodied in the Reserve notes was something far different. As pointed out in the previous chapter, they were designed as self-liquidating currency secured by, and varying with, the prime commercial paper held by our banks.

There is an interesting contrast between the dynamics of the Reserve notes and the commodity-backed currency. The Federal Reserve notes were expected to increase in volume as business grew more active and to contract in step with a shrinkage in business volume. This arrangement was based on the plausible theory that the quantity of money should fluctuate with the needs of business. But the "needs of business" may comprise something beyond a mere proportioning of currency to commercial borrowings. An argument may be made for the opposite policy. If business contracts in a depression, it may be wholesomely stimulated by a timely increase in the money supply. And an unduly rapid advance in the tempo of business might well be offset by a reduction in circulation, somewhat in the same way as by a tightening of money rates.

The mechanics of the commodity-unit currency will operate along these lines. For units will tend to accumulate, and the currency issue to increase, when business falls off; and conversely when a business upswing makes for higher prices. Because of the great change in the character of the assets of the Federal Reserve system—with its enormous holdings of gold and government securities and its relatively minor concern with commercial paper—it does not appear likely that the original flexible-currency idea, grounded on rediscounts of eligible commercial paper, will again be operative in any substantial degree. On the other hand, it may well be true that the opposite type of flexibility, which is inherent in our proposal, will prove better adapted to the needs of the business cycle for offsetting controls.[8]

The Federal Reserve notes remain flexible in the sense that they can retire themselves by the process of being deposited in a Federal Reserve bank. (The depositor is presumably either a member bank or the Treasury.) This is fortunate, since it means that the commodity-unit currency can replace an equivalent amount of Federal Reserve notes, instead of adding to the total of money in circulation. The question of the volume of currency in existence is one which is important not in itself but in its effect upon the credit structure. This will be the subject of our next chapter.

Chapter XIII

THE RESERVOIR PLAN AND CREDIT CONTROL*

"The responsibility for drastic control of expansion has never yet
been undertaken. Still I think the control of expansion is more feasible
than the control of contraction, and that the only safeguard against
future depressions is the control of inflation."
—E. A. GOLDENWEISER[1]
Director of Research and Statistics,
Board of Governors of the Federal
Reserve System

THERE is widespread agreement among economists that
abuse of credit constitutes one of the chief unwholesome
elements in business booms and is mainly responsible for the
ensuing crash and depression. The boom of 1919–1920 was
accompanied by unprecedented borrowings of commercial
enterprise to finance an insensate speculation in inventories.[2]
Eight years later the emphasis had shifted from commodities
and inventories to stocks and real estate.[3] It can hardly be
denied that the extreme intensity of the depression that
followed was due directly to the enormous volume of loans
on securities and on real estate, and to the unsound valua-
tions and other questionable policies that accompanied this
inflation of credit.

It is essential to both our economic and political stability
that the swings of the business cycle be held within saner
limits than those we have just experienced. This is a major
objective of our Monetary Storage plan. It will be attained,
on the one hand, by impounding and neutralizing the surplus
of raw materials that proves the chief demoralizing factor in

*This chapter is addressed primarily to economists, and may be
omitted by the non-technical reader.

depression and, on the other hand, by preventing the unwholesome speculative price advances that often characterize boom periods. But this mechanism bears no *direct* relation to the problem of credit control. Apparently it would have exerted little if any repressive influence on the disastrous speculation of the late 1920's in securities and real estate. Furthermore, the increased currency supply that would grow out of our proposal might interfere with the technique of credit control.

It is proper to inquire, therefore, into the various relationships between our commodity-unit proposal and the credit structure. We should, then, carry this study further and ask whether, independent of but supplementary to our plan, there are at hand feasible methods of influencing the volume of credit in the direction of soundness and stability. Let us first give brief attention to the present status of credit control in this country.

The volume of credit depends upon three factors: the desire to borrow, the ability to lend and the desire to lend. (The *ability to borrow* is essentially the same as the desire to lend.) In the past four years we have witnessed an ability and a desire to lend rendered largely ineffective by an absence of suitable borrowing demand.[4] This is an unusual condition, and one which, however protracted, is unlikely to prove permanent. With the return of normal business psychology, borrowers are certain to come forward for whatever funds are offered on reasonable terms. As prosperity develops into boom, even a decided stiffening of interest rates is not likely to repress the demand for funds by those who play for quick and heavy speculative gains.

Hence we cannot look to the self-control of borrowers to keep the volume of credit within safe bounds. The next line of defense lies in the voluntary conservatism of the lending banks. Experience teaches us that lenders as well as borrowers are apt to set the desire for profit above the dictates of safety—or rather that their ordinary business prudence is likely to become clouded in an atmosphere of optimism and attractive interest rates.

It is well recognized, therefore, that some measure of control of credit must be imposed by outside authority upon both lender and borrower. These controls now operate through the reserve requirements stipulated in the Federal Reserve Act and the discretionary powers vested in the Board of Governors of the Federal Reserve system. The reserve ratios set up a mechanical or arithmetical relationship between the quantity of gold in the country and the maximum permissible volume of Federal Reserve notes and of bank deposits. Limitation of bank deposits acts as a limitation upon bank loans. Under the *minimum* requirements of the law, a dollar of gold may serve as a base for $2.50 of currency or between $20 and $40 of demand deposits. Based on the average situation, this would mean that each dollar of gold in the country may support well over $10 of bank loans.

To clarify the discussion let us remind the reader that the reserve mechanism operates in two distinct parts. There is first the required relationship between the gold holdings of the Reserve banks and their own liabilities, consisting in part of Federal Reserve notes and in part of member bank deposits. These deposits of the member banks with the central banks in turn constitute the legal reserve that must be held against the deposits of the public in the member banks.[5] The first ratio—that within the Reserve banks themselves— may conveniently be termed the "central-bank ratio." The ratios between member banks' reserves and the public's deposits may be referred to as "member-bank ratios."

The reserve ratios originally grew out of the traditional requirement of the gold standard that both paper money and deposits be freely convertible into gold. It was not necessary, of course, that enough gold be at hand to redeem all the currency and all the deposits. But it was equally true that if the gold reserves were relatively inconsequential it would be impossible to maintain that confidence which in turn maintained convertibility. Some middle course had to be chosen. The ratios decided upon were chosen by rule of thumb. Arbitrary as they were, they have seemed adequate and reasonable. Prior to the panic of 1932–1933 every-one thought we had enough gold to support the free con-vertibility of all our currency and all our bank deposits.

Once these minimum ratios were established the amount of the gold reserve set an upper limit to credit expansion. This credit-control function of gold is a derivation—and a rather accidental one—from the original emphasis upon unquestioned convertibility. The point at which the *deposits* grew too large for the gold reserves that supported them was assumed to be the very point at which the *loan structure* was expanding beyond the limits of sound credit policy.

The newer developments in gold-standard technique seem pretty well to have abandoned the objective of free internal convertibility. Gold bars become mere counters in inter-national settlements, to be shoved to and fro as needed to maintain (reasonably) fixed foreign-exchange rates. It can hardly be suggested that the gold holdings needed for *that* purpose are in any way comparable with those formerly required to maintain internal convertibility of currency and deposits. The maximum ratios of bank deposits to gold, set up to keep the old gold standard operative, have practically no relevance at all to the new dispensation. Hence we find that the original purpose of the gold-reserve mechanism, like several of the original uses of the metal itself, has all but disappeared. Control of the total volume of credit, formerly the accidental and secondary function of the reserve ratio, has now become its chief *raison d'être*.

But nothing could be cruder or less scientific than this idea of relating permissible business activity to the amount of gold that happens to be in the country at a given moment. Like so many other aspects of our economic structure it derives what virtue it has from the principle of *faute de mieux*. An arbitrary and erratic safety valve on the credit boiler (or speed governor on the credit engine) may be better than no device at all. Our actual experience with credit expansion and contraction since passage of the Federal Reserve Act in 1913 is not such as to generate much confidence in the reserve ratio as a smoothly working engineering mechanism for credit control.

This is particularly true at the moment because of the enormous quantity of gold held in the United States. Our gold store of 12 billions could, under present law, support a superstructure of perhaps 150 billions in deposits and loans. This would be *three times* the volume of deposits existing at the peak of the unwise credit expansion of the 1920's. It is true that by 1936 the deposit total had again climbed past the 1929 figure, without any accompanying overexpansion of commercial, security, or real-estate loans.[6] But the current situation is recognized as anomalous and impermanent. Unless effective external checks are imposed, other than merely the maximum permissible ratios of deposits to gold, the country's enormous hoard of gold may generate—or at least facilitate—a new credit inflation far beyond anything hitherto experienced.

The real meaning of this situation is that the gold-reserve ratios can no longer be relied upon to provide even a crude and hit-or-miss control over the volume of credit. If we are to have any control at all—and some measure of control is absolutely essential—it *must* arise from the exercise of discretionary powers by the Federal Reserve Board.

A *managed currency* may or may not be a necessity. We believe it is not, and have proposed an automatic, unmanaged supplement to our present currency system. But *managed credit* is inescapable. Since 1913 the Federal Reserve Board has been vested with certain discretionary powers. These powers in recent years have been greatly enlarged. Whether or not they can or will be wielded with entire success is, at bottom, beside the point. We *must* give wide power to the Board; we *must* select the best men available to exercise it; and the rest must lie in the lap of the gods.

The methods now available to the Federal Reserve Board for checking undue expansion of bank credit embrace the following:[7]

a. Raising the rediscount rate.

b. Sale of Reserve banks' holdings of government securities or commercial paper (open-market operations).

c. Increase in the reserve requirements of member banks (by not more than 100 per cent above the statutory minima).

d. Raising the margin requirements on security loans.

e. Restricting the total volume of loans on securities, and prohibiting individual banks from increasing their collateral loans.

f. Denying credit facilities to any member bank which is making "undue use" of bank credit for the speculative carrying or trading in of securities, real estate or commodities.

A rise in the rediscount rate is the traditional first means of discouraging further credit expansion. The rate applies to the borrowings by the member banks from the Federal Reserve banks, but it influences in turn the rate which the member banks will charge their customers. For the rediscount rate to exert an appreciable effect it must be assumed that there is a substantial volume of rediscounts, *i.e.*, that the member banks are leaning heavily upon the central banks for the funds they advance to their own customers. Under our present setup this condition might not develop until credit expansion had already progressed to a dangerous point. Rediscounts today are virtually nil.[8] The combination of enormous gold (certificate) holdings by the Reserve banks and huge holdings of government issues by the member banks means furthermore that an extraordinarily large extension of bank loans can take place without any general necessity for rediscounting to create reserves. Hence the rediscount rate "weapon" is not a particularly serviceable one in the present state of affairs. It is also true that even extremely high interest rates do not seem to have much of a repressive influence upon borrowing during the full tide of a speculative boom.[9]

The open-market operations are a technical method of improving or reducing the member banks' reserve position. Purchases of securities by the Reserve banks result in corresponding increases in the reserves held by the member banks. Conversely, by selling out these security holdings the Reserve banks can bring about a contraction in the member-bank reserves, which in turn will reduce their power to make loans. Given a condition where the Reserve banks hold *both* a substantial volume of rediscounts and a substantial portfolio of open-market securities, liberal sales of the latter could have an appreciable effect in tightening credit. Again it must be remarked that the present banking situation permits so much leeway to the member banks that the open-market weapon, like the rediscount rate, has very limited utility.

A further limitation arises from the desire of the government to maintain high prices and low interest rates for its obligations. Sales on a large scale of the Reserve banks' holdings of government issues might have a seriously depressing effect upon market levels. Hence it has been pointed out that such open-market sales are not likely to be resorted to as a device of credit control unless and until the government has balanced its budget and is comparatively free of financial problems.[10]

These considerations may explain why the only positive step thus far taken to discourage credit expansion has not been along either of the traditional lines just discussed. Instead it has invoked a third and newly granted power, *viz.*, the right to raise the reserve requirements. As of Aug. 1, 1936 the minimum reserves that must be held against demand deposits were raised by 50 per cent, and in January 1937 they were advanced an additional 50 per cent of the base amount. The second advance was applied in two equal steps, becoming finally effective May 1, 1937. Requirements now amount to 14, 20 and 26 per cent of the demand deposits, depending on the location of the member bank. Reserves against time deposits have been similarly advanced from 3 to 6 per cent to all banks. These rulings have increased the required reserves by just three billion dollars (as of June 1937) and have consequently decreased the "excess reserves" (the difference between the amount required and the reserves actually on deposit with the Reserve banks) by the same amount. This means that the potential expansion of credit has been sharply reduced—though the maximum possibilities are still very great indeed.

It is obvious that if the Federal Reserve Board had *unlimited* powers to raise the reserve requirements, it could exercise a direct and decisive control over the total volume of credit. By setting the required percentages sufficiently high it could make it impossible for the member banks as a whole to increase their loans beyond any figure thought suitable. Further than that, it could compel a contraction in the amount of loans already outstanding.

The power now vested in the Board is limited to an advance of not more than 100 per cent in the statutory ratios. This is a considerable discretion, and any extension thereof is likely to be sharply opposed by the member banks, who might fear over-drastic measures of repression. Yet a study of the entire banking situation as it now exists may lead to the conclusion that a further widening of the Board's power to raise reserve requirements is essential to make its control over credit expansion really effective.

Superficially considered, the flexible reserve ratio is a means of making more effective the braking force of the gold supply upon credit expansion. At bottom, however, it means the *replacement* of the automatic gold-supply brake by a discretionary control under the management of the Federal Reserve Board. The whole mechanism is operated without any direct reference to the gold reserve. (The ratio actually prescribed is that between the public's deposits in the member banks and the member banks' deposits with the Reserve banks.) The indirect influence of changes in the gold supply can be neutralized to any extent desired by appropriate changes in this ratio. (If we should lose a tremendous part of our gold, the ratio between the gold supply and the deposit structure might conceivably get down again toward the minima prescribed by the Federal Reserve Act, in which case the mechanical braking effect of the gold reserve would again become operative. Such a development seems most improbable; and this improbability compels the conclusion that the gold supply *per se* is no longer a practical instrument of credit control.)

This longish discussion of the mechanics of credit control is a necessary preliminary to any appraisal of the effect of the Monetary Storage plan upon the credit structure. Insofar as our plan creates additional currency it generates an inflationary influence and further reduces the effectiveness of the three traditional methods of limiting credit expansion, *i.e.*, through the gold-reserve ratios, the rediscount rate and open-market operations.

If these traditional devices were operating satisfactorily under present conditions, and could be relied upon to meet the challenge of future credit demands, this particular feature of the proposed Reservoir system might well be regarded as unfavorable. (In this respect, of course, it would be no more unfavorable than the currency increases resulting from the silver program, and much less unfavorable than the continuous additions to our gold supply.) But since the premise is entirely incorrect, the conclusion is quite irrelevant. Our supply of money—particularly of gold—is already so unwieldy in its credit-control aspect that the whole idea of relating the volume of credit to the supply of gold and other currency is no longer practicable. The battle for credit control must be fought with other weapons, which are capable of neutralizing the inflationary effects of an unprecedently large currency base. With the problem shifted in this direction, the advent of the commodity-backed currency will not be found to add any new difficulties of importance. As we shall point out, its price-stabilization feature should be of prime assistance in the newer system of credit control.

There remains one point to be made in passing as to effect of the commodity-unit currency upon the *total* volume of money. Of some 6.4 billions of currency in circulation, over 4 billion dollars consists of Federal Reserve notes, which can be readily retired if not needed. Assuming no other changes in the currency and credit situation, the practical result of emitting a substantial amount of commodity-backed currency would be the substitution of this new currency for an equivalent amount of Federal Reserve notes. Similar substitutions, unnoticed by the public, have been going on for some time—in particular, the replacement of gold certificates and national bank notes by additional amounts of silver certificates and Federal Reserve notes.

To the extent that Federal Reserve notes are replaced by either silver certificates or commodity-unit notes, there will be a tendency for member-bank reserves to expand. (Another reason for such expansion would be a further increase in our gold holdings.) If the Reserve Board is given much wider powers to raise member-bank reserve requirements—which we think may prove necessary *in any event* for adequate credit control—then such expansion in the member-bank reserves will not create any new or more difficult problem than already exists. It would simply mean that the member-bank ratios will have to be stepped up higher than would otherwise be necessary.

Let us pass now from our discussion of the total volume of credit and currency to some consideration of the various kinds of business operations which may give rise to undue credit expansion. These may be usefully grouped in three categories: commercial loans, security loans and real-estate loans. Expansion of commercial loans during a period of business prosperity is both a natural and a wholesome thing, *provided* such expansion remains proportionate to the increase in the physical volume of trade. In the typical business cycle, however, a rise in trade activity is accompanied by a rise in commodity *prices*. This twofold advance is accompanied by an expansion in commercial borrowings at a substantially greater rate than the physical growth of production and consumption. The credit expansion reflects, therefore, a considerable element of voluntary or involuntary speculation in commodity prices and in inventories. This is the unsound aspect of the growth of commercial credit in boom times.

Our proposed Reservoir system, with its accompanying stabilization of the price level for basic commodities as a group, should interpose an effective barrier to the purely speculative expansion of commercial loans. Without a substantial upward move in prices there can be little inducement to speculate. With speculation checked in the normally volatile raw-materials group, it is unlikely that any spectacular advances will take place in the inherently more stable category of fabricated goods. We suggest, therefore, that under the Monetary Storage plan we are likely to see perpetuated the stable conditions of 1923–1929 in the field of commercial loans, rather than the hectic inflation of 1919–1920.

The danger to the credit structure would lie in the future, as it did in the late 1920's, in the sphere of real-estate and security loans. With these our Reservoir plan has no connection. Fortunately, ample powers have now been given to the Federal Reserve Board to deal with the collateral-loan situation. The percentage of margin required can be raised; the total volume of loans on collateral, in relation to banking capital, can be restricted; the loan policies of individual member banks can be scrutinized and made the subject of disciplinary action. As far as the Federal Reserve system is concerned, unsound expansion of security loans can undoubtedly be prevented by an alert and determined Reserve Board. While nonmember banks are free from some of these potential restrictions, they do not constitute a sufficiently powerful financial group to present any serious threat to the efficacy of Federal Reserve Board control. So-called "bootleg loans" on stock-exchange collateral—made by non-banking corporations and individuals, on an enormous scale in 1928–1929—are now prohibited by law.

The final category of real-estate loans may present greater difficulties of control than the other two. The national banks are subject to legal restrictions in this field, relating both to the percentage of appraised value that may be loaned on any particular property and to the total volume of such loans for the individual bank.[18] There is need for a much more stringent attitude in the matter of appraised values than prevailed before the crash. The state banks outside the Federal Reserve system are subject only to the legislative restrictions of their individual state. Those within the system may be controlled to some extent by the blanket power now vested in the Federal Reserve banks to scrutinize the credit policies of member banks asking for credit, and by the additional power of the board of governors to deny the credit facilities of the system to a member bank making undue use of its borrowings from the central bank.

Viewing the credit picture as a whole, we see that, on the one hand, it contains arithmetical possibilities of enormous and highly dangerous expansion; but, on the other hand, discretionary powers of control are now vested in the Federal Reserve Board which appear adequate to cope with this threat of overexpansion and ensuing catastrophe. As regards our Monetary Storage proposal, this would add measurably to the difficulty of controlling the credit volume *by reference solely to statutory reserve ratios*. But this traditional method of control is no longer efficacious in any case. On the side of facilitating credit control, our Reservoir plan will have the signal merit of greatly reducing those speculative fluctuations in the price level of basic commodities that have been at once the cause and the result of unsound conditions in the field of commercial borrowings.

PART IV

Agricultural Relief and the Ever-normal Granary

"An unprecedented condition calls for new means to rescue agriculture."

—President Franklin D. Roosevelt
in Message transmitting the
Agricultural Adjustment Act,
Mar. 16, 1933

"The community, indeed, could not advance in prosperity and civilization if it were to continue indefinitely a policy of restricting agricultural production with a view to adapting it to dwindling demand. . . . Instead of leveling down, it must begin to plan coordinated expansion for employing the services of science and technique to the satisfaction of human needs."

—Report of the International
Institute of Agriculture
Sept. 1, 1937

Chapter XIV

FARM PROBLEMS AND REMEDIES

"The Nation needs to build permanent defenses for agriculture against two directly opposite kinds of hazard. One kind of hazard is the danger of price collapse resulting from production in excess of market demands. The other is the danger of shortage of marketable supplies resulting from crop failure."

—H. R. TOLLEY, Agricultural
Adjustment Administrator
Annual Report for 1936.

THE Reservoir plan deals predominantly with the products of agriculture, and its direct benefits will accrue chiefly to the American farmer. (Products of the American farm make up about 70 per cent of the value of the commodity unit, about one-half of the total value being represented by the three major staples: wheat, corn and cotton.[1]) Hence the Reservoir plan may be viewed, in large measure, as a proposal for the support and relief of agriculture. At this point it will be pertinent, therefore, to inquire briefly into the nature of the farm problem and the various types of solutions which have been advanced. Our discussion will lead us to a consideration of the Roosevelt Administration's Ever-normal Granary proposals, for these are part of a comprehensive farm relief program.

The farm problem, so-called, consists of at least four distinct and separate problems. These may be called, respectively, the problem of price and income parity, the problem of the business cycle, the problem of the weather and the problem of the export surplus. There are, of course, many other difficulties facing our farm population—among which the question of tenant farming has recently attracted widespread attention. But the four problems we have mentioned are the chief underlying factors in the composite problem of farm income. They are tied together in the sense that they all may be referred to as "price problems."[2]

The relationship between agricultural and nonagricultural prices has been a central point in the discussion of farm relief. For a number of years prior to the depression of the 1930's there seems to have been a moderate tendency for farm prices to lose pace with other prices. The farmer could buy less for what he had to sell.[3] This tendency had developed independently of the business cycle itself, but it was greatly accentuated in the depth of the depression. For at that time farm prices had fallen a great deal more than other prices.[4] One of the announced purposes of the Agricultural Adjustment Act was the reestablishment of pre-war "parity" between the prices of agricultural and industrial products.[5]

The business cycle itself affects agriculture predominantly in the factor of price changes. Unlike industrial production, the output of farm products as a whole has shown comparatively little change during the more recent periods of prosperity and depression.[6] It is also true that the consumption side has been subject to only minor phases of expansion and contraction. By contrast we find that the fluctuations in the *price* of agricultural materials are far wider than those of fabricated goods.[7] Apparently a relatively small reduction in consumptive demand—or perhaps a mere contraction in middlemen's stocks, which causes the demand at the primary markets to fall short of the actual current consumption—may have a devastating effect upon the price structure. This weakness is characteristic of products such as staple foods, in which both the supply and demand are highly inelastic, *i.e.*, insensitive to moderate changes in price and therefore requiring drastic price variations to induce offsetting adjustments in production or consumption, or both.[8]

Fluctuations in agricultural production are chiefly due to the weather. Since weather conditions may be quite divergent in different parts of the enormous area of the United States, we frequently find that a short crop in one region is offset by a bumper crop somewhere else. In such cases the vagaries of the weather will create problems for individual groups of farmers rather than for agriculture as a whole. Bad weather may reduce the total yield of one or two staple crops while others are comparatively unaffected. The droughts of 1934 and 1936 were exceptional in the huge area they covered, but even in those years of visitation a few of our important crops did reasonably well.[9]

Prior to a generation ago the weather cycle and the business cycle were interrelated. General prosperity was definitely associated with splendid crops, supplying a generous export surplus, while short crops were likely to prove a causal or intensifying factor in depressions.[10] In recent times this simple and logical connection appears to have been dissolved. Satisfactory agricultural *prices* now seem to be a more important requisite to prosperity than does an ample agricultural output. And since the latter tends to induce a severe decline in farm prices, we now observe a paradoxical tendency for large farm output to count more as a depressing than as a stimulating factor in general business.

The problem of the weather thus divides itself into several component problems, *viz.*, (*a*) the threat of bad weather to the well-being of the individual farmer, (*b*) the danger of a national food shortage resulting from protracted drought, and (*c*) the unsettling effect of extreme fluctuations in price resulting from abnormally large or abnormally small agricultural yield.

The export-surplus question is now almost as important in its effect upon the domestic price structure as it is upon our international trade position. This is particularly true in respect to wheat. Formerly, when we were a debtor nation and primarily agricultural, a large export surplus of wheat sold abroad at good prices could pull us out of depression into prosperity.[11] But in 1935 and 1936 we witnessed the phenomenon of an energetic domestic recovery coupled with the complete disappearance of our wheat exports. In 1937 the return of the United States to an export position coincides fortunately with a generally small world supply. But looking forward to future years, our agricultural leaders are greatly concerned with the threat to the price of wheat and to the position of the wheat farmer that is likely to arise from the presence of a "normal" export surplus amounting to about 20 per cent of the total crop.

There is something paradoxical in the fact that by establishing an export market we subject our entire domestic production to the vagaries of that market. It is in line with the soundest principles of international trade that our fertile acres should produce food and fibers for people who dwell on poorer soil. These exports, so essential to other nations, should give us a certain meed of strength and power in the world's economy. But instead of our enjoying such strength from this export position, it seems to afflict us with a peculiar vulnerability. This is the outgrowth of the extraordinary role which the price level has come to play in our economic life.

For under open-market conditions, whenever any part of a crop must be sold at the world price, then all the crop will be sold at the world price. A tariff may prevent foreign wheat from entering the United States, but it will not provide the farmer with a higher price for the four-fifths of the wheat normally sold here than he receives for the one-fifth which is sold in the markets of the world. The world price may become an uneconomic price for the American farmer through any one of several reasons. There may be a general price collapse associated with depression; there may be unusually large export crops in competing countries; some of the importing nations may follow the autarchic principle and replace foreign purchases by more expensive domestic production; or, finally, a "currency war" might react against the dollar price. If any of these things happen, the American farmer finds the realization diminished on his entire crop, including its domestic as well as its export component.

The farmers contend vigorously that the world price is likely to be an unduly low price for their entire output. Most of our American manufacturers, they claim, are able to utilize tariff protection so as to obtain higher prices here than exist abroad. Even those fabricated articles which we sell in some quantity to other countries are not at the mercy of international price developments, because our industries can and will sacrifice their exports and reduce production to a domestic basis rather than subject their entire output to an unprofitable international price. Because of these contrasting conditions in agriculture and industry, our farm leaders assert that the mechanism by which the world price for the export component establishes the same price for the larger domestic consumption is both injurious and unfair to agriculture.

In the case of cotton it is scarcely logical to speak of the price problem as arising from an export *surplus*. For our exports generally represent more than half of our total crop,[12] so that the cotton farmer is really in the business of producing for a world market. Limitation of our wheat production to a strictly domestic basis is feasible though scarcely desirable; but a corresponding restriction of cotton output is entirely out of the question. The problem of low cotton prices, based upon unfavorable competitive developments abroad, must be considered as arising from an *unfortunate* rather than an *unfair* situation confronting the cotton farmer.

Having thus stated the various major aspects of the farm problem, let us now consider with equal brevity the remedial measures which have engaged the attention of Congress in recent years. We shall omit references to legislation liberalizing farm credit, encouraging cooperative marketing and dealing with farm tenancy; and discuss solely the measures directly affecting farm prices. These may be divided into five sections as follows:

I. The Equalization-fee (McNary-Haugen) and Export-debenture plans, 1924–1928.

II. The Federal Farm Board, 1929–1933.

III. The (first) Agricultural Adjustment Act, 1933–1936.

IV. The Soil Conservation Act, 1936–.

V. The (proposed) Crop Insurance and Agricultural Adjustment acts of 1937.

I. In the years prior to the depression the question of farm relief centered largely on the adverse effect of the export surplus. The chief remedial measure was known as the McNary-Haugen Bill which was twice passed by Congress (in February, 1927, and May, 1928) only to be vetoed by President Coolidge and to fail of passage over his veto. The McNary-Haugen plan provided for an export bounty on the portion of the crop sold abroad, sufficient to maintain a fair differential between the domestic and the foreign market prices. The bounty would be raised by a tax on the producers themselves.

For example: If 200 million bushels are to be sold abroad at $1.00 and 600 million bushels sold in the United States at $1.42, this could be accomplished by an export subsidy of 42 cents per bushel requiring 84 million dollars. This sum in turn could be raised by a tax of 10½ cents per bushel on the entire crop. The result would be that all producers would net $1.31½ per bushel regardless of whether they sold it at home or abroad.[13]

The second Coolidge veto message listed six objections to the measure, *viz.*, (1) it aims at price fixing; (2) it taxes producers; (3) it sets up a bureaucracy; (4) it invites profiteering and wasteful distribution methods; (5) it stimulates overproduction; (6) it aids foreign competitors. In addition the attorney general pronounced the measure unconstitutional.[14]

An alternative proposal was known as the Export-debenture plan. It originated in 1924, was introduced into Congress in 1927, and passed the Senate but not the House in 1929.[15] This plan proposed in effect that tariff money collected on imported goods should be used to pay a bonus on farm exports. The mechanism consisted of paying an export debenture—similar to a cash subsidy—to the exporting farmers. The farmer in turn could sell the debenture to any importer, who could deliver it to the government in lieu of a corresponding amount of import duties. The total amount of the subsidy was to be limited to one-half of the total import duties collected.

A modified form of this idea has been actually incorporated in the 1935 amendments to the Agricultural Adjustment Act. Section 32 provides that 30 per cent of the import duties are to be turned over to the Secretary of Agriculture to be used to divert agricultural commodities from the "normal channels of trade and commerce"—one method being the payment of export benefits or indemnities.

II. The Federal Farm Board was set up in 1929 in accordance with Republican promises during the presidential campaign of 1928. Originally designed to stabilize prices through promoting orderly marketing of crops,[16] it soon found itself engaged in the task of supporting prices in the face of an unprecedented economic collapse. The extent of its operations and losses was summarized in Chap. II.

III. The Agricultural Adjustment Act of 1933, together with the amendments thereto adopted in August 1935, was an omnibus measure with multifarious purposes.[17] In its farm relief sections it aimed to avoid the embarrassment of the Farm Board by making financial aid to farmers dependent upon restriction of output. The money paid to the farmers under the curtailment program was to be raised by processing taxes collected from wheat millers, cotton manufacturers, etc. The Commodity Credit Corporation was also set up, as part of the program, to make loans to cooperating farmers against their surplus holdings (chiefly) of corn and cotton.

In 1934 and 1935, following referenda among farmers, restriction of output was made virtually compulsory with respect to cotton, tobacco and potatoes by the imposition of a heavy tax on marketings in excess of an allotted quota. All of these arrangements were adopted as temporary measures, being limited either to the period of the "national economic emergency in relation to agriculture," or for one or two years after passage.

In January, 1936, the Agricultural Adjustment Act was declared unconstitutional by a 6 to 3 decision of the United States Supreme Court.[18] The nub of the decision held that the act "is a statutory plan to regulate and control agricultural production, a matter beyond the power delegated to the Federal Government." The benefit payments to the farmers and the processing taxes on the manufacturers were declared to be invalid means to an unconstitutional end. This decision was conceded by the government to invalidate the cotton-, tobacco- and potato-control acts.

IV. The Soil Conservation and Domestic Allotment Act of February 1936,[19] passed promptly after invalidation of the Agricultural Adjustment Act, endeavored to maintain the underlying idea of crop control, while avoiding the machinery held unconstitutional by the Supreme Court. It provides for benefits to be paid to farmers in return for soil-building and soil-conserving practices, including in the latter diversion of acreage from soil-depleting crops, *e.g.*, wheat, corn and cotton. It states as a specific purpose the reestablishment of 1909–1914 relationship in the per-capita net income of farmers and nonfarmers. Powers given the Secretary of Agriculture are not to be used to discourage production of food and fibers sufficient to maintain normal domestic human consumption. Expenditures under the act are limited to 500 million dollars per annum. Funds may be used for the expansion of foreign and domestic markets, or for seeking new markets, or for the removal and disposition of surpluses of agricultural commodities.

After Jan. 1, 1942[20] payments under this act are to be made as grants-in-aid to the various States, which are required to devise suitable plans complying with the purposes of the Act. Prior to 1942, however, the benefit payments are to be made directly by the Treasury to the farmers, unless a State plan is put into operation. In the first year of operations under the Soil Conservation Act of 1936 the farmers received about $380,000,000 of benefit payments.[21] These sums were paid for carrying out soil-building practices on approximately 53 million acres of land and for diverting about 31 million acres from soil-depleting to soil-conserving crops.

V. The New Farm Legislation of 1937. Beneficial as the Soil Conservation Act has been to the farmer, neither the Department of Agriculture nor the farm leaders have felt that it supplies an adequate mechanism for preventing over-production of agricultural staples, given a return of favorable weather conditions. Following a conference of farm leaders in February 1937, there was prepared and introduced into Congress—as a quasi-Administration measure[22]—a new and comprehensive measure for farm relief, entitled the Agricultural Adjustment Act of 1937. In February 1937, also, there was introduced into Congress the Administration's

Crop Insurance Bill, designed to protect the individual farmer against weather hazards.

These two measures embody for the first time the underlying idea of the Ever-normal Granary, which for many years has been close to the heart of Secretary of Agriculture Wallace.[23] Because of the similarities existing between the granary concept and our own Reservoir plan, we shall consider the pending farm legislation in some detail in the next chapter.

Chapter XV

THE 1937 FARM LEGISLATION—THE EVER-NORMAL GRANARY

"From the standpoint of the national interest, the consuming interest, and the agricultural interest, the increased stability of supply and price that would come with the ever-normal granary is essential."

—SECRETARY OF AGRICULTURE H. A. WALLACE[1]

THE proposed Crop Insurance Bill[2] and the proposed Agricultural Adjustment Act of 1937 are entirely independent measures, either of which may be enacted without reference to the other. Widely as they differ in their scope, they share two objectives with our own proposal, namely, the stabilization of farm prices and the impounding of surplus production.

THE INSURANCE-GRANARY PLAN

The Crop Insurance plan would be applied to wheat only in the first year, and then extended gradually to other staples. All-risk insurance would be provided by a government agency at rates worked out on actuarial lines from the detailed records of the Department of Agriculture. The farmer would be indemnified for the amount by which his output fell short of a certain percentage "to be determined by the Board," of his base output per acre. Indemnities would be paid to the farmer in kind or in cash at the current value of the wheat due him. Hence insurance would run in terms of wheat and not in terms of money.

The Ever-normal Granary feature arises from provisions relating to the payment of premiums by and indemnities to the wheat farmer. He would be permitted to pay his premiums in the form of wheat instead of money, and these premiums might be made payable only in years of production above the average figure.[3] The premium payments made in wheat would be held in storage by the insurance agency. When indemnities were due for insufficient output they would also be made in the form of wheat turned over to the farmer (or sold for his account) out of the grain reserve.

Assuming that crop insurance is found to be feasible from the actuarial side, the provisions for payments in kind would constitute an ingenious and appealing extension of the utility of the crop insurance mechanism. In its insurance aspect, it would mean indemnifying the insured not in terms of money but in terms of property. This is sound from the standpoint of the beneficiary; and by the storage arrangement it becomes practicable, *i.e.*, nonspeculative, from the standpoint of the insurer. As in every comprehensive storage system, its further effect would be to conserve the surplus of fruitful years for use in times of shortage. Finally, by taking surplus off the market and holding it until really needed, this granary plan would contribute toward more stable price levels for the commodities affected.

It is natural that we should be highly sympathetic towards this special type of Crop Insurance plan, since it parallels our own objectives. Whether or not it can be operated successfully depends, in our opinion, on the magnitude of the difficulties obtruded by its insurance or actuarial elements.[4] Without seeking to dilate on these difficulties in detail, we might point out that crop insurance must deal with two fundamentally different kinds of hazards—which may be called the recurrent and the eventual. In normal years certain individual farmers or regional groups would suffer weather damage for which they would be indemnified out of the current premium fund. In addition there would be the large-scale benefits to be paid in crop-failure years out of the reserves accumulated during a prior period. This second type of protection is the hardest to establish on a scientifically dependable insurance basis. (The same obstacles are faced in connection with unemployment insurance, bank-deposit insurance, real-estate mortgage insurance, and other types where a huge amount of claims are likely to be made simultaneously at unpredictable times.) Unfortunately it is this long-term, or "catastrophe," insurance which is of chief interest in the present discussions of crop insurance, and it is exclusively in this part of any crop insurance system that the ever-normal granary feature can be incorporated.

Assuming the actuarial problems may be solved, and an all-risk Crop Insurance plan established containing the "ever-normal granary" provision, how nearly would such an arrangement duplicate the advantages sought by our Commodity-reservoir proposal? The insurance scheme is necessarily more limited in its scope than our own, so that there must be considerable differences in their respective consequences. Of these the more important are the following:

The insurance plan deals solely with variations caused by the weather. Its purpose is confined to leveling out the effects of the weather cycle. Taking any fairly long period of time, the storage reserves accumulated during surplus years must all be drawn down in the years of subnormal output. Otherwise, the farmers could rightfully complain that the premiums charged them are excessive.

Hence the Insurance-granary idea would afford no protection against the disruptive effects of business depressions, except to the extent that a depression might be caused or aggravated by supernormal crops. While this proviso is not so contradictory as it sounds, it is evident that the disturbing effects of the business cycle upon agriculture are substantially independent of weather conditions.

The Insurance-granary plan does not deal with the general problem of surplus from the standpoint of purchasing-power deficiency. It does not turn surplus into purchasing power, or provide a groundwork by which accumulated surplus may be utilized to advance the national living standard. Since the reserves must come and disappear with the weather cycle, the insurance plan sets up no permanent store. It safeguards the country only against drought.

The insurance plan must deal with each commodity separately. Its storage mechanism can be applied only to those products which are found eligible for a comprehensive crop insurance system. Its benefits may have to be confined to a few agricultural commodities and to those producers who voluntarily participate. Of course it must completely exclude nonagricultural raw materials.

The Insurance-granary idea and our Monetary Storage plan can hardly be regarded as competitive or alternative proposals. They are alike chiefly in their emphasis upon storage as the most logical means of dealing with surplus. If the Insurance-granary plan is found feasible, its adoption should be of great value to the thesis advanced in this study. It might well pave the way for a more comprehensive mechanism such as we are recommending.

It is quite possible that the Insurance-granary arrangement might function soundly for one or more individual commodities at the same time as our more comprehensive Reservoir system is in operation. The insurance granary might have a special advantage in reducing price fluctuations arising solely from the weather cycle. Our own proposal, however, has a feature of similar character which may be found to supply as much weather-price stability as is needed. We refer to the arrangement under which an individual commodity may be withdrawn from the stored units and replaced by futures contracts. At bottom this should operate in the same way as the insurance-storage mechanism, except that our sequence begins during a period of shortage and then carries over into the ensuing years of larger output. In other words, the insurance plan would first acquire and store a "weather-caused" surplus and then send it out into consumption during a "weather-caused" shortage. Our arrangement would first draw on a permanent reserve during the shortage and then replenish that reserve out of later surplus.[5] Over several weather cycles, the price-stabilization effects of both systems on individual commodities might well prove broadly similar.

THE PROPOSED AGRICULTURAL ADJUSTMENT ACT OF 1937

Comprehensive farm legislation, including an ever-normal granary provision, was presented before Congress in May 1937.[6] This legislation states that it is the policy of Congress to maintain both "parity of prices" and "parity of income" to producers of the "major agricultural commodities"—here defined to comprise wheat, corn, cotton, rice and tobacco. Parity is defined as that price of the commodity which holds the same relationship to the prices of "articles the farmers buy" as existed during the period August 1909 to July 1914 (in the case of tobacco, August 1919 to July 1929). Parity of income is that net income of farmers which bears the same relationship to the income of nonfarmers as existed from August 1909 to July 1914.

Additional aims include provision of an ever-normal granary for each major agricultural commodity and conservation of soil resources and fertility. The third aim appears only in certain references to the Soil Conservation Act of 1936.

The bill proposes to guarantee cooperating farmers a price for their product ranging from 100 per cent of the parity price (when the total supply does not exceed "normal") down to 82 per cent of parity (when the total supply is 114 per cent or more of normal). These guarantees are made effective by direct parity payments by the government of the difference between the average farm price and the guaranteed income rate. There are also made available Surplus Reserve loans at certain percentages of parity price, the rate being also dependent upon the percentage that actual supply bears to a stated normal. If the loan rate exceeds the farm price, the parity payment is reduced correspondingly. These benefits are paid in lieu of the "soil-conserving" (acreage-diversion) payments under the Soil Conservation Act of 1936. However, cooperating farmers may still receive "soil-building" (Class II) payments with respect to the crops covered by this bill, and both soil-conserving and soil-building payments with respect to other crops.

The farmer becomes a cooperator, eligible for these various benefits, by signing an adjustment contract. This obligates him to do any of the following when so required by the Secretary of Agriculture: (a) store under seal up to 20 per cent of his output, (b) reduce his acreage by a prescribed percentage, (c) limit his marketing to a specified quota.

As a safeguard for the consumer, whenever the price advances to 110 per cent of parity, the Secretary is required to call Surplus Reserve loans, or release and dispose of stored supplies, to the extent necessary to stabilize the price at parity. Also, when such an advance takes place the tariff on the commodity shall be reduced by the difference between the market price and the parity price. Similarly, the tariff is to be raised in the same amount when the price falls below 90 per cent of parity.

The bill establishes a national "soil-depleting base acreage" for each of the commodities affected. This national acreage is to be divided first among the States, then regionally and locally, and finally among the individual producers in proportion to their production over the preceding 10 years, with certain adjustments. Cooperating farmers must limit their acreage to their allotment; and this acreage and the average yield therefrom will form the base for computing acreage diversion and marketing quotas.

Non-cooperators shall not receive any benefits either under this act or under the Soil Conservation Act. When marketing quotas are in force, all producers—whether or not coopera-tors—shall be subject to a heavy penalty upon marketings in excess of their quota. All producers, purchasers or pro-cessors of the major agricultural commodities must keep such records (as to acreage, yield, storage, marketing, etc.) as may be prescribed by the Secretary.

In the balance of this chapter we shall consider critically the Ever-normal Granary feature of the proposed Agricul-tural Adjustment Act of 1937, reserving a discussion of its farm relief aspects for the following chapter. Will the new legislation establish a satisfactory ever-normal granary or reservoir? The answer must be a reluctant, "No."

While a stated purpose of the bill is "to provide an ever normal granary for each major agricultural commodity," there is nothing in the legislation itself which makes direct or positive provision for a granary of any size whatever. Although the Secretary of Agriculture is directed to take steps to restrict production in the event of an excessive supply, there is no provision requiring him at any time to encourage production, or to build up surplus stocks. The ever-normal granary is mentioned in only one paragraph in the body of the bill, and then in an extremely ambiguous form. This provision states (Section 9 *a*) that after the "total supply" of a commodity for a given marketing year has been ascertained, then the Secretary shall "establish and proclaim the following:

"First, the ever normal granary for each major agricultural commodity during each marketing year. The ever normal granary shall be such supply, in addition to the normal supply but not in excess of 10 per cent thereof, as will maintain a surplus reserve adequate to meet domestic consumption and export need in years of drought, flood, or other adverse conditions, as well as in years of plenty."

It might be thought that this means the Secretary is actually to "establish" an ever-normal granary by acquiring and storing a reserve supply. But a study of the remainder of the bill indicates that nothing of the sort is intended. Instead it means merely that the *point of compulsory curtailment of acreage* is to be set at a figure which includes the above discretionary and limited allowance for a granary. But even this allowance, if made up to the 10 per cent maximum specified, will not permit—much less require— the creation of any really substantial granary or reservoir supply. The fact is that in the case of wheat and corn, the point at which curtailment *must* take place, even with the supposed allowance for the granary, is actually less than the average supply during the 1921–1930 decade.

The appurtenant figures are given in the table opposite.

The much-publicized Ever-normal Granary feature of the new Farm Bill is thus found, upon analysis, to be unimportant as to extent and indefinite as to execution. The loans to be made by the Surplus Loan Corporation are not likely to create much of an increase in supply. They are intended rather to prevent an existing liberal supply from breaking the price. Ordinarily such loans would constitute an inducement to larger production, but these are conditioned on the borrowers' acceptance of measures to *reduce* production. The provision for lowering tariffs if the price advances may be helpful to the consumer but it does not in itself create or encourage a larger domestic supply.[8] On the other hand,

MAXIMUM SUPPLY OR CURTAILMENT POINT AND MARKETING QUOTA POINT, AS PROVIDED IN THE FARM BILL OF 1937

(Approximate figures, based on 1927–1936 averages, in millions)

Commodity	A "Normal annual consumption and exports" (10-year average)*	B Allowance for carryover		C Normal supply (Cols. A+B)	D Maximum allowance for ever-normal granary (10 per cent of Col. C)	E Maximum supply or curtailment point (Cols. A+B+D)	F Marketing-quota point		G Actual average supply,[7] 1921–1930
		Per cent of Col. A	Amount				Per cent of Col. C	Amount	
Corn, bushels..........	2300	5	115	2415	242	2657	110	2657	2800
Wheat, bushels........	680	20	136	816	82	898	120	980	1008
Cotton, bales.........	13.1	40	5.2	18.3	1.8	20.1	115	21	18.4
Rice, barrels.........	11.4	5	0.6	12	1.2	13.2	110	13.2	12
Tobacco, pounds.......	1300	†	1700†	3000	300	3300	110	3300	3118

*The 10-year average is to be "adjusted for current trends."

†One hundred and eighty per cent of domestic consumption plus 50 per cent of exports.

the machinery for reducing the acreage planted by cooper-
ators, and for imposing marketing quotas on all producers,
represents a practical means of reducing this supply and
preventing it from ever exceeding by much the very modest
figure which is supposed to give us a granary.

If we compare the granary provision of the Farm Bill with
our own Reservoir proposal, we see that the concept of
storage is the central feature of our plan, while it is minor
and almost incidental in the Farm Bill. The Reservoir system
is prepared to absorb and impound a really substantial
quantity of commodity units and to hold them indefinitely
until called out by an emergency, or successfully translated
into a higher standard of living for the American people.
The underlying philosophy of the Farm Bill is hostile rather
than sympathetic to the creation of a liberal granary.[9] The
prospective carryovers aimed at are very modest, indeed,
and as soon as they are exceeded restrictive measures are to
be employed which may easily reduce the supply well below
a comfortable minimum.

Despite its announced purpose "to provide an ever normal
granary" the Farm Bill is in reality directed primarily
against abundance.

Chapter XVI

THE RESERVOIR PLAN VERSUS CROP CONTROL AS
A METHOD OF FARM RELIEF

"Now be it therefore resolved by the Senate and the House of
Representatives in Congress assembled, that abundant production of
farm products should be a blessing and not a curse."
—Resolution adopted by both
Houses of Congress, August 1937[1]

IN this chapter we shall consider to what extent our
Monetary Storage proposal may be relied upon to solve
the major problem besetting American agriculture—the
maintenance of an adequate price level. We shall then compare its essential character with that of the proposed Agricultural Adjustment Act of 1937, which in our opinion
involves drawbacks far outweighing its benefits.[2]

As pointed out previously the preponderance of domestic
farm products in our proposed commodity unit makes our
plan in effect a mechanism for taking a composite agricultural surplus off the market and for stabilizing the average
price level of farm products. Hence it may properly be
viewed as a farm relief measure with substantially the same
basic objectives as those of the proposed Farm Bill. But
similar as are their aims, the two plans differ greatly in
their philosophy and their method.

These differences may be listed under four primary heads,
as follows:

I. The Farm Bill seeks to stabilize separately the (relative)
price of each major agricultural product. The Reservoir
plan will stabilize only the price level of farm products as a
whole.

II. The machinery of the Farm Bill turns primarily upon crop restriction. The Reservoir plan encourages unlimited, if balanced, production.

III. The Farm Bill subsidizes the farmer by direct bonuses and "loans" paid out of the Treasury. The Reservoir plan finances itself (except for storage cost) by monetizing the composite commodity units.

IV. The Farm Bill introduces a highly complicated form of governmental regimentation and control over the operations of each (cooperating) farmer. The Reservoir plan is completely automatic and impersonal; by comparison with the Farm Bill, its mechanism is simplicity itself.

Let us consider these various points of difference in order.

I. A STABILIZED PRICE LEVEL VERSUS INDIVIDUAL PRICE FIXING

Under this heading our thesis is, first, that the Reservoir plan will, in fact, substantially assure an adequate price level for farm products generally; secondly, that such assurance is nearly as beneficial to the farmer as the stabilizing of individual prices; and, thirdly, that our objective is economically sound while individual price fixing is not.

The Reservoir plan definitely fixes the 1921–1930 price level for a group of commodities of which American farm products make up about 70 per cent in value. It may be objected that the domestic farm products could conceivably sell at much less than their 1921–1930 values, while the other items sell proportionately higher. As a practical matter this is most unlikely. The nonfarm component is made up about equally of American minerals (including petroleum) and imported products. Practically all these commodities have faced the same problem of price weakness as has vexed the American farmer. The price record shows that periods of depression have almost the same proportionate effect upon the nonfarm as upon the farm component.[3] There is no reason to believe that the relative position of the two components is likely to suffer a serious adverse change from the standpoint of the farm group. It is fair to assume, also, that whatever variations take place in favor of one group or the other are likely to cancel out in the long run.[4]

The arithmetic of the case is also strongly on the side of relative stability for the farm group. Any decline in this part of the unit must produce an advance more than twice as large proportionately in the other products. If the farm component in the dollar should fall, say, 10 per cent, from 70 to 63 cents, this must produce an advance in the nonfarm component from 30 to 37 cents, or fully 23 per cent. It follows that a relatively small decline in the farm price level will create a sufficient rise in the other prices to stimulate production and reestablish a balance in the supply of both components.

If it be granted that our Reservoir plan will assure substantial stability for farm products as a whole, and at an adequate level, will not this go so far as necessary in solving the price problem of the American farmer? "No!" says the cotton farmer, "because I need an adequate price for cotton. The 1921–1930 level for farm products generally will not help me if I am getting only 50 per cent of that level while other farm products sell proportionately higher."

It will readily be admitted that, if other things were equal, the farmers would prefer the assurance of a fair price of each individual farm product to that of a fair price for farm products as a whole. But, on the one hand, it is not essential to the farmer's prosperity that he have the former assurance rather than the latter. And, on the other hand, the guarantee of individual prices can be effected, if at all, only at a prohibitive cost to the nation, and even to the farmers themselves.

True it is that a large crop may often hurt the farmer rather than help him, but the extent of that difficulty should not be exaggerated. As compared with the disaster of a price collapse in a general depression, the vagaries of farm-price and farm-yield relationships in times of normal business do not create any intolerable burden that cries for an extreme solution. A study of all the important crop statistics for the 1923–1929 period will reveal instances when a crop above normal has been sold at an excellent price; more numerous instances when the large crop depressed the price disproportionally; still other instances of the old-fashioned sort when the farmer suffered badly as the result of a short crop. Few impartial students would conclude that the 1923–1929 record proves the need for complete governmental control over farming operations to prevent the disaster of bumper crops.

If the price of farm products as a group is kept at a fair level, the variation in the individual prices is likely to cancel out over a reasonable period of time. If the corn farmer is at a disadvantage in one year he is likely to make it up a year or two later. After all, the farmer is in business, too, and he must take some of the businessman's risks. A guarantee of a fair price every year to every individual farmer on every individual major product does sound like a great deal more than any group has a right to expect. If the farmers are assured a fair price for their products generally, on a permanent basis—as our Reservoir plan provides—they will be receiving a degree of assistance far greater than is accorded to other lines of business.

An important consideration in comparing the benefits to the farmer under the Reservoir plan and under the crop-control proposal is the fact that in the former case farm production may increase considerably while in the latter it is strictly limited. The Reservoir plan aims directly at a substantial expansion of both the production and consumption of farm products. Hence the *aggregate* money income of the farmers—or their aggregate purchasing power—is almost certain to be far greater under the reservoir arrangement than under a system of controlled and limited crops. This very real advantage should more than offset the difference between the individual-price and the group-price guarantee. Hence we are confident that the Reservoir plan will offer more concrete benefits to the farmers of the nation than they will derive from the proposed Farm Relief Act.

The wheat and cotton farmers may contend they are in an especially adverse position because of their dependence upon world prices, and that therefore they are in particular need of an individual-price guarantee. But let us recognize clearly *that the problem of inadequate world prices does not arise basically from excessive production here, and its solution is not to be reached by production control.* Unless, indeed, we are prepared to reduce our cotton acreage by more than half and to give up our export market altogether—a proposal that no one would advance seriously. It follows therefore that the specific problem of the export surplus falls outside of either the Reservoir or the crop-control scheme. The question at issue is whether we wish the American people to pay, and the American farmer to receive, a higher price for the domestically consumed portion than for the exported portion of certain crops.

Because that issue is not really at stake in a choice between the Reservoir and the crop-control proposals, it is not necessary to discuss its pros and cons at this point. But assuming that the idea of a price differential is accepted, then the McNary-Haugen "equalization fee" method, or something similar, is undoubtedly the simplest and fairest method of bringing it about. The payment of a subsidy on exports, to be raised by a tax on the crop itself, will result automatically in a spread between the domestic and the world price about equal to the subsidy. Although the McNary-Haugen plan is not without its objections, they are far less serious than those inherent in a crop-control plan. It is not at all necessary to embrace the latter proposal, with all its complexities, in order to provide specific relief from the export-surplus problem. Nor is it to be forgotten that crop control may threaten us with a progressive diminution, and perhaps the virtual extinction, of our agricultural exports.

We have argued in the previous paragraphs that individual price fixing is not essential to the farmer's well-being, and that he is not entitled to that degree of assurance against ordinary business hazards. Let us now point out that the whole idea of permanently fixed prices, or price relationships, for a number of individual products is economically unsound because it fails to take into account variations in costs of production and other supply-and-demand factors that may develop over a period of time. The freezing of the relative prices of several major products on the basis of the 1909–1914 situation proposes to perpetuate the situation of a quarter century ago. That such relationships may not always be right is shown in the Farm Bill itself by the fact that the 1909–1914 price of tobacco was not considered representative, so that the 1919–1929 average was used as a basis instead. Must the 1909–1914 price ratio of corn to cotton remain inviolate regardless of all the developments since then and in the future? What of the effect of bringing new and better land into cultivation, e.g., in California? What of the effect of new methods, e.g., possibly a mechanical cotton picker?

In Chap. III we pointed out that the absolute fixing of separate prices for a number of different commodities is an economic impossibility. Assuming it were possible to fix *minimum price or income ratios* for a number of farm products, as is proposed by the Farm Bill, it would still be true that such an arrangement would soon be found wanting in fairness.

II. CROP RESTRICTION VERSUS BALANCED PRODUCTION

Let us pass on to the methods by which the rival proposals would reach their objectives. The Farm Bill makes its guarantee of individual-price ratios dependent upon production control. This is a necessary consequence of the price-fixing idea. For otherwise certain farm products, which turn out to be especially favored by the guarantee arrangement, would be produced in such quantities as to create an unbalanced and embarrassing surplus. (Furthermore, the Farm Bill scheme could not handle even a well-balanced surplus of farm products generally, of really substantial proportions, for lack of a method of monetizing these holdings.)

Crop control means crop reduction, through cutting down acreage at the government's direction. The objections to any permanent crop-curtailment policy are numerous and cogent. They spring from both logic and sentiment. It must be fundamentally wrong to reduce production of food and fiber while one-third of our population is still ill fed and ill clothed. It is also true that a policy of crop control is almost certain to work out imperfectly because, while acreage can be planned, the weather cannot. Hence we may find a drought year coinciding with and unduly intensifying an acreage reduction campaign—as in 1934 and 1936—or else especially favorable weather creating a tremendous increase in the output from a small expansion of acreage as happened to cotton in 1937.

Even if crop restriction were sound in theory and could work out smoothly in practice—neither of which is true— it would still be politically inexpedient, because of the ingrained popular aversion to such a policy. Intelligent or not, this popular prejudice against crop control will prove the nemesis of its proponents. They will receive grudging credit for whatever turns out right, and they will be abused unmercifully for whatever goes wrong. (One has but to recall the vitriolic nature of the criticism visited upon the AAA's restriction policy as the drought developed in 1934 and in 1936.)

The instinctive objection to crop control is nowhere better expressed than by Secretary Wallace himself in his famous pamphlet, *America Must Choose:*

> We shall have to go on doing all these things we do not want to do. The farmer dislikes production control instinctively. He does not like to see land idle and people hungry. The carriers dislike production control because it cuts down loadings. The processors dislike it because of the processing tax. The consumer dislikes it because it adds to the price of food. Practically the entire population dislikes our basic program of controlling farm production; and they will do away with it unless we can reach the common intelligence and show the need of continuing to plan. We must show that need of continuing if we are to save in some part the institutions which we prize (p. 1).

The crop-destruction and crop-restriction program of the 1933 AAA was resorted to as a desperate and temporary measure impelled by a desperate and baffling emergency. The emergency supplied its justification and its temporary nature supplied its saving grace. But the proposed farm legislation of 1937 raises the fundamental issue whether crop control—*which means crop restriction*—shall be made a permanent and dominant element in our economic system. Surely every other possibility must be explored to the full before the United States can commit itself to this sinister path.

III. GOVERNMENT SUBSIDIES VERSUS A SELF-FINANCING PLAN

The proposed Farm Act undertakes to pay cooperating farmers a direct subsidy equal to the difference between market prices and not less than 82 per cent of parity prices.

In addition it supplies the farmer with "loans" which, in effect, permit the farmer to speculate on a price advance with government money and completely at the government's risk.

What the Farm Bill means to the United States Treasury may be illustrated concretely by the case of cotton. In October 1937 the new crop was estimated at 17,500,000 bales (of about 500 lb.); the world carryover of American cotton was about 5,700,000 bales, the price for December delivery was 8 cents (equal to about 7.7 cents on the farm) against a parity of 16.5 cents. Since the total supply of about 23,200,-000 bales was more than 114 per cent of normal, the government would be obligated under Section 8 of the act:

a. To make a parity payment to cooperating cotton producers equal to the difference between the market price and 82 per cent of parity, or 13.5 cents. Assuming the farmers eventually sold all their cotton at 7.7 cents, the government would have to pay out 5.8 cents per pound, or $29 per bale. If this payment is applied only to the normal production of 13,200,000 bales,[5] it would mean a government subsidy of over $380,000,000 on this single crop.

b. To make Surplus Reserve loans at the rate of 52 per cent of the parity price, or 8.6 cents per pound. (The rate of interest and period of such loans are left to the discretion of the Agricultural Administration.) If such loans are made on a third of the crop (the rest going into consumption) the government would lend the cotton farmers about $250,000,-000 on the sole security of their cotton. The farmers would get the benefit of any price advance during the life of the loan; but if the price remains below the loan rate (plus accrued interest), the government would take the loss.[6]

It is impossible to forecast how much this subsidy and loan program would cost the United States Treasury. Proponents of the bill have estimated the probable annual parity payments at an average of about $400,000,000, part of which would replace payments now being made under the Soil Conservation Act.[7] Other estimates ran as high as $1,000,000,000 for the five crops covered, with a very much larger sum involved if the act were extended to all farm crops, and not allowing for any loans.[8]

A permanent system of bonus payments by the government to certain classes of producers is inherently objectionable for considerations beyond its money cost. It inspires similar demands from other classes and ever-increasing demands from the beneficiaries themselves. It adds greatly to the purely political aspect of the State's economic policy. These objections are intensified when the bonuses are paid to encourage curtailment instead of expansion of production.

The Reservoir plan pays no bonuses or subsidies to anyone and lays no burden upon the Treasury except such part of the storage charges as may not be defrayed in other ways. It is true that under our plan complete commodity units may be acquired in unlimited quantities at a fixed value or price, and then used as the physical backing for the money issued against them. But the issuance of paper dollars in exchange for commodity units loses all aspects of a subsidy, once the complete equivalence of the commodity unit and the paper dollar is accepted as the basis of a sound monetary system.

IV. REGIMENTATION AND COMPLEXITY VERSUS A SIMPLE AND
AUTOMATIC MECHANISM

Control of production is a complicated matter. Estimates must be made out and quotas assigned. The cooperating farmers are regimented in that the extent of their planting and perhaps of their marketing is to be prescribed by the government. It may be that the fears of such regimentation have been exaggerated. The Department of Agriculture has had elaborate dealings of this sort with millions of farmers since 1933 and it seems to have carried out its difficult job with commendable efficiency and fairness. It has been greatly aided by the device of having local committees handle the problems of the individual farmers on a neighborhood basis.[9]

Nevertheless, regimentation of the sort envisaged in the bill is undeniably a wide departure from the traditional independence of American agriculture. Neither the farmer nor the American people generally could view the advent of this new dispensation without the gravest apprehension.

Just how complicated is the machinery set up in the proposed legislation may best appear from the following schematic summary:

PROVISIONS OF THE PROPOSED AGRICULTURAL ADJUSTMENT
ACT OF 1937

1. There is permanently established for each major agricultural commodity a national soil-depleting base acreage.

2. There is to be established for every crop and for each year:

   a. A normal supply level.

   b. A total (prospective) supply for the year.

   c. Possibly, a national marketing quota.

3. There is to be established for every farm and for each major agricultural commodity:

   a. A soil-depleting base acreage.

   b. A normal yield per acre.

   c. Possibly, a marketing quota.

4. Farmers may receive the following payments from the government:

   a. Soil-building payments.

   b. Parity payments.

c. Surplus Reserve loans.

d. Soil-conservation payments with respect to other than major agricultural commodities.

5. The farmer may be required:

a. To store up to 20 per cent of his crop.

b. To divert acreage from a major crop to some other use.

c. To keep records and furnish proof of his acreage, storage and marketing.

6. The farmer may be subject to a specific penalty tax for marketing in excess of his quota.

7. The government is required:

a. To prepare and tender adjustment contracts to all producers of all the major commodities.

b. To make the various determinations, payments, and loans already referred to.

8. The government may be required:

a. To call Surplus Reserve loans or to sell out commodities acquired thereby.

b. To increase or decrease the duty on the major agricultural commodities.

9. Purchasers or processors of major agricultural commodities shall keep records and furnish information on forms prescribed.

10. The "soil-depleting base acreage" and the "individual marketing quotas" shall be subject to determination and review successively by (1) a local committee, (2) a review committee, (3) a reviewing officer, (4) a United States district court.

As compared with the complexity of governmental operations under the Farm Bill, our Reservoir proposal is simplicity itself. The commodity unit is established by merely dividing the average quantity of each component commodity by the average dollar value of all the components taken together. The operating machinery consists merely of delivering paper money in exchange for commodity units and commodity units in exchange for paper money.

Finally, the question of constitutionality is not involved in our proposal as it is in the Farm Bill of 1937. The reasoning by which six justices of the Supreme Court declared unconstitutional the original Agricultural Adjustment Act of 1933 would certainly invalidate the new legislation as well. The latter might be upheld, it is true, but only through a direct reversal of the sentiment of the court. On the other hand, our proposed Reservoir system is merely an application of the power of Congress "to coin money and regulate the value thereof." It poses no constitutional problem of any kind.

That the government must extend substantial aid to the farmers is now all but universally recognized. The proposed Farm Bill is a sincere and well-considered attempt to place agriculture on a sound economic footing. There is logic in its underlying principle that *if* individual prices are to be maintained then production must be controlled. But it is our thesis, first, that the disadvantages inherent in this combination of maintained prices and controlled output are so serious as far to outweigh its benefits; and second, that by means of the reservoir mechanism the farmer can receive adequate protection, without curtailment, regimentation or government subsidies.

The adoption of the Reservoir plan will not preclude additional measures on behalf of individual crops, if these should seem desirable. The present cotton situation is a case in point. That staple is faced this year by the loss of a good part of its foreign market and an enormous increase in the yield per acre. Assistance in such an emergency might follow any of the Farm Bill devices or it could be of a different type—such as the two-price system embodied in the McNary-Haugen plan or the equivalent processing tax-producers bonus arrangement.

There are obvious advantages in first adopting a sound plan of general farm relief and then considering whether any individual crop may require special treatment. The technique of the Farm Bill may gain popular acceptance if it is limited to special or emergency situations, such as we have in cotton, and particularly if its effect is mitigated by the adoption of a more important general plan which looks to coordinated expansion instead of to contraction.[10]

CONCLUSION

The issue of permanent crop control, now directly and dramatically before the nation, turns in essence upon a conflict of economic viewpoints which can be resolved only by recourse to a new concept of storage. The gist of the argument for crop control is that a prosperous nation depends upon a prosperous agriculture; that the farmer's prosperity depends upon fair prices; and that he can obtain a fair price only if his output is regulated. The gist of the argument against crop control is that national well-being cannot be attained through scarcity. These statements, while opposed, are not contradictory. They apply to different parts of the economic structure, and their variance is one of emphasis rather than of fact.

The only way in which these two viewpoints can be reconciled is by giving the farmer a fair price without requiring curtailment. The only feasible way to bring this about is to impound and store his surplus production. But such storage must be more than the mere intermediate stage in a continuous process of production and consumption, and more even than a temporary and emergency withholding of output from market. To avoid depressing the price level such surplus must be neither a current nor an overhanging factor on the market; it must be almost as effectively eliminated as a bearish market factor as if it had been destroyed and never produced.

But this is precisely the function of a true granary when viewed not merely as a repository of grain for sale but as a safeguard against "years of drought, flood or other adverse conditions"—including war. Such were the granaries of Joseph, of the Incas, of the Chinese, and of Rome. Such, most emphatically, were not the grain holdings of the Farm Board or the coffee holdings of the Brazilian valorization schemes.

Ostensibly this is the very function of the ever-normal granary provided as part of the Crop Control Bill. If that were really so, it might well make the crop control itself unnecessary. Actually, as we have pointed out, the Farm Bill allows a maximum granary equal to only 10 per cent of a normal year's production plus carryover, and it may be less, or nothing at all. If we compare the 10 per cent maximum, say, $1\frac{1}{2}$ months' supply, with the reserve of several years regarded as necessary in ancient times, we see at once why the granary provided in the Farm Bill cannot be expected to solve the problem of surplus, and why the bill must necessarily resort to crop curtailment as its chief weapon for dealing with abundance.

If our Reservoir plan can effectively impound a composite farm surplus for future use, as we believe is the case, then it stands forth as the logical solution of the present basic conflict between the advocates of fair farm prices and the advocates of expanding rather than limiting production.

PART V

Other Aspects of the Reservoir Plan

"It would perhaps be a permissible simplification to say that the economic problem with which the civilized world is grappling is, in substance, that of adjusting production and consumption so as to avoid both want and glut. All the disputes over currencies, debts, tariffs, prices and trade are phases of the central riddle, since the aim of monetary efforts, price-raising and taxation is, or should be, both to stimulate production and to facilitate the consumption of what is produced."

—HAROLD CALLENDER
New York Times, Apr. 8, 1934

Chapter XVII

INTERNATIONAL ASPECTS OF THE RESERVOIR PLAN

"The economic activities of the United States and England combined represent more than half of total world activity; and these countries are in normal times the main sources of capital. World booms and depressions are more likely to spring from changes originating in them and carried outward than by the reverse process."
—Prof. JOHN H. WILLIAMS[1]

IN considering the Monetary Storage proposal from the international standpoint we should discuss in turn its effect upon the foreign-exchange value of the dollar, upon the volume and character of our foreign trade and upon the settlement of debts due us from abroad. A foreign-exchange rate represents the relative value of two currencies. The external value of the dollar will depend, therefore, as much upon the policies of other countries as upon our own. At the moment these foreign monetary policies are quite indefinite and unpredictable. If the United States should stabilize the dollar in terms of the 1921–1930 level for basic commodities, it is by no means impossible that other countries may follow a similar course. In that case stable external values for the important currencies will follow as the result of stable internal values. Declarations made at various times respecting the British monetary policy have made it clear that the establishment and maintenance of a reasonable internal price level are regarded as more important objectives than a fixed gold standard.[2] England may ultimately return to gold because of the advantages of fixed gold parities in conducting international trade; but in any event it seems probable that the far-flung "sterling bloc" (including the

Scandinavian countries) will endeavor to manage a new gold standard in the interest of domestic price stability. It thus appears that the monetary policy of a good part of the commercial world will harmonize very closely with our own objective.

Let us assume, however, that the leading foreign nations return simply to a fixed gold standard at about today's values for their respective units. Is there any reason why the United States would be unable to do likewise, and at the same time maintain the fixed value of the commodity unit? We have already expressed the view that the predepression price level for basic commodities is by no means too high in relation to a $35 price for gold.[3] It is a customary remark that we must choose between external and internal stability for the dollar.[4] In other words, we must either fix the foreign, *i.e.*, the gold, value of the dollar and permit the domestic price level to fluctuate, or else stabilize at home at the cost of fluctuating foreign-exchange rates.

In our opinion this dilemma need exist only in times of considerable economic disturbance. In another emergency such as that of 1931–1933 there is little doubt that we should be willing to sacrifice the gold or foreign-exchange value of the dollar to prevent a collapse of domestic prices. (This is what England did under compulsion in 1931 and we did semivoluntarily in 1933—both times with satisfactory results.) But given reasonably normal world conditions, involving only moderate fluctuations in the general price level, it should not be difficult for us to maintain both the fixed gold value and the fixed basic-commodity value for the dollar.

If we were on a free-trade basis, such a double standard would probably be impracticable. We should face the same difficulty that is involved in the attempt by any one nation to establish bimetallism. If the commodity unit were overvalued in terms of world prices we should have a large influx of commodities with a corresponding loss of gold. (In the same way the adoption of "the free and unlimited" coinage of silver at $1.29 per ounce would result in sending an enormous part of the world's silver to our shores, for which we should have to pay with our gold.)

The effect of our protective tariff, however, has always been to permit the maintenance of a domestic price level substantially higher than that in other countries. Most of the items in the commodity unit are subject to import duties at fairly stiff rates. Hence our fixed price level for the commodity unit is reasonably well insulated against variations in world prices.[5]

It is conceivable, of course, that the world price level may decline to a point which will permit commodity units to flow in from abroad across the existing tariff barriers. If that should occur we should have a choice of two policies, either of which may be defended. First, we might elect to accept a substantial volume of commodity units from abroad, to be added to our commodity reservoir. Presumably these would be paid for out of our gold supply. The net cost of these commodity units to the nation would be less than their fixed dollar value by the amount of tariff duties collected upon their entry.

The possible advantages of such an exchange are threefold. In the first place a trade of some of our gold store at $35 per ounce for commodity units at considerably less than their 1921-1930 average cost might well be regarded as good business from the standpoint of national well-being. We should be getting things worth more than the gold given up. It is essential to bear in mind that these foreign commodities would not come into competition with our own in the domestic markets, but would simply flow into monetary storage, increasing our reservoir supply.

In the second place, the transfer of some of our plethora of gold to other nations might assist in restoring a more wholesome international economic and political situation. We have too large a share of the world's gold supply, for the good either of the rest of the world or of ourselves.[6] Finally this interchange of gold and commodity units, as between ourselves and other countries, might prove a useful mechanism for the stabilization of world prices. Our gold holdings are probably large enough to act as a balance wheel for the international price level. If a moderate portion of our gold goes out into the world in exchange for commodity units, the receipt of this gold by other countries may have inflationary effects sufficient to reverse the downward trend of prices. The opposite situation (import of gold here against export of commodity units) is also conceivable, though not so likely.

Secondly, we may decide as a matter of national policy against the acceptance of commodity units from abroad in exchange for part of our gold. If that is our decision, and if the world price level should fall to a point resulting in an influx of commodity units, we can end this inflow by raising our tariff rates. This has been our traditional defense against international threats to our domestic price structure. While the best economic thought would undoubtedly favor the other alternative, political sentiment is likely to favor the exclusion of foreign additions to our store of commodity units.

The general question we have been discussing comes down to this: Can the United States control its domestic price level and at the same time maintain a fixed foreign-exchange (gold) value for the dollar? The answer is that this can be done either by using its large gold hoard as a means for stabilization of world prices, or else by continuing to employ the tariff as a barrier between internal and external prices.

We have thus left unsettled the question whether we should accept foreign commodity units in exchange for our gold. But there can be no doubt at all that we should gladly accept these units *in settlement of trade and financial balances due us from abroad*. The Reservoir plan offers us a convenient solution for the "creditor-nation dilemma" which has been perplexing us ever since the war. With substantial amounts due us annually on private investments abroad and on inter-government war debts, we have still insisted on exporting more than we import. This required either continuous additions to our foreign lending, or persistent imports of gold, or both, in order to balance the accounts.[7]

Foreign governments have excused their failure to maintain payments under the war-debt settlements by pointing out that we refuse to accept their merchandise and that they cannot afford to ship us additional gold. Similar justification has been offered in part for defaults on foreign obligations privately held by our investors.[8]

It would be greatly to our interest to facilitate payment of amounts due us from abroad by accepting commodity units for addition to our reservoir supply. Undoubtedly we should be better off with those commodities in our possession and safely impounded, than with a mass of unpaid claims against foreign debtors.[9]

The war-debt question has been in abeyance for some time; but many in this country are reluctant to let the matter lapse entirely, and it remains a highly unsatisfactory element in our international relations. Our Reservoir plan should permit new settlements to be reached which could provide for payments in the form of commodity units which would be assembled and delivered by the debtor nations. As a desirable concession under the circumstances, we might well waive the import duties on commodity units sent in on war-debt account. This arrangement would permit the debtor governments to pay us "in kind"; but the goods received will have a currency value similar to gold payments, and they will not compete with any products in our domestic markets.

A final word may be added on the matter of the future development of our foreign trade. No one who is realistically minded can be hopeful for the return either here or abroad of free competition, on the basis of merit only, between domestic and foreign products. Our imports are likely to be pretty well limited to raw materials which we do not adequately produce here, or to articles of luxury or of special quality which are in good part noncompetitive with domestic manufactures. Similarly we cannot expect to sell either our raw materials or our manufactured goods to countries which can readily produce a sufficient supply for themselves. Our automobiles, typewriters, etc., have been able to compete with domestic products in industrialized countries because of the efficiency and economy of our mass-production methods. It is doubtful whether we shall be allowed to hold this advantage, and we may find our sales of manufactured goods restricted more and more to the less developed countries.

If we wish to maintain and extend our exports of finished products we must become increasingly liberal with either our foreign loans or our imports of raw materials. The Commodity-reservoir plan offers a sound basis for offsetting exports by imports in a manner least upsetting to our domestic markets or our investment structure. We can, in fact, trade our surplus output of manufactured goods for foreign raw materials which, by entering into the stored commodity units, will create simultaneously an essential reserve for the nation and a corresponding quantity of currency available to pay our manufacturers for their exports.

Summarizing the above discussion, we think it a demonstrable fact that the Monetary Storage arrangement need not create any serious problems as regards foreign-exchange stability; but, on the other hand, it should contribute most effectively to the maintenance of our foreign trade and to the settlement of foreign-debt problems.

Chapter XVIII

PRECEDENTS AND RELATED PROPOSALS

"There is no reason why the farmer should not finance himself, as the gold miner does, by turning his output into money directly."
—Thomas A. Edison[1]

OUR Reservoir system, or Monetary Storage plan, has been developed as a logical solution of the central problem of "poverty amid plenty." Basically, the suggested mechanism represents an adaptation to modern conditions of early ideas for State acquisition and disposal of surplus. The commodity-unit arrangement was devised to meet the difficulties created by the advent of a fairly large number of primary commodities in place of the one or two dominant ones of the distant past. The use of these commodity units as the backing for currency becomes possible because of their inherent qualities, and also as a result of the emergence of newer concepts in the monetary field. The price-stabilization feature of the plan is a consequence of the monetary mechanism; but in view of the overshadowing role of the price structure in present-day economics,[2] the stabilization aspect assumes an importance only slightly inferior to that of the surplus-conservation element.

As previously stated, the Monetary Storage plan is in reality a synthesis of three quite distinct ideas: (a) storage of surplus for future need, (b) the use of basic commodities as the backing for money, and (c) the stabilization of the price level. Some claim for originality may be made on behalf of the completely articulated proposal herein presented. But its component parts, separately considered, deserve neither the acclaim nor the reproach of novelty.

Each is solidly grounded in precedent and authority. It may aid not a little in the understanding of our own contribution if we seek now to relate the proposal to other suggestions and to actual practice.

Chapter II, on government and surplus, contains numerous references to State activities directed toward conserving surplus. The examples given include Egypt and Rome in ancient times, Peru in the medieval period, China from the sixth century B.C. to modern days, France under the Bourbons and under Napoleon. We have contemporaneously the State grain reserve of Switzerland and the very recently projected food reservoir of Great Britain.

The most important recent proposals along storage lines are, of course, the two legislative measures setting up an Ever-normal Granary system, which were discussed in the preceding section. Another idea of considerable interest is that advanced by Thomas A. Edison in 1921. Since this contained monetary and price-stabilization features as well as the storage element, it may be best to consider the Edison scheme comprehensively toward the end of this chapter.

From the monetary side, the precedents for our proposal fall into two divisions: those relating to the use of commodities as physical money and those relating to the deposit of commodities as a reserve against, or backing for, paper money. In theory our plan is more closely allied to the first arrangement than the second. For our commodity-unit certificates are in all technical respects similar to the old-style gold certificates. These were not regarded as being "secured" by gold, but rather as directly representing a certain amount of gold, which to all intents and purposes was actually in circulation. (The certificate device, with the actual gold held in trust thereagainst, was adopted mainly for convenience in handling and to save loss through abrasion.) The commodity-unit certificates are, of course, the

only feasible method of monetizing the actual commodities—
but this procedure may properly be regarded as turning the
physical units into physical money.

The use of commodities other than gold and silver as
physical money has an ancient history. The Chase National
Bank collection of moneys of the world presents a bewildering variety of commodities that have served as money in
various times and places. These include not only metals
such as iron, copper, bronze and platinum, but also such
products as grain, spice, salt, nails, soap, cheese, cocoa, silk
and cotton cloth and countless others.[3] As late as the seven-
teenth and eighteenth centuries we find that paper money
backed by tobacco was well established as a monetary medium in several of the American colonies.[4]

The joining together of two or more physical commodities
to form a composite money—as is envisaged by our commodity unit—has an ancient counterpart in the coins made
of *electrum*, a metal consisting of 73 per cent by weight of
gold and 27 per cent by weight of silver. Electrum was found
in a natural state in Asia Minor, and the earliest coins of this
metal seem to have appeared in India and Lydia.[5] Some
centuries later (about 400 b.c.) similar coins were minted by
Carthage out of artificial or fused electrum.

In recent times the idea of joining the two precious metals
together has been revived in a well-defined monetary proposal known as "symmetallism." It is a special form of
bimetallism, designed to avoid the difficulties arising from
fluctuations in the relative price of gold and silver. Under a
symmetallic standard, the dollar might be defined as equivalent, say, to about $1/47$ oz. of gold plus about $1/5$ oz. of silver.
(This would correspond to a 75 per cent component of gold,
taken at $35 per ounce, and a 25 per cent component of silver,
taken at $1.28 per ounce.) For monetary purposes the two
metals would always be taken together in the fixed propor-

tion. Coins would consist of the two metals fused together; currency would be issued and redeemed only against deposit and through delivery of the two metals combined. The currency value would not be affected by change in the relative market price of the two metals and the Treasury would be concerned only in keeping the value of the dollar fixed in terms of the *composite* value of the two metals.

It will be recognized that the underlying principles of symmetallism and of our commodity-unit currency are identical. Our monetary proposal may therefore be defined as symmetallism applied to a fairly large group of basic commodities, instead of to gold and silver. We are not disposed to enter here upon a detailed discussion of the merits and defects of the original symmetallic proposal embracing the two precious metals, for it does not appear that gold will return to free circulation in the predictable future, either alone or tied to silver. It may be remarked that there is respectable authority behind the statement that symmetallism is the only really practicable form of bimetallism.[6] Bimetallism itself is not regarded in economic circles as quite the heretical notion that it seemed in the days of Bryan. We do not favor gold-and-silver symmetallism, because we see no necessity in the modern world for building our economy around two essentially unimportant commodities. However, the admission of the symmetallic idea to serious consideration by economists may be regarded as a helpful preliminary to the similar but more comprehensive suggestion which we are advancing.

The idea of using basic commodities as part of the monetary reserve—rather than as a direct monetary equivalent—has been advanced quite recently by the English authority, Dr. Paul Einzig.[7]

To sum up our discussion of monetary precedents, we may point out that there is at least one parallel for each aspect of our monetary proposal, *e.g.*, (*a*) gold certificates, as an example of paper money representing a physical commodity held in trust against it; (*b*) various commodities, other than gold and silver, formerly used as money; (*c*) symmetallism, as a scheme for combining two commodities into a single monetary unit; and (*d*) the ideas of Edison, Einzig *et al.*, for using stored basic commodities as a backing for currency.

The third facet, or division, of our proposal relates to the stabilization of the price level. This concept has inspired tremendous interest, numerous concrete proposals and searching criticism. Joseph Stagg Lawrence's scholarly work, entitled *Stabilization of Prices* (published in 1928), described and analyzed about a dozen different plans for eliminating or reducing variations in general prices. Most of these plans turn upon one or more of three devices: changing the gold content of the currency unit, controlling the amount of currency in circulation and controlling the credit supply. The more important proposals discussed in Lawrence's study may be briefly summarized as follows:

THE FISHER PLAN[8] (THE COMPENSATED DOLLAR)

This provides for raising or lowering the gold content of the dollar to offset advances and declines in the price level. This plan was incorporated in the Goldsborough Bill introduced in Congress in 1922 and again in 1924. A closely similar plan was presented by D. J. Tinnes, and incorporated in a bill introduced in Congress in 1924.

THE STRONG AMENDMENT TO THE FEDERAL RESERVE ACT

This bill, introduced in Congress in 1926, provided that "all the powers of the Federal Reserve System shall be used for promoting stability in the price level." The amendment was revised and amplified in 1927 and 1928, but the underlying idea remained the same.

THE SNYDER PLAN[9]

This plan, presented by Carl Snyder in 1923, aims "to keep the amount of currency and credit in balance with the price level, and maintain the latter at as nearly a constant figure as is practically possible." The means employed is to be a combination of automatic changes in the rediscount rate and automatic changes in the Federal Reserve banks' holdings of securities and acceptances, to offset changes in the price level as measured by the Bureau of Labor Statistics index of wholesale prices. (Dr. Snyder now favors a more inclusive measure of the "general price level."[10])

THE KEYNES PLAN[11]

L. M. Keynes's proposal, published in 1924, was a combination of the Fisher and the Snyder idea, as applied to Great Britain. It suggested that the government and the Bank of England together should achieve stability of prices by discretionary variations in the price of gold, in the bank rate and in the rate of emission of Treasury bills.

THE HAWTREY PLAN[12] (1923)

On the one hand, this provides for international agreements setting up a gold-exchange standard and a fixed "aggregate circulation of (uncovered) paper money in the international system." In addition it required that the central banks in the various countries utilize their credit-control powers to offset deviations in the price level.

THE GENOA PLAN[13]

This was embodied in the Resolutions on Currency of the Financial Commission at the Genoa Conference in April 1922. It suggests an international convention to "centralize and coordinate the demand for gold, and so to avoid these wide fluctuations in the purchasing power of gold which might otherwise result from the simultaneous and competitive efforts of a number of countries to secure metallic reserves." The means proposed include a gold-exchange standard or an international clearing system. It also suggests control of credit in each country with a view to stabilizing prices.

Lawrence also discusses two other ideas of a different character, *viz.*

THE LEHFELDT PLAN

This proposal, advanced before Congress in 1928, required international cooperation for the purpose of acquiring all the gold mines in the world and then controlling the annual output in order thereby to regulate and stabilize the world price level.[14]

THE LEWIS PLAN[15]

This plan, described in 1925, set up a convertible composite money, representing appropriate amounts of wheat, cotton, iron and silver. The government would be prepared to issue money against "warrants" for the four commodities when presented together, and to deliver a set of such warrants in exchange for currency.

It would appear adequate for our purpose if we direct our own discussion, first, to the Fisher plan for the compensated dollar; second, to the Lewis plan, because of its points of similarity to our own; and, finally, to the general idea of stabilizing the price level by controlling the volume of credit and currency.

To Prof. Irving Fisher must go the major credit for calling popular attention to the disadvantages of the unstable dollar, for developing the use of index numbers to measure changes in the price level, and for advancing a concrete plan for price stability which has been a central point in the discussion of the subject.[16] Fisher's scheme provides for changing the gold content of the dollar to counteract a change in the price level. If prices decline, the gold content of the dollar is to be increased proportionately; if prices rise, the gold content is to be reduced.

This plan depends for its success on either or both of two assumptions: (*a*) Changes in the gold content of the dollar will affect prices directly, because people will ask a higher or lower price for their goods according as the dollar they receive contains fewer or more grains of gold. (*b*) The price level will be corrected *indirectly* by changes in the weight of gold in the dollar, through the effects of such changes upon foreign exchange, foreign trade and international gold movements, on the one hand, and on the domestic credit structure, on the other.

That the first assumption is incorrect has been amply demonstrated by the monetary history of the past few years. The price level of all commodities has shown no tendency to respond directly and proportionately to the reduction of 41 per cent in the gold content of the dollar.[17] It is quite clear that the prices charged by the individual manufacturer or merchant will not be governed in his own calculations by the number of grains of gold to which the paper dollar happens to be actually or theoretically equivalent. Hence, were the Fisher plan in operation, there is no reason at all to expect that small changes in the gold content of the unit will have a definite countervailing effect upon the price level.

There is a better theoretical reason for expecting the Fisher plan to gain its objective through its indirect effects. A cut in the gold content of the dollar should lead to a higher price level by stimulating exports and curtailing imports, and also by increasing the gold reserves, thus making credit easier. For opposite reasons an increase in the gold content should make for lower prices. But even if the plan were operating under the most favorable conditions, we could scarcely expect these corrective changes to take place automatically and immediately.

The required favorable conditions are, first, a definite and reasonably stable international price level which can readily affect domestic prices by means of substantial exports or imports and, secondly, a close-knit credit structure which is quickly responsive to any change in the amount of the gold base. We are very far from having either of these conditions at the present time. There is no chance at all of our being allowed by other nations to use a definite international price level as a fulcrum against which to raise or lower our domestic level by means of variations in the foreign-exchange value of the dollar. (In all probability this idea was never really feasible except for some comparatively small country whose domestic price developments would have practically no effect upon the general international situation.) As for the second point, in view of our present enormous stock of gold in relation to total credit, it is quite clear that changes in that stock—whether through revaluation, imports or exports—are likely to have a much smaller effect upon credit than the various control measures within the authority of the Federal Reserve Board, to which reference has already been made in the chapter on credit control.

The writer must express grave doubts, therefore, as to the practicability of the Fisher plan under present-day conditions.[18] While a generation ago there may have been good reason for believing in the efficacy of controlling the price level through the gold content of the currency unit, the status of gold has since grown so completely artificial (or metaphysical) as to make it a thoroughly undependable agency for influencing any important sector of our general economy.

The plan put forward by Prof. G. M. Lewis in 1925 has attracted comparatively little attention, but its points of resemblance to our own proposal entitle it to discussion here. Under this proposal the currency unit would be made equivalent to a composite commodity unit consisting of fixed amounts of wheat, cotton, iron and silver. The government would issue currency in exchange for "warrants" representing the four commodities and, conversely, deliver "warrants" upon presentation of the currency for redemption.

If the commodities tendered for currency were to be held in storage by the government, then the Lewis plan would be basically identical with our own. Yet this was not at all the author's idea, as is indicated by the following paragraph from his presentation of his proposal.[19]

> In countries which might possibly be cut off from the supply of one or more of these basic commodities, it might be desirable to establish Government warehouses for storing one or more of the basic commodities, but this is no essential part of the plan, and indeed it is usually found best not to tax the Government with duties which can equally well be performed by the existing machinery of private enterprises. The fact that the Government possesses no reserves will not affect the value of its money as long as the people are confident that the Government will fulfill its obligations to convert its money into the basic commodities.

The text is far from clear as to the actual mechanics of the plan, but Lewis apparently considered that the commodities brought in for money should be sold out by the government in the open market. Conversely, the government would have to buy them in the open market when they were demanded in exchange for money. Such an arrangement would be entirely impracticable, since it would mean continuous and unlimited sales of commodities at a loss when there was a surplus at the standard price level, and similar unlimited purchases at a loss when there was a shortage at the standard level.

The Lewis plan was evidently devised solely as a device for stabilizing prices, without reference to the disposition of a possible surplus. The latter problem is the starting point of our own proposal and leads us to the Commodity-reservoir plan, with price stabilization as a derived and secondary effect. With full acknowledgment of the extent that Professor Lewis's ideas parallel our own,[20] we cannot avoid the conclusion that the Lewis proposal as presented is incomplete and quite unworkable.[21]

At the present time the price-stabilization idea that enjoys the greatest vogue is that of "managed money" and "managed credit." It is widely held that a monetary authority vested with sufficient control over the creation of money and credit could so employ its powers as to keep the internal price level of the country on an even keel.[22] This concept was embodied not only in the Strong amendments to the Federal Reserve Act, already referred to, but also in a new Goldsborough Bill, which passed the House of Representatives in 1932, in the following form:[23]

Be it enacted . . . That the Federal Reserve Act is amended by adding at the end thereof a new section to read as follows:

Section 1. It is hereby declared to be the policy of the United States that the average purchasing power of the dollar as ascertained by the Department of Labor in the wholesale commodity markets for the period covering the years 1921 to 1929, inclusive, shall be restored and maintained by the control of the volume of credit and currency.

Section 2. The Federal Reserve Board, the Federal reserve banks, and the Secretary of the Treasury are hereby charged with the duty of making effective this policy.

Section 3. Acts and parts of Acts inconsistent with the terms of this Act are hereby repealed.

Whether or not such a course is practicable is a highly controversial question. In Chap. XII, having discussed the various methods of credit control now available to the Federal Reserve Board, we expressed the tentative view that they might be adequate to cope with the threat of overexpansion and resultant catastrophe. But control of credit is by no means coextensive with control of the price level. In a broad sense it is true, of course, that a widely expanded credit structure will make for higher prices; and conversely. But the relation between credit volume and the price structure is an extremely irregular one at best. In 1928–1929 we had enormous credit expansion accompanied by an actual decrease in the commodity price level—the price advance having been concentrated on securities and real estate. In 1933 we had a spectacular increase in the commodity price level without any credit expansion.[24] From March, 1933, to the end of 1936 the value of stocks listed on the New York Stock Exchange has increased from 19.7 to 60 billion dollars, with an addition of only 700 million dollars in brokers' loans.

Price-level control through monetary management is subject, therefore, to doubts of a twofold nature. It is by no means certain—though it is fairly possible—that a monetary authority can effectively and satisfactorily control the credit structure. It is much more uncertain whether even an effective control of credit can be so exercised as to result in a high degree of stability throughout the price structure. The experience of Sweden since 1931 is pointed to as evidence that such results can be accomplished. No one will claim, however, that Swedish conditions are comparable to ours;[25] nor does the period during which the control policy was operative necessarily indicate that it is bound to be equally successful in the future.

Our Commodity-reservoir proposal is not open to the doubts that attach to currency and credit management as a means of stabilization. The latter rests on certain assumptions as to the effect upon prices of various moves in the field of money and credit. Our mechanism is as direct and as unequivocal as was the fixing of the price of gold under the old gold standard. We do not try to fix the price level by *changing* other things, *e.g.*, the value of gold, the rediscount rate, or the holdings of government securities by the Reserve banks. Instead we fix the price level—for the composite group of basic commodities—*by establishing a complete equivalence and a continuous physical interchange between this commodity group and the dollar.*

It seems improbable in any case that the problem of burdensome surpluses can be solved by monetary management alone, without the use of a commodity reservoir. We should have to assume that these banking devices alone can maintain a continuous equilibrium between supply and demand. Without such an equilibrium the price level must rise or fall, regardless of any other measures that may be invoked. Our Commodity-reservoir plan does create such a balance in the field of basic materials by the mechanism of impounding a temporary surplus and releasing it when needed. Furthermore, it has the unique quality of establishing a physical reserve which can function as national wealth and as the means for improving our national living standard.

Our final discussion of alternative proposals will be devoted to the Edison Commodity-dollar plan, which was first published in December 1921.[26] Under this proposal the farmers (and other producers of raw materials) may borrow without interest against deposit of basic commodities in a government-controlled storage system. The amount borrowed is to be limited to one-half of the average price of the commodity over the preceding 25 years. The money borrowed is to be created in the form of new currency secured by the deposited commodities. Each loan is to be repaid within a year, presumably by the sale of sufficient of the deposited commodity, and upon such repayment a corresponding amount of the new currency is to be retired.

There are striking resemblances and striking differences between the Edison plan and our own. In both cases there is to be storage of basic commodities by the State. In both cases also a new form of currency is to be issued, backed by and redeemable through the stored commodities. But Edison's idea is to be carried out by means of non-interest-bearing *loans* against individual commodities. In our plan the commodity unit is monetized directly in the same way that gold and silver have been coined into currency.

The loan feature compelled Edison to introduce serious restrictions into the operation of his proposal. Most important is the requirement that the loans be liquidated within a year. This is needed because otherwise the borrower could speculate for an indefinite period, without cost, on a rise in the price of his product. It was necessary also to limit the borrowing to one-half of the average market price in the past, in order to protect the government as much as possible against loss through a severe price decline accompanied by nonpayment of the loans.

These two restrictions would seem to reduce the practical effect of the Edison plan to a scheme for facilitating the orderly marketing of crops during the full crop year. It deals only with *seasonal* surplus, and offers no solution to the problem of cyclical and secular oversupply. Its price-stabilizing element arises solely from the help it extends to the producer towards extending his marketing season over a full year, instead of concentrating it in a brief period after bringing in the crop.

We must add, however, that Edison's monetary philosophy was much broader than his specific plan. The inventor insisted, as we do, that basic raw commodities afford a sounder backing for modern money than does gold. He emphasized the need for a nonfluctuating monetary unit, and attempted to replace a gold currency of variable value by a commodity currency of stable purchasing power. We should like to claim for our plan that it carries out the fundamental concepts of the great inventor, which his own detailed proposal would fall short of realizing.

Chapter XIX

THE RESERVOIR PLAN AND THE DEMOCRATIC TRADITION

"The important changes that have been made peacefully have always been made by an expanding economic system. Where there is expansion, there is security; and where there is security, there are the time and the opportunity for men to give reason its right to empire. . . . Accommodation is always possible in a society where new material benefits can be continually conferred."
—HAROLD LASKI[1]

"Political freedom is the condition of all freedom."
—DOROTHY THOMPSON[2]

IN this concluding chapter we wish to consider some of the political implications of our Monetary Storage proposal. Superficially and in the narrower sense, it may seem that we are adding to an already excessive weight of political interference with business. Upon reflection our plan will be found, we think, to offer comparatively little in the way of political spoils or partisan advantage. But when we consider political significance in its broader meaning, this aspect of the Reservoir plan may well be found to constitute a far-reaching and valuable contribution to the solution of the deepest problems of today.

Let us speak first of the plan and politics. In this field two questions suggest themselves. Is the purpose or effect of our proposal to benefit one economic group at the expense of others? Will the machinery of the Reservoir system offer wide opportunities for political pressure, controversy or chicanery?

On the first point we have acknowledged, or rather asserted, that the primary benefits of the Monetary Storage plan will accrue in largest measure to agriculture. In the present era when such strenuous efforts are being made to assist our farm population, this characteristic of our proposal will scarcely need to be defended. Yet an important distinction should be drawn between the agricultural aid which we have formulated and the various types of farm relief recently adopted or now under consideration.

Farm relief has been approached hitherto as an unavoidable resort to group legislation. The farmer has been singled out to receive many kinds of help not accorded other sections of the population. He has been granted cash bonuses of various sorts, special credit facilities and powerful assistance in controlling total production; his output has been purchased by the government; a special price-level objective has been formulated for his benefit; he will soon receive, no doubt, protection against weather hazards at less than commercial cost. There is now in prospect a comprehensive relief measure looking to the guarantee of suitable (relative) prices for each important product.

It can scarcely be claimed that the nation's farm relief policies have been the result of any reasoned political philosophy, under which we have established just why the farmer is entitled to special benefits at the hands of the government and the exact extent of his preferential claims. We have, rather, felt instinctively and somewhat vaguely that the farmer has a special status (a) because he produces indispensable raw materials, (b) because farming is a way of life as well as a business, and (c) because farm prosperity or depression appears to affect other areas of business more directly than the other way around. For these reasons—and perhaps others, including his voting strength—the country as a whole is quite ready to see the farmer get help from the government. But the nature and extent of this help—in the absence of any coherent economic theory—have been left largely to generalized judgment, to the urgings of necessity and to political pressure.

The approach of the Monetary Storage plan to the farm problem is completely different. It does not seek to aid the farmer as such. It does not deal with the farmer at all, but with his products. It recognizes in a concrete and limited manner the special status of these products as basic raw materials—this being the peculiar economic merit of agriculture, on which its claim to distinctive consideration has long been made and recognized.

The benefits conferred on the farmer by the Reservoir system are highly important, but they are strictly limited to what his product can contribute in return, and they are not confined to the farm population as a class. (The oil producers loom larger in our picture than the wheat growers.) In an oversimplified phrase, we may say that we are placing the farmer and other raw-materials producers in the same category as the owners of gold mines, by according the same monetary status to basic commodities as a group that has long been conferred on gold. But this extension of the coinage privilege is not proposed as a favor, or as a relief measure, or as a convenient means of stimulating business by creating more purchasing power. It is based on the considered principle that the primary raw materials are really primary throughout the economic sphere. Not only do all the material things of life begin with and develop from them; but the complex and delicately interrelated organization of business receives its first impetus and its controlling tone from this area. The economic flow has a definite *entropy*, or permanent direction, from raw materials outward. Thus our identification of the monetary medium with raw materials as a group is merely a logical synthesis of the two primary elements out of which our elaborate economic fabric is constructed.

If the farmer receives most, though by no means all, of the benefit of this synthesis, it is because his product entitles him to it. Hence we assert that it is not the *political* but the *economic* status of agriculture that is here given its carefully measured recognition.

To what extent may the machinery of our plan be tampered with by purely political efforts? Will the make-up of the commodity unit be subject to group pressure, or special pleading or reciprocal logrolling? It seems to the writer that there are cogent reasons for minimizing this threat. The chief of these is the difficulty of obtaining special favors for one commodity in a mutualized arrangement wherein what is given to one is necessarily taken directly from all the others. The second reason is that the partiality would have to be extreme and glaring to be of manifest practical benefit to the producers who might press for it.

These assertions may appear more persuasive if the method of setting up the commodity unit be contrasted with that involved in a tariff bill—the notorious arena for the exertion of political pressure. Each tariff schedule is virtually independent of every other. Except for the rather indefinite concept of "difference in cost of production" there are no principles or formulas by which the correct rate of duty may be objectively determined. Hence tariff making inevitably inspires an avalanche of pressures from interested groups. And since one group does not feel injured by favors accorded another, their combined influence is toward mutual support and stimulus rather than as a mutual check.

Our commodity unit, on the other hand, is constructed on an objective and fairly scientific basis, in the same way as weighted index numbers have been constructed for many years. Its make-up is far more a matter of arithmetic than of judgment. Discretion may, indeed, enter to some extent into the selection of the base period, but the decision on this point is scarcely one on which the adherents of any single commodity could exercise any effective pressure in their own interest. But the chief check against undue pressure is the mutual opposition of all the component products. Favoritism could be shown an individual item only over the combined protests of all the others, and in defiance of a definite and reasonable principle of allocation. Favors accorded all the component commodities would, of course, cancel each other and be entirely meaningless.

The analogy, if one is to be sought, is therefore not to be found in tariff making or pork-barrel allocations, but rather in such well-established and nonpolitical methods as those of apportioning government subsidies for road building among the states, or the state appropriations for education among its subdivisions. In such instances the presence of a logical formula and the mutual check imposed by contrary interests are sufficient to ensure a fair division of the benefits.

The other intrinsic feature which should tend to minimize objectionable political maneuvers is the fact that any moderate change in the composition of the commodity unit would exert an indirect and unimpressive effect upon the commodities involved. An increase, say, of 10 per cent in the quantity of wheat as against other commodities would represent a quite considerable change in the make-up of our unit. Yet such a change would be unlikely to have an important influence upon the status of the wheat farmers. It would mean only a fractional increase in that minor portion of their output which flows into monetary storage. The influence upon the price, while real enough, would not be distinguishable from the many other and more important factors that determine the day-to-day quotations for wheat. Nor would such a change involve any benefits directly conferred upon the individual farmer, and thus sufficiently manifest to inspire the determined effort necessary to obtain an unjustified advantage against the opposition of all the other producers affected.

But these are political considerations in the narrower and the lesser sense. The significant political aspects of the Reservoir plan lie in its relationship to those portentous stresses and changes which now hold almost the entire world in their grip, and have not failed to cast their shadow across our own land. That there is a world-wide challenge to democracy may not be denied. That this challenge has its roots in economic instability[3] and that its danger increases as prosperity diminishes are now equally manifest. What would happen to American democracy in another depression similar to the last is a none too pleasant question.

The Reservoir plan is an engineering mechanism applied to the field of economics, and in its essence it has nothing to do with democracy or any other political philosophy. It will operate with equal efficiency and value under capitalism or communism; in a democratic, fascist or oligarchic state. In sum, it is suited to any economy which uses money and is capable of creating a surplus of raw materials above immediate consumptive requirements.

But while this proposal is not inherently identified with the American system of democracy and competitive capitalism, it is peculiarly apt and serviceable for the preservation of that system. The weakness of capitalism is its inability to deal efficiently with its own production. The weakness of democracy appears in economic crisis, when the emergency seems to call for an unlimited concentration of power. Few will doubt that if the economic collapse of 1932–1933 had continued here much longer it would have eventuated in some form of political dictatorship. The ultimate direction of such a dictatorship, and its effect upon our civil as well as our economic liberties, would have rested in the lap of the gods.

It is probably superfluous to argue that the Reservoir plan should be adopted because by preventing a repetition of economic collapse it will safeguard our democratic heritage. It may seem quite enough to claim that our proposal will avoid the catastrophe of deep depression; for this would surely be sufficient merit in itself and hardly needs to be buttressed by reference to political dangers. Yet this added emphasis may not be amiss, in view of our ingrained tendency to forget the nightmare of depression as soon as the sun of prosperity has risen once again. Now in 1937 is really the best time to consider the challenge of the business cycle— while the rigors of the receding disaster are still fresh in our memory, but the lifting of the pressure gives us the opportunity for quieter and clearer thought.

The imperfect and ambiguous nature of our returning prosperity makes the need for such pondering all the more evident. With the index of general business risen above normal, we still find unemployment and relief a major burden. The balancing of the federal budget is yet to be accomplished. The banking situation is artificial and replete with explosive possibilities. Great irregularities persist in the rate of recovery in various areas of business. The economic machine has still to show even the deceptive smoothness of former prosperous eras. Although we have not yet fully emerged from the penumbra of the last depression we can already descry upon the horizon the ominous shadow of the next.

As we look back upon the recent troubled years, which strained our economic and political structure so nearly to the breaking point and which called forth such vigorous and novel remedial measures, it is natural to ask what policies and techniques have now been developed to prevent the recurrence of such disaster. The answer is none too reassuring. We have, indeed, created new controls of credit, particularly in the field of securities; and we may thus believe, though hardly be certain, that the credit abuses which accentuated the business cycles of the past will now be eliminated. (Against this improvement in procedure stands the fact that our gold reserves and the deposit totals created by government deficit financing have together laid the foundation for potential credit expansion on a tremendous scale.)

But even if we were able to prevent undue expansion of bank loans, the inherent character of our business organization would still seem to threaten us with cyclical swings of dangerous intensity. Contraction and prostration are once again giving way to expansion on all fronts. That this expansion will graduate into overexpansion, and culminate in collapse, seems just as inevitable in 1937 as it was prior to 1930. The demand for capital goods will again make itself felt insistently, but impermanently; the production of raw materials will again be overstimulated by higher commodity prices. Purchasing power and consumption will eventually fall short of production, and the now familiar paradox of poverty through plenty will again hold us in its grip.

This prospect we may not face down with the old comfortable platitudes. It will not do to say smugly that the business cycle is a natural and salutary process and that variations in trade conditions are the price of progress. The risk is too great that the next depression will resemble the last. If that should happen we shall have more to worry about than bad business. The people of the United States will not tolerate another deep depression that arises not from any lack of natural resources, productive capacity or man and brain power, but solely from imperfections in the functioning of the system of finance capitalism.

Those who would retain the merits of capitalism and individual initiative are challenged to make that system workable. If within a short time it should fail miserably once again, it may give way quite suddenly to something else. That "something else" may turn out to be no better economically, and far worse politically, than what it replaces. But when a people will no longer bear the ills they have, they fly to others that they know not of. For that truth we have example, and to spare, in recent history.

Whatever be our view of the ultimate evolution of our economic structure—whether or not we perceive an underlying tide bearing us inexorably towards some form of collectivism—it is essential to the preservation of the American way of life that sudden economic metamorphosis be avoided and that our destiny be permitted to unfold itself by gradual steps. At this stage collectivism seems quite incompatible with democracy. We lack the settled and unanimous conviction necessary for its peaceful acceptance. We lack, too, the tradition of efficient and unselfish public service without which collectivism might well mean a ruthless and crushing bureaucracy. We need time to develop much further that sense of social responsibility which has been growing apace in recent years.

It is not the least merit of the Commodity-reservoir plan that it enables us to deal with the challenging problems of surplus production and the distribution of income within the traditional framework of American democracy. It does not require regimentation to adjust supply to demand, nor does it invoke confiscation to raise the living standard of the underprivileged. It supplies a sorely needed mechanical improvement to an economic system which, after demonstrating a marvelous efficiency on the side of production, has recently revealed a glaring weakness in the field of distribution.

CHAPTER NOTES

Chapter I

1. Quoted by Chen Huan Chang, *Economic Principles of Confucius*, p. 358, New York, 1911.

2. John I. McFarland, quoted in the *Wall Street Journal*, October 1935.

3. About 10 million acres of cotton were plowed under, equivalent to 25 per cent of the total planted. Cotton destroyed was estimated at 4,257,000 bales. Cash payments made by the government under this destruction program totaled 110 million dollars. The AAA purchased for slaughter four million pigs and one million sows "soon to farrow," resulting in an estimated reduction in the 1934 supply of 1800 million pounds (see summary in *The Agricultural Situation*, September 1933).

4. In the six crop years ending in 1936, coffee destroyed in Brazil totaled 36,700,000 bags. From July 1936 to March 1937 nine million bags additional were destroyed (see *Annual Coffee Supplement of the New York Coffee and Sugar Exchange*, July 1936).

5. Brief references to all these meetings and agreements (except as to coffee) can be found in *World Production and Prices* 1925–1933, pp. 20–44, published by the League of Nations in 1934. The intergovernmental coffee conference took place in 1936, in Bogota, Colombia (see reference in the *New York Sun*, Dec. 7, 1936).

6. See Annual Report of Bank for International Settlements, 1936, *Federal Reserve Bulletin*, June 1937.

7. Note the following from an address by P. H. Johnston, president of the Chemical National Bank of New York quoted in the *Commercial and Financial Chronicle* (referred to below as *Chronicle*), Jan. 22, 1931, p. 316:

"The most serious obstacle confronting us in the present situation is the fact that our productive capacity is geared up to about 30 per cent more than home consumption. Our national prosperity will be measured by our ability to develop stable foreign markets for our surplus production."

8. See reference to issuance of 40 million dollars of 8 per cent secured notes by Copper Export Corporation in *Chronicle*, Feb. 12, 1921, p. 655.

9. This viewpoint is illustrated by the following quotation from an editorial, Cycles and the Influence of War, *Chronicle*, Oct. 29, 1926, p. 1811. "Nor can the hectic, the 'illusory' prosperity experienced *during* the war be allowed to seemingly overcome what was in reality the abyss of depression, the sudden cataclysm of destruction which almost instan-

taneously fell upon the natural march of increase towards overproduction. We did not, if this be true, enter upon a decline *after* the war, but *in* and *during* and *because* of the war."

10. See, for example, the discussion of the economic consequences of the war in *Report of the Gold Delegation of the Financial Committee*, pp. 17–20, League of Nations, June 1932.

11. For a summary of the causes of depressions from 1798 to date, see E. C. Bratt, *Business Cycles and Forecasting*, pp. 81–210. Money panics, due to bank failures, loss of gold, etc., played a large part in ushering in depressions.

12. "Overbuilding of railways was the primary cause of the English crisis in 1847 and the American crisis of 1873" (see W. C. Clark, *Business Cycles and the Depression of* 1921). Bratt also ascribes the United States depression of 1883–1885 in part to overbuilding of railroads (*ibid.*, pp. 189–193).

13. *Cf.* the following from an editorial in the *Journal of Commerce* of June 22, 1937. "We live in an era in which public interest has been diverted in large measure from the problems concerned with the creation of wealth and directed to those arising from its distribution."

14. See Genesis XXVII, 13, 14; XXXVI, 6, 7, etc.

15. See *Salammbô*, Chap. V.

16. For a comprehensive study of liquidity see Berle and Pedersen, *Liquid Claims and National Wealth*, in particular, Chap. II on Liquidity and Modern Economics. The authors bring out the distinction between the classical concept of liquidity as depending on the character of the underlying assets, *i.e.*, *moving into consumption* and the new idea of liquidity as arising from "shiftability," *e.g.*, *the ability to sell in the stock market*.

17. See *Wealth of Nations*, Vol. II, p. 6.

18. See Benjamin Graham and David L. Dodd, *Security Analysis*, p. 151, McGraw-Hill Book Company, Inc., New York, 1934.

19. This tendency is well illustrated by the contrast between inventory and sales of General Motors Corporation in the 1920–1921 period and the 1929–1932 period, *viz.*,

(Amounts in Millions)

	1919–1920				1929–1932			
	Year	Sales	Inventory at year end	Ratio of inventory to sales, %	Year	Sales	Inventory at year end	Ratio of inventory to sales, %
Prosperity..	1919	$567.3	$164.7	29.1	1929	$1504.4	$188.5	12.5
Depression..	1920	304.5	108.8	35.9	1932	432.3	75.5	17.4

20. These observations apply particularly to farming in western and southern regions. The New England farmer belongs to a somewhat different category. For a discussion of this point see an article by Frank Money, The Horse-and-Buggy Farmer, in the April 1937 issue of the *American Mercury*. It is interesting to note that in 1787, 95 per cent of our population lived on farms and produced almost exclusively for themselves. The 25 per cent of our population now on farms produce mainly for others and sell 85 per cent of their product for cash.

21. Note that world manufacturing activity in 1932 is computed at 78 per cent of the 1925–1929 average, while world agricultural production for 1932 was 104 per cent of the 1925–1929 average (League of Nations, *World Economic Survey*, 1934–1935, pp. 74, 113).

22. See paragraph headed "Low Prices Forced High Production," *Achieving A Balanced Agriculture*, p. 16, published by the U.S. Department of Agriculture, August 1934. See also remark to the same effect in B. Nogaro, *Les Prix Agricoles Mondiaux et la Crise*, 1936, p. 159.

Chapter II

1. References to the varying relationship between European governments and cartels can be found in K. E. Pribam, *Cartel Problems*.

2. The Industrial Recovery Act was to lapse at the end of two years after enactment or sooner if the President or Congress declared that the "emergency has ended" (Second 2c).

3. Most of our references to governmental price-fixing and crop-restricting activities can be located in *Control of Production of Agricultural Products by Governments*, Department of Agriculture, Agricultural Economics Bibliography 23, 1927. Separate page references will not be given because of their number, except in some important instances. Certain additional authorities will be referred to below.

4. See *Chronicle*, Oct. 30, 1926, p. 2208.

5. *Ibid.*, Dec. 11, 1926, pp. 2957–2958.

6. In 1921 the Open Competition plan of the American Hardwood Manufacturers Association was declared illegal by the United States Supreme Court "because it reduces competition by concerted action in curtailing production and raising prices." (*Cases on the Federal Anti-trust Laws of the United States*, pp. 314–331, ed. by J. N. McLaughlin, 1930.) Similar actions were being pushed against the Maple Floor Manufacturers Association and the Cement Manufacturers Association in 1925, but these were finally decided against the government (*ibid.*, pp. 339–380).

7. See V. J. Wyckoff, *Tobacco Regulation in Colonial Maryland*, for an exhaustive study of the numerous control measures affecting this staple.

8. It may be of interest to point out that in past centuries the power of the State has frequently been used to compel production as well as to

curtail it. We find laws on the statute books requiring the raising of flax-or hempseed in England (1532) and in Connecticut, Massachusetts and Virginia during the 1600's. At the same time some of the colonies required the planting or storage of corn, also the growing of vines and of mulberry trees for silk. So, too, the Irish farmer was compelled by English statute to grow a certain amount of corn and plant a quota of trees.

9. See R. G. Hampton, Export Control Board in New Zealand, in *Commodity Control in the Pacific Area*, pp. 320–322.

10. See The Story of Bawra, p. 1228, *Commerce and Finance*, June 23, 1926.

11. See Oliver Lawrence, International Control of Rubber, in *Commody Control in the Pacific Area*, pp. 431–440.

12. See *Report of International Conference* called by "Fight the Famine Council" in London, Nov. 4–6, 1919, by Lord Parmoor *et al.*, Swarthmore Press, London, 1920.

13. For an account of the protracted Russian famine see F. C. Hulbert, *Feeding the Hungry in Russia*, 1919–1925.

14. So-called "Russian dumping" appears to have begun in November 1929 with barley and was soon extended to wheat. The following quotation from a London despatch to the *Chronicle* of Sept. 20, 1930, p. 1792, is of interest: "It is recalled here that whereas a few weeks ago there was talk of the United States organizing food relief for Russian cities, grain is now pouring in out of South Russian ports and glutting the European markets."

15. See references to production bounties for sugar in England (1925), for cotton in Australia (1931) and for wheat in Switzerland (1914–1929), in *Agricultural Price Supporting Measures in Foreign Countries*, U.S. Department of Agriculture, Bureau of Agricultural Economics, 1932.

16. On the other hand, sugar production in Cuba was curtailed 10 per cent by law in 1926, and cotton production in Egypt was restricted between 1914 and 1929. (See Control of Production, etc., *Agricultural Economics Bibliography* 23, pp. 4–6, 34, U.S. Department of Agriculture, 1927.)

17. For destruction of tobacco in Greece, see Agricultural Price Supporting Measures, etc., p. 125, U.S. Department of Agriculture, Bureau of Agricultural Economics. There is also a reference to 26,500,000 lb. of United States tobacco "rendered unmarketable by growers in compliance with AAA contracts in 1934." See *Survey of Current Business*, 1936 Supplement, p. 172, note 13.

18. See Agricultural Price Supporting Measures, etc., pp. 248–250, U.S. Department of Agriculture, Bureau of Agricultural Economics, 1932. Bounties were also paid on the export of a variety of products. See also statement by Chester Davis, Administrator of the AAA, quoted in the *U.S. News*, June 8, 1936 that "France has spent $150,000,000 in dumping the non-salable portion of their crop in foreign markets."

19. See A. Erman, *Life in Ancient Egypt*, trans. by S. Tenard, pp. 107–108.

20. See article in *La Grande Encyclopédie* under "annône."

21. *Ibid.*, under "approvisionnement," Prof. J. E. Boyle in an article in the *Saturday Evening Post*, May 8, 1937, entitled That Ever-normal Granary, gives other instances of State granaries, but expresses a highly adverse opinion as to the results of all of them.

22. Control of Production, etc., p. 25, *Agricultural Economics Bibliography* 23, U.S. Department of Agriculture, 1927.

23. See Bland, Brown and Tawney, *English Economic History*, 1914.

24. See Genesis, XLI; XLVII, 13–26.

25. See Josephus, *Antiquities of the Jews*, Book I, Chap. V.

26. *Ibid.* ("without discovering to anyone the reason why he did so").

27. W. H. Prescott, *History of the Conquest of Peru*, Book I, Chap. 2, p. 60.

28. *Ibid.*, p. 60.

29. P. Ondegardo, quoted by Prescott, *op. cit.*, p. 61.

30. The description of the Chinese Granary system is taken from Dr. Chen Huan Chang's monograph, *The Economic Principles of Confucius*. For a less favorable view of the Chinese experience, see J. E. Boyle, That Ever-normal Granary, *Saturday Evening Post*, May 8, 1937, p. 14.

31. Dr. Chen, *op. cit.*, p. 358.

32. *Ibid.* p. 570.

33. *Ibid.* p. 572. Dr. Chen's book was published in 1911. J. E. Boyle says, "Eventually the Chinese gave up the idea." However, there are references in the *Chinese Economic Bulletin* to granary activities in 1925, 1930, 1931 and 1935.

34. For a summary of the various Brazilian valorization operations see *Agricultural Price Supporting Measures in Foreign Countries*, pp. 36–37, U.S. Department of Agriculture, Bureau of Agricultural Economics, 1932.

35. The profit to the State of Sao Paulo in the first and second operations is estimated at 50 and 20 million dollars, respectively; that on the third operation to the federal government is estimated at 40 per cent (*ibid.*).

36. See *World Production and Prices* 1925–1936, published by the League of Nations, p. 32.

37. For the terms and results of the Buffer-stock proposal, see Oliver Lawrence, International Tin Restriction, in *Commodity Control in the Pacific Area*, pp. 376–398.

38. Author's translation. The French text is as follows (Paragraph 1 of Article 23 of the Swiss Constitution, voted by the Swiss people Mar. 3, 1929):

"La Confédération entretient les réserves de blé nécessaires pour assurer l'approvisionnement du pays. Elle peut obliger les meuniers à emmagasiner du blé et à faire l'acquisition du blé de réserve pour en faciliter le renouvellement."

39. The quantity held in 1932–1933 averaged 77,385 tons (*Swiss Bank Corporation Monthly Bulletin*, September 1934). The French government set up a national reserve of six million quintals (22 million bushels) in December 1934. (*World Economic Survey*, 1934–1935, p. 39.)

Other governments have recently embarked on the policy of accumulating a reserve of foodstuffs as a war measure. Great Britain has announced formation of a Foods Defense Plans Department, to work out methods of storing a year's food supply (*New York Times*, Nov. 29, 1936). The same despatch refers to a reputed two years' supply of canned meat put in storage by Germany. An editorial in the *Wall Street Journal*, Dec. 15, 1936, stated, "Today Russia is reported to be aiming at a year's grain supply in its military reserve." Our own War Department is behind the Faddis Bill authorizing the acquisition of a reserve supply of strategic metals, including ferromanganese ore, chrome ore, tungsten ore and pig tin (*ibid.*, May 19, 1937).

40. See summary of the Canadian wheat experience by J. E. Boyle in Wheat Out of Politics, *Barron's Weekly*, Sept. 21, 1936.

41. See article by S. G. Hanson, The Argentine Wheat Board, *Journal of Political Economy*, April 1936. Also reference to termination of the price guarantee in the *Wall Street Journal*, Dec. 3, 1936.

42. See E. S. Haskell, The United States Federal Farm Board, in *Commodity Control in the Pacific Area*, pp. 104, 113. The losses on wheat and cotton are stated to be 313 million dollars of which part is due to donations to the Red Cross. The operations of the Federal Farm Board are succinctly summarized in the *World Almanac* for 1934, pp. 160–161. The estimated loss is there put at 350 million dollars. The cotton holdings were transferred to the AAA cotton pool in the fall of 1933, and were finally liquidated in July 1936 (see the *Wall Street Journal*, July 20, 1936).

43. Outstanding loans of the Commodity Credit Corporation at various dates are shown in *The Agricultural Situation*, May 1935, p. 18. The maximum amount loaned on corn was 117 million dollars in June 1934, and this was reduced to 4 million dollars in December 1934. On the other hand, cotton loans rose from 47 million dollars in September 1934 to 285 millions in March 1935. On Dec. 31, 1936, cotton loans amounted to about 183 millions. There were also certain loans of minor amount against rosin, turpentine and tobacco (see also the report of Agricultural Adjustment Administrator, H. R. Tolley, pp. 141–142, dated June 15, 1937). The large cotton crop of 1937 with its resultant price decline halted the program of cleaning up the old cotton loans and led to a new loan program at a base

level of 9 cents per pound. (*Wall St. Journal*, Aug. 31, 1937). Resumption of large-scale loans on corn in the fall of 1937 has also been under consideration. (*Ibid.*, May 5, 1937; Oct. 13, 1937.)

44. Failure of state control operations may have been due frequently to lack of continuity in administration, preventing the managers from adjusting their policy in the light of experience as is done in private business.

Chapter III

1. That Ever-normal Granary, *Saturday Evening Post*, May 8, 1937, p. 71.

2. This characterization is not exact, of course, since it ignores the additional function of our gold hoard as "backing" for our currency. But with our paper money inconvertible, this "backing" is a psychological or metaphysical concept, except in so far as it becomes actual through the operation of foreign exchange. In other words, our dollar is equivalent to 13.8 gr. of gold only by virtue of the fact that certain foreign central banks or stabilization funds may exchange their dollars for domestic gold at this rate. (The newly arisen "burden" of maintaining the gold price is discussed in Chap. X.)

3. The average annual farm value of wheat for 1921–1930 was 824 million dollars, while the value of petroleum output at the wells in the same period averaged 1120 million dollars. (*Statistical Abstract of the United States*, 1933, pp. 595, 682.)

4. This statement was true as to gold until the recent emergence of doubts as to its monetary future.

5. See Table VII in the Appendix for data as to the relationship between stocks of commodities and production or consumption.

6. Between Sept. 20, 1931, when England left the gold standard and Mar. 31, 1937, the gold holdings of the Bank of England increased from 1100 to 2584 million "new" dollars (*Federal Reserve Bulletin*, January 1932, p. 52, and May 1937, p. 486). In addition the British stabilization fund held 933 million dollars on that date (*New York Times*, June 29, 1937).

Chapter IV

1. Quoted in the *New York Times*, Aug. 14, 1936.

2. The location of the chief futures markets for the various commodities is as follows:

Wheat, corn, oats, rye.................. Chicago Board of Trade
Barley............................. Minneapolis Chamber of Commerce
Cocoa............................. New York Cocoa Exchange
Coffee, raw sugar...................... New York Coffee and Sugar Exchange

Cotton.............................	New York Cotton Exchange, New Orleans Cotton Exchange
Wool (tops).........................	New York Cotton Exchange
Silk, rubber, hides, copper, lead, tin, zinc, gasoline, petroleum..................	Commodity Exchange, Inc.
Flaxseed............................	Minneapolis Chamber of Commerce
Cottonseed meal.....................	Memphis Merchants Exchange
Cottonseed oil, tallow, tobacco, pepper, linseed oil.......................	New York Produce Exchange
Lard, ribs, bellies, mess pork, soybeans....	Chicago Board of Trade
Eggs, butter, potatoes.................	Chicago Mercantile Exchange
Mill feeds (bran, gray shorts, standard middlings).........................	St. Louis Merchants Exchange
Field seeds (clover, alsike).............	Toledo Board of Trade
Live hogs..........................	Chicago Live Stock Exchange
Canned corn, peas, tomatoes............	Commercial Exchange of Philadelphia

See G. W. Hoffman, *Futures Trading upon Organized Commodity Markets*, pp. 54–55, 1932.

3. These reasons are (*a*) non-storability—live hogs, (*b*) article not a raw material—canned goods, (*c*) lack of statistical data on production or consumption—feed seeds and mill feeds, (*d*) insufficient value of production or consumption during the base period (1921–1930)—soybeans and pepper. (Linseed oil is already represented by flaxseed.)

4. Hides are stored under refrigeration, but they do not offer the same problems as cold-storage *foods.*

5. Of the 37 commodities listed, only 15 were traded in before the war (Hoffman, *op. cit.*, pp. 54–55).

6. Additional commodities previously traded in on United States exchanges and evidently technically eligible for such trading include burlap, molasses, refined sugar (in contrast with raw sugar) and silver (see Hoffman, *op. cit.*, p. 53). As to previous trading in burlap see J. E. Boyle, The New York Burlap and Jute Exchange, *Annals of the Academy of Political and Social Science*, May 1931. For information regarding various additional products traded in on foreign exchanges, including rice, see a group of articles in the same issue of the *Annals*. See also, in particular, the article by C. A. Kulp on Possibilities of Trading in Organized Exchanges, in which he suggests that trading be carried on in lumber and soft coal (in addition to petroleum and wool, which were admitted to dealings after his article). For remarks as to possible trading in pig iron, sisal and hemp, onions and apples, see J. B. Baer and C. P. Woodruff, *Commodity Exchanges*, pp. 204–205, 1929.

7. Data as to imports and exports of the component commodities are given in Table VIII, page 276.

8. *Statistics Bulletin 453, Revised Index Numbers of Wholesale Prices, U.S. Bureau of Labor,* September 1927, gives the detailed weightings as well as an explanation of the method used.

9. Moody's has published a mimeographed explanation of the weightings used. Dow Jones & Company also publishes a daily weighted index of the futures prices of 11 important commodities.

The commodities and weights (in per cent) are as follows:

Commodity	Moody	Dow Jones
Wheat..............................	13	19.5
Cotton..............................	13	23
Hogs..............................	13	
Steel Scrap..........................	10	
Sugar..............................	10	12.5
Wool..............................	7	
Copper..............................	5	
Hides..............................	5	4
Corn..............................	4	8
Rubber..............................	4	6
Silk..............................	4	9
Coffee..............................	4	5
Lead..............................	3	
Silver..............................	3	
Cocoa..............................	2	5
Oats..............................	...	4
Rye..............................	...	4
Total..............................	100	100

The Associated Press computes a daily weighted price index of 35 basic commodities. The National Fertilizer Association publishes a weekly wholesale price index, also weighted.

10. However, if the futures price of about 78 cents were taken for corn, the value of the unit in June 1937 would be only 85.3 per cent of the 1921–1930 average. This corresponds to the Bureau of Labor Statistics index of raw-materials prices, which in June 1937 stood at 86.1 per cent of 1926.

11. The 1921–1930 price level for raw materials as given in the Bureau of Labor Statistics index was 141 per cent of the 1913 figure. Adjusted to the 59-cent dollar, the gold value of 1921–1930 level becomes only 83.2 per cent of the 1913 level.

12. For convenience, to avoid tendering and receiving less than, say, 1000 bushels, such odd amounts may be settled for in cash at current market prices. Over a period these cash adjustments should tend to cancel out.

13. See, for example, quotations for Standard Oil of New Jersey "old" and the 39 constituent companies, *Chronicle*, June 27, 1914, p. 1985.

14. Wall Street history includes a number of other examples of similar nature, such as the simultaneous trading in Guggenheim Exploration Company stock and the numerous mining shares into which it was divided, and the more recent arbitrage operations between "fixed-trust" shares, or units, and the individual issues into which they could be split up upon tender of a certain minimum amount.

15. See the author's article "Stabilized Reflation" in *The Economic Forum*, Vol. 1, No. 2, Spring 1933; also a summary of his proposal in various newspapers, *e.g.*, the *Los Angeles Times*, Feb. 26, 1933.

16. A lower price level was then being recommended by various economists, *e.g.*, Sir Arthur Salter.

17. A special device connected with bank credit might be resorted to for the purpose of keeping prices *down* to the standard level even after all commodity units had been redeemed. This is discussed briefly in Chap. VI.

18. See headline in the *New York Times*, Aug. 10, 1937: "Huge Cotton Crop and Market Drop Alarm Congress." The August crop estimates resulted in a successful demand for renewed crop loans, which in turn brought Presidential pressure for crop-control legislation.

Chapter V

1. Statement at the Imperial Economic Conference, Ottawa. *Chronicle*, Sept. 3, 1932, p. 1574.

2. It is not our purpose to assert that *any* decline in the price level of raw materials generally is due to the presence of a burdensome surplus requiring remedial measures. A price decline might be occasioned by purely monetary developments, *e.g.*, a relative shortage of gold, or by lower costs through technological improvements.

But our proposal seeks to make the monetary unit correspond with the commodity unit. Hence a decline in the price level is made to produce a flow of commodity units into storage as a *monetary* corrective measure, in the same way as a fall in the exchange value of the dollar formerly produced a corrective flow of gold abroad as part of the monetary mechanism. The operations of our mechanism will *always* be appropriate to maintain monetary stability, and they will *frequently* be essential to assure business stability.

3. Actually, of course, we should not first have a jump of the commodity-unit value to 1.07 and then a readjustment to 1.00. The declines in the rest of the unit would commence before the advance in wheat had been completed.

4. The price range for 16 commodities between 1911 and 1936, given in Table IV, page 272 while showing wide variations as between different

products, bears out our main contention as to the improbability of completely disproportionate price advances.

5. On June 30, 1937 the price for spot corn was $1.24¾, a premium of more than 60 per cent above the price of 70½ cents for December delivery. For additional examples see Table X in the Appendix.

6. Monthly price records show only the following instances over the last 25 years in which any commodities in our unit would have been subject to suspension under the proposed arbitrary rule:

a. Zinc reached a price of 22 cents in 1915 against an average of 5.11 cents in 1914 and about 6 cents for 1906–1914.

b. Coffee reached a price of 23 cents in 1919 against an average of 9.75 cents in 1918 and about 11 cents in 1909–1918.

c. Silk reached $14.50 in 1919 against an average of $7.12 in 1918 and about $4.50 for 1909–1918.

d. Refined sugar reached 22½ cents in 1920 against an average of 8.94 cents in 1919 and about 6 cents in 1910–1919.

e. Rubber reached $1.03 in 1925 against an average of 24½ cents in 1924 and about 44 cents in 1915–1924.

In addition, the prices of $2.06 for corn and $2.97 for wheat reached in 1917 would have come under our rule, but these prices were controlled by special war measures of our own government.

7. This point is advanced by H. D. Gideonse in his article "La Stabilisation des Prix de Gros" in *Revue Economique Internationale*, July 1936, pp. 65–99.

8. Our silver policy is discussed further in Chap. X.

9. B. Nogaro points out that only a slight degree of "overproduction" of agricultural raw materials was responsible for the price collapse of 1930 (*Les Prix Agricoles Mondiaux et La Crise*, p. 54). The following data,

WORLD PRODUCTION AND CONSUMPTION OF WHEAT (EXCLUDING RUSSIA)
Millions of Bushels

Crop years beginning August	Average production plus Russian exports	Average consumption	Average surplus or deficit		World Stocks		Per cent change
			Amount	Per cent of consumption	Beginning of period	End of period	
1923–1927	3490	3460	+ 30	+1	551	693	+26
1928	4030	3777	+261	+7	693	954	+38
1929–1933	3850	3812	+ 38	+1	954	1149	+20
1934–1936	3510	3720	−210	−6	1149	520	−55

summarized from *Wheat Studies* of Stanford University for December 1935 and January 1937, show the large effect upon world stocks of wheat created by relatively small annual disparities between production and consumption.

10. That a dormant futures market in a commodity may come to life through favorable trade developments is well illustrated by copper on the Commodity Exchange of New York. In all of 1930 total trading was only 5400 tons. In the first four months of 1937 trading aggregated 208,000 tons (*Monthly Bulletins* of the Commodity Exchange, Inc.).

11. "The qualities of uniformity, imperishability, uncertainty of demand and supply must be inherent in the commodity or connected with its use, if it is to lend itself to the organization of an exchange. . . . It is evident that the adaptability of the commodity and adaptability of the market must coexist before futures trading in a commodity can take place." J. B. Baer and G. P. Woodruff, *Commodity Exchanges*, pp. 207–208.

Chapter VI

1. Radio address, Oct. 22, 1933.

2. This policy was first stated in President Roosevelt's message to the American delegation at the London Economic Conference, July 3, 1933 (*Chronicle*, July 8, 1933, p. 222).

3. See articles of Dr. Anderson, A Planned Economy and a Planned Price Level, *Chase Economic Bulletin*, June 1933; On the Practical Impossibility of a Commodity Dollar, December 1933.

4. It may be found simpler to attain this objective by imposing a special tax on profits from commodity sales whenever the Commodity reservoir is exhausted. This would correspond to the 50 per cent tax on profits from trading in silver imposed by the Silver Purchase Act of June 19, 1934.

5. See the four studies published under the general title of *The Distribution of Wealth and Income in Relation to Economic Progress*, particularly the last volume, *Income and Economic Progress*.

6. Commodity Prices versus General Price Level, *American Economic Review*, September 1934, p. 391.

7. *Prices*, p. 24.

8. This point is fully discussed in Carl Snyder's article referred to in note 6.

9. For an argument in support of our own on this point, see P. W. Martin, Chief, Economic Group, International Labour Office, *Some Aspects of Economic Planning, Essays in Honor of W. C. Mitchell*, p. 339, 1935.

10. Snyder's study demonstrates that while all commodity prices at wholesale have shown no definite secular trend in either direction, other price elements, *e.g.*, retail prices, wages, real estate, etc., reveal a very

marked upward tendency during the past century. There is no evidence that this *gradual advance* has been harmful to business or to the general welfare. The stabilization of basic commodities at wholesale, which we propose, should not introduce any *new factor* so far as long-term trends of prices are concerned.

Considerable stress has been laid upon the harmful effects, especially during depression, growing out of the coexistence of "administered" and inflexible prices for industrial products alongside of highly flexible and fluctuating prices for raw materials (see report of G. C. Means, transmitted to the U.S. Senate by the Secretary of Agriculture, pursuant to *Senate Resolution* 17, Jan. 15, 1935). Professor Means calls for a monetary policy which will "bring the prices of the more flexibly priced commodities into line with the rigidly priced commodities." (Report, p. 38.) Our proposal should go far to accomplish this objective.

11. The following data, from the U.S. Department of Labor Index of Wholesale Prices, are significant:

1926 = 100

Average for	Raw materials	Finished goods
1916	82.6	82.3
1917	122.6	109.2
1920	151.8	149.8
1921	88.3	103.3
1929	97.5	94.5
1932	55.1	70.3
April 1937	88.7	87.4

Chapter VII

1. Commodity Prices versus General Price Level, *American Economic Review*, September 1934, p. 400.

2. This viewpoint is illustrated by the following remark of E. A. Goldenweiser, Director of Research and Statistics in the Federal Reserve System: "I am inclined to think that even business stability—which is a vague term describing the goal toward which, in a general way, everyone should try to work—is not necessarily desirable. Stability has an implication of stagnation. A growing economy is not a stable economy" How can Credit Be Controlled? *Proceedings of the Academy of Political Science*, May 1936, p. 8.

3. From April 1926 to September 1929, the New York Stock Exchange Index of all listed shares advanced from 105 to 173.3; but during this

period the Department of Labor Index of Raw Materials Prices actually declined slightly from 100.6 to 98.9.

4. The Federal Reserve Board's Index of Industrial Production rose from 107 to 121 during the above period.

5. See J. A. Hobson, *The Economics of Unemployment*, 1922.

6. See Major C. H. Douglas, *Social Credit*, 1924.

7. See report of G. C. Means, referred to in Note 9 of chapter notes for Chap. VI.

8. Note the significant decline of stocks of raw materials from July 1933 to December 1936 as shown in the chart on page 7.

9. The studies of the Department of Agriculture show a striking correlation between total farm income and total industrial wages. See article by L. H. Bean in *The Agricultural Situation*, February 1933. Also article by Mordecai Ezekial in the *American Statistical Association Supplement* of March 1933, pp. 182–189. Dr. Ezekial stated that "increase in employment among city workers depends, to a considerable degree, upon increase of income among farmers" (*ibid.*, p. 189).

10. As of January 1937 unemployment was estimated at 8,403,000 by the National Industrial Conference Board (*Chronicle*, Mar. 20, 1937, p. 1872). Works Progress Administrator Hopkins estimated that unemployment would be between 6½ and 7½ millions in 1937 even with return of 1929 level of production (*ibid.*, Jan. 30, 1937, p. 707). In his message to Congress on Jan. 11, 1937 President Roosevelt estimated that 2,580,000 would be employed on relief in the coming winter, *ibid.*, Jan. 16, 1937, p. 376). See the article on Unemployment in *The Index*, published by The New York Trust Co., August 1937, pp. 163–170.

11. For detailed quantitative estimates of the development of technological unemployment see D. Weintraub, The Displacement of Workers, etc., *Journal of the American Statistical Association*, December 1932, pp. 383–400.

12. "Maladjustments can also be corrected more easily in a society enjoying high investment activity and moderately rising prices." Alvin H. Hansen, Gold Today in Relation to World Currencies, *American Economic Review*, March 1937, p. 131.

Chapter VIII

1. Quoted in an editorial of the *New York Times*, May 17, 1937.

2. The following references to rationing in wartime among many others are to be found in the *Chronicle:* Heatless Mondays, Feb. 9, 1918, p. 545; Meatless Tuesdays, Wheatless Wednesdays, Oct. 27, 1917, p. 1667; restrictions on use of sugar, Dec. 15, 1917, p. 236.

3. L. L. B. Angas expresses the same view in *The Problem of the Foreign Exchanges*, p. 165. He ends by saying "Indeed for a food-importing country

like England, it would, I think, certainly be much better for the Government to hold its war-chest in the form of food rather than gold." See similar doubts as to the value of gold as a war reserve in Whittlesey, *International Monetary Issues*, pp. 228–229.

4. See the article by Senator Vandenberg, That $47,000,000,000 Blight, *Saturday Evening Post*, Apr. 24, 1937.

5. This fact is acknowledged in the Social Security Act, for the government is required therein to pay interest of not less than 3 per cent on obligations held in the Reserve fund (Section 201b). Thus dealings between the government and its own Social Security agency may be independent of the market rate of interest.

6. For a discussion of the workings of the British unemployment insurance scheme, see A. C. Hill, Jr., and I. Lubin, *The British Attack on Unemployment*, The Brookings Institution, 1934.

Chapter IX

1. Note the following from the report of the President's Committee on Crop Insurance, December 1936, p. 18:

"In the case of corn, if a plan should be developed for that commodity, farm storage would not only be practicable but highly desirable because a large percentage of the corn crop is fed on farms near the point of production."

Note also the following from Governor Landon's Des Moines address, Sept. 22, 1936: "I shall propose an amendment to the Federal Warehousing Act so that reserves of feed, such as corn, can be carried on the farm." Dr. Alvin Johnson has made the helpful suggestion that the problem of loss of weight of grain in storage, due to evaporation, may be met by placing the quantity of each grain in the unit on a moisture-free basis. In other words, receipts into and deliveries out of the Reservoir will be adjusted for variations in moisture content. Dr. Johnson also suggests that rat-proof cribs can be supplied for corn at a relatively small annual expense.

2. "It is doubtful that farm storage of wheat would be practicable in all areas." Report of President's Committee on Crop Insurance, December 1936, p. 18.

3. See statement on this point in the article on Crop Insurance published in the *U.S. News*, Aug. 3, 1936, p. 6.

4. Report of President's Committee on Crop Insurance, December, 1936, p. 8.

5. Total stocks of tobacco on Dec. 31, 1936 were 2210 million pounds against the estimated year's production of 1153 million pounds. Cigarette manufacturers calculate their tobacco costs on a three-year moving average basis. (See article in *Wall Street Journal*, Dec. 9, 1936.)

6. The feasibility of long-term storage of oil is supported by the following statement of Federal Trade Commissioner A. F. Myers, made in 1928: "Millions of gallons of crude oil have remained in storage untouched since 1921." From Present Plans for Stabilizing the Oil Industry, *Annals of the American Academy of Political and Social Science*, September 1928, p. 88.

A total of some 20 million barrels of oil from the Salt Creek field was held in storage at Caspar and Clayton, Wyo., between 1921–1923 and the end of 1936. The president of the Midwest Oil Company estimates that the shrinkage in quality and quantity over the 15-year period was about 10 per cent, or 0.7 per cent per annum (from a letter to the author).

7. The market value of a commodity unit in February 1933 was only about 35 per cent of the 1921–1930 average. See calculation based on a differently constituted unit in the author's article entitled Stabilized Reflation, *Economic Forum*, Spring 1933, p. 192. Moody's Index of Staple Commodity Prices stood at 80 in February 1933, or 31 per cent of the 260.4 average for the year 1926.

8. See reference to seigniorage profits on silver in Note 25 to chapter notes for Chap. X.

9. Total expenditures of the federal government for the six years ended June 30, 1938 will have amounted to some 47 billion dollars. Of this amount, 23 billions are defined as regular expenditures, and 3 billions represent debt retirement. The balance, representing emergency expenditures related to the depression, exceeds 21 billions (figures taken from the President's annual budget messages of Jan. 1935, 1936 and 1937).

The net debt of the federal government on June 30, 1937 was $33,872,-000,000 against about $15,500,000,000 on Dec. 31, 1930.

10. The following figures are based chiefly on estimates of national income 1929–1936 appearing in the *Survey of Current Business*, July 1936, p. 15:

(Dollar Figures in Billions)

Year	National income produced	General price level*	National income produced, in 1929 dollars	Shrinkage from 1929 level
1929	$81	100	$81	
1931	54	83.8	65	$ 16
1932	40	73.7	54	27
1933	42	72.1	58	23
1934	48	76.6	63	18
1935	53	81.1	65	16
Total for five years......				$100

* Dr. Carl Snyder's Index Number, supplied by the Federal Reserve bank of New York.

The aggregate shrinkage in the national income from the 1929 level, in terms of 1929 dollars, for the five years 1931–1935 totaled 100 billion dollars.

11. President's budget message of Jan. 6, 1937 (*Chronicle*, Jan. 9, 1937, p. 164).

Chapter X

1. *Federal Reserve Bulletin*, August 1937.

2. The dollar was devalued to $15\frac{5}{21}$ grains, nine-tenths fine, by Presidential Proclamation of Jan. 31, 1934, in accordance with Section 12 of the Gold Reserve Act of 1934, dated Jan. 30, 1934.

3. Executive orders of President Roosevelt dated April 5, April 20, and Aug. 28, 1933, in accordance with Section 11 (*a*) of the Federal Reserve Act, as amended by Act of Mar. 9, 1933.

4. See Section 5 of Gold Reserve Act of Jan. 30, 1934.

5. E. C. Simmons in his article, The Gold Certificate, *Journal of Political Economy*, August 1936, points out that the original act of 1863 creating these certificates gave the Secretary of the Treasury power to issue certificates in an amount exceeding the deposited gold by 20 per cent; but this right was never availed of, and was annulled in the Gold Reserve Act of 1934.

6. This action was taken pursuant to Section 26 of the Federal Reserve Act, added Mar. 9, 1933.

7. See *Federal Reserve Bulletin*, August 1937.

8. See Section 43 (*b*) of the Farm Act of 1933, added June 5, 1933.

9. Section 16 (2) of the Federal Reserve Act.

10. *Ibid*. This permission was to expire originally May 3, 1935, but was extended to Mar. 3, 1937 and then to June 30, 1939 (*Chronicle*, Mar. 6, 1937, p. 1524).

11. Section 18 (*b*) of the Federal Reserve Act amended Mar. 9, 1933. The maximum amount of Federal Reserve Bank Notes reported as issued under this amendment was $208 million, on Dec. 31, 1933 (*Federal Reserve Bulletin*, December 1934, p. 787).

12. Federal Reserve Act, Section 27 (2).

13. Retirement of National bank notes was effected by calling, on Mar. 9, 1935, the U.S. government bonds with circulation privilege, funds therefor being appropriated out of the Treasury's profit from dollar devaluation. At date of call there were about 823 million dollars of National bank notes in circulation (*Federal Reserve Bulletin*, April 1935, p. 202).

14. The acquisition of large amounts of silver under the Silver Purchase Act of June 19, 1934 is discussed in the next chapter.

15. On Sept. 7, 1917, President Wilson placed an embargo on the export of gold (*Chronicle*, Sept. 15, 1917, p. 1047). This promptly resulted in the

dollar selling at a discount in neutral countries, ranging from 5 per cent in Switzerland to 17 per cent in Madrid (*Ibid.*, Oct. 27, 1917, p. 1661). Sales of gold to jewellers and others by the New York Assay Office were suspended on Aug. 30, 1918 and resumed subject to regulation shortly thereafter (*Ibid.*, Aug. 31, 1918, p. 844; Sept. 7, 1918, p. 939; Sept. 14, 1918, p. 1047).

16. The average price of silver by decades for 1881–1930, and for 1931–1935, was as follows:

Period	High, cents	Low, cents	Average for period, cents
1881–1890	113.9	93.6	104.6
1891–1900	99.0	59.1	70.6
1901–1910	54.2	52.2	53.2
1911–1920	135.0	51.9	80.4
1921–1930	80.5	38.7	64.1
1931–1935	63.9	32.0	44.6

17. The Secretary of the Treasury may use the net earnings derived by the United States from the Federal Reserve banks to supplement the gold reserve against United States notes (Federal Reserve Act, Section 7*b*).

18. See text in *Chronicle*, Oct. 3, 1936, p. 2134.

19. See the excellent account of the assignats in A. D. White, *Fiat Money Inflation in France*, reprinted by D. Appleton-Century Company, Inc., New York, 1933.

Chapter XI

1. *Conquest of Peru*, Vol. 1, p. 510.

2. "The possession of gold and silver ornaments gave distinction and social prestige to the owners. Everyone prized the precious metals therefore, and in consequence their general acceptability made them most desirable commodities for monetary purposes." Norman Angell, *The Story of Money*, p. 65.

3. A table given on page 101 of Berle and Pedersen, *Liquid Claims and National Wealth*, estimates that from 1880 to 1929 gold and silver coin and bullion in the United States increased from 600 to 5200 million dollars, or about ninefold, while total bank deposits increased from 2 to 54 billions, or twenty-sevenfold.

4. "Gold jewelry is out of fashion, so that industrial needs now absorb 5 per cent of current output against a former 20 per cent." From Seventh Annual Report of the Bank for International Settlements, as summarized

in the *Wall Street Journal*, May 4, 1937. Complete text of the report appears in the *Federal Reserve Bulletin*, June 1937, pp. 540–575.

5. The extraordinary dominance of the monetary use of gold over its other uses is shown by a calculation reproduced in the *Bulletin of the New York Stock Exchange*, June 1936. During the six years 1930–1935 the world output of gold is set at 151,670,000 oz., or 5300 million dollars at present value. Of this total only 3,900,000 oz. net, or less than 3 per cent, is estimated to have been absorbed in the industrial arts. Even these small takings were far more than offset by the net release of 33 million ounces from the hoards of India, China and Egypt. Hence appreciably *more* than the six years' production was added to the world stocks of *monetary* gold.

The increase in the holdings of central banks and treasuries totaled 144 million ounces, or 95 per cent of the total output of the mines. Thus, despite all the reasons for individual hoarding of gold coin during this period, there was only a negligible increase in gold used for every purpose—ornament, industry, circulation or personal hoards—outside of the central reserves.

6. Total bank deposits on Dec. 31, 1928 were about 57 billion dollars against some 4.1 billions of gold (*Federal Reserve Bulletin*, April 1929, pp. 247, 306).

7. See the discussion of "flights of capital" by Robert B. Warren, The International Movement of Capital, *Proceedings of the Academy of Political Science*, May 1937, pp. 66–67.

8. See Note 15 of chapter notes for Chap. IX.

9. This viewpoint is well summarized in the letter of James Warburg to Senator Borah, Nov. 28, 1933, published in *Chronicle*, Dec. 2, 1933, pp. 3937–3938.

10. This power was given to the President by the Thomas Amendment to the Farm Bill of 1933; in Section 43 (*b*). It has been extended to June 30, 1939 (*ibid.*, Jan. 30, 1937, p. 702).

11. This discretionary power was given to the Secretary of the Treasury in Sections 9 and 10 of the Gold Reserve Act of 1934.

12. The Monetary Report of the Ottawa Imperial Economic Conference issued in August 1932, stressed the need for a rise in the general level of commodity prices to equal the cost of production (see summary in *Journal of Commerce*, Aug. 13, 1932).

13. The rise in wholesale prices generally was not proportionate to the cut in the gold value of the dollar. However, the rise in basic raw materials, important in international trade, was in fairly close relationship to the increase in the price of gold (see N. L. Silverstein, American Devaluation, Prices and Export Trade, *American Economic Review*, June 1937, pp. 279–293).

14. The seventh Annual Report of the Bank for International Settlements says there is now no country which has not devalued or else imposed exchange restrictions (see summary in the *Wall Street Journal*, May 4, 1937).

15. Historians of the future should chuckle over the following amazing headline in the *New York Herald Tribune* of Apr. 20, 1933 following our departure from the gold standard:

"Britain Expects Retaliatory Act to Save Pound." "Saving" the pound, in this case, meant preventing it from advancing.

16. See references on this point in Note 3 of chapter notes for Chap. VIII.

17. Gold production for 1936 amounted to 35,254,000 oz., worth 1215 million dollars, compared with 19,673,000 oz. in 1929. Seventh Annual Report of Bank for International Settlements, *Federal Reserve Bulletin*, June 1937, p. 555.

18. Since Dec. 24, 1936 gold imports have been placed in an "inactive fund," which is included as part of the Treasury's cash balance, but against which no gold certificates are issued to be added to the credit base. In September 1937, 300 millions of this "sterilized" gold was released, but by Oct. 5, 1937 the "inactive gold" held by the United States Treasury amounted to 1231 millions.

19. Gold coming in from abroad could be added to banking assets (in the form of gold certificates held by the Federal Reserve banks), but both these gold certificates and the member bank deposits thereby created could be segregated and earmarked as 100 per cent reserve against a corresponding amount of foreign short-term balances. This would obviate the "inactive gold" device as a means of sterilizing gold imports.

20. From address of Chairman John Martin at annual meeting on May 7, 1937, quoted in *London Economist*, May 15, 1937. For a summary of doubts as to the future of gold see Whittlesey, *International Monetary Problems*, especially page 207. R. H. Brand, of Lazard Freres, London, a supporter of the gold standard, admits its metaphysical character in the following statement: "Gold has, and should keep, a certain mystic quality, which would be destroyed if the world treated gold as if it were rubber or tin" (*The Times, London*, London, June 16, 1937).

21. Germany, for example, has carried on an expanding national economy with virtually no gold on hand since June 1934. Its holdings on June 30, 1937 were only 28 million dollars (*Federal Reserve Bulletin*, December 1934, p. 801; August 1937, p. 768).

22. "Up to the sixth century B.C. no gold was coined in the Greek cities. They adhered to silver." Angell, *op. cit.*, p. 95.

23. This "monetary" value is taken at $1.29 per ounce for silver and $35 per ounce for gold, subject to legislative change. Stocks of gold and

silver are defined as the amount owned by the United States, and also the silver contained in United States coins at the time outstanding. Silver Purchase Act, June 19, 1934, Section 10.

24. See address of George B. Roberts, The Silver Purchase Program and Its Consequences, *Proceedings of the Academy of Political Science*, May 1936, pp. 18–25, also article entitled Silver: Two Years' Experience, *The Index*, published by the New York Trust Company, September 1936.

25. See data supplied by Secretary Morgenthau in the *Wall Street Journal*, Mar. 4, 1937.

26. The annual report of the Secretary of the Treasury for the year ended June 30, 1936 indicates a total seigniorage profit on silver certificates issued to that date of $315,901,000. At the end of the previous year the profit was $140,111,000 (*Chronicle*, Jan. 16, 1937, p. 352). In addition thereto, there are profits on domestically acquired silver, which are reported as income in the Treasury statements, and which totaled $146,-200,000 from July 1, 1934 to June 30, 1937. (*Ibid.*, July 11, 1936, p. 217; July 17, 1937, p. 303.)

27. The maximum emission of greenbacks was 447 million dollars at the end of 1864; their lowest value in terms of the gold dollar was 35.09¢ reached in July 1934 (see W. C. Mitchell, *History of Greenbacks*, p. 179). The unsecured or greenback component in the silver or silver-backed currency outstanding June 30, 1937, valuing silver at 45 cents per ounce, amounts to over 950 million dollars.

Chapter XII

1. *Monetary Reform in Theory and Practice*, p. 209.

2. Money in circulation jumped from 4426 million dollars in July 1920 to 7532 millions in March 1933, during the bank holidays. After receding to 5325 millions in August 1933 it again expanded to 6543 millions in December 1936 (*Federal Reserve Bulletin, passim*).

3. In the three years from February 1930 to February 1933, the U.S. Department of Labor's index number of wholesale prices fell from 92.0 to 59.2. In the four years to February 1937 the index number recovered to 86.1.

4. In terms of gold, the February 1937 price level was only 51 per cent of the 1926 average and about 73 per cent of the 1913 average.

5. This is evident from the numerous proposals for stabilizing the dollar made prior to the depression (see J. S. Lawrence, *Stabilization of Prices*, 1928, referred to in Chap. XVIII. See also Irving Fisher, *Stable Money*, 1934).

6. In the technical sense, the issuance of huge amounts of currency backed by *silver* should constitute a severer threat to the maintenance of a gold standard, since the silver currency is clearly overvalued, and by

Gresham's law the poorer money should drive out the better. While anything but an advocate of the present silver policy, the writer must voice a doubt whether Gresham's law would really operate in this case, where (a) the stock of gold is so enormous and (b) there is so little popular interest in the intrinsic character of the currency. It would take a huge foreign drain of gold to expose the weakness of the silver currency, and this would be quite unlikely in view of our tremendous financial strength coupled with our comparative isolation.

This reasoning would apply to the commodity-unit currency as well, if we were to make the assumption—quite contrary to fact—that this money would be intrinsically much weaker than our other kinds.

7. Section 13 (7) of the Federal Reserve Act permits member banks to accept drafts secured by a warehouse receipt, etc., covering "readily marketable staples." Section 16 (2) makes such acceptances eligible as collateral for Federal Reserve notes.

8. For a critical examination of the flexibility of the Federal Reserve notes, see E. C. Simmons, Elasticity of the Federal Reserve Notes, *American Economic Review*, December 1936. His conclusion reads: "The present collateral requirements do not provide elasticity, but they may provide embarrassment to those who are vested with the responsibility of formulating monetary policy."

Chapter XIII

1. From How Can Credit Be Controlled? *Proceedings of the Academy of Political Science*, May 1936, p. 6.

2. Loans and investments of all member banks of the Federal Reserve system increased from 13,420 million dollars on Dec. 31, 1918 to 18,076 millions in June 1920. The degree of speculation in inventories is indicated by the following (from a study by the author, published in 1921):

TWELVE INDUSTRIAL COMPANIES, 1919–1920

Earned for common stock	$148,000,000
Added to surplus	30,000,000
Inventories increased	141,000,000
Other (net) current assets decreased	*101,000,000*

Summarized in Graham and Dodd, *op. cit.*, p. 534.

3. Borrowings by Stock Exchange members increased from 3,569 million dollars in June 1927 to 8,549 million dollars in September 1929. During the same period loans of all member banks not secured by stocks and bonds or real estate actually declined slightly, from 12,050 to 11,988 million dollars. (*Federal Reserve Bulletin, passim.*) Total urban mortgage debt increased from 8,968 million dollars in 1921 to 27,616 millions in 1929 (*The Internal Debts of the United States*, p. 66, Twentieth Century Fund).

4. Between June 30, 1933 and Dec. 31, 1936 deposits of all member banks increased from 21.1 to 32.6 billion dollars, or more than 50 per cent. During the same period total loans to customers increased only negligibly —from 11.3 to 11.6 billion dollars (*Federal Reserve Bulletin, passim*).

5. The *minimum* amount of such member bank reserves varies with the location of the member bank, being set by law as 13 per cent of demand deposits in New York and Chicago ("central reserve cities"), 10 per cent in 65 other "reserve cities," and 7 per cent for banks located elsewhere (these being known as "country member banks"). The reserve against time deposits must be 3 per cent for all banks. These minima may be increased by the Federal Reserve Board by an amount not exceeding 100 per cent. This has been done, in three steps, so that present reserve requirements are now twice the legal minima.

6. The following figures from the reports of all member banks are significant:

(In Millions)*

	Dec. 31, 1929	Dec. 31, 1936
Loans on securities................	$8,488	$3,051
Loans on real estate...............	3,191	2,405
Other loans to customers...........	11,514	6,172
Total loans....................	23,193	11,628
U.S. government securities.........	3,863	13,545
Cash and reserves................	2,932	7,269
Total deposits..................	29,880	32,635

* *Federal Reserve Bulletin, passim.*

7. These may be found in the Federal Reserve Act, Sections 13 (8); 12*A*; 114 (6); 11 (25); 4 (8); also Securities Exchange Act of 1934, Section 7 (*a*).

8. On May 29, 1937 the total "bills discounted" by the Federal Reserve Banks amounted to only 15 million dollars, out of total assets of 12,524 millions. (In November 1920 bills discounted aggregated 2,826 millions, out of total resources of 6,413 millions.)

9. Interest rates on prime commercial paper at New York ranged between 5½ and 6 per cent during the entire boom period of 1919. Call-loan rates averaged about the same rate and reached as high as 30 per cent in November 1929 (*Federal Reserve Bulletin*, May 1920, p. 479). Call-money rates held consistently above 6 per cent from June 1928 on and reached 10 per cent at the end of 1928. The crash of October 1929 did not

take place until 18 months after the first definite tightening of money rates.

10. This point was made by Prof. J. H. Rogers in Prospects of Inflation in the United States, *Proceedings of the Academy of Political Science*, May 1936, pp. 134–139.

Chapter XIV

1. See Table VI in the Appendix.

2. The problem of income parity is by no means identical with that of price parity, although they are closely related. Per-capita income available for living in 1929 increased 58 per cent over 1909–1914 in the case of farmers, as against an increase of 98 per cent in the case of nonfarmers (L. H. Bean, Parity Income from Farm Production, *The Agricultural Situation*, May 1937, p. 20). This disparity was due in only small part to the changes in relative prices (see next note); but seems to have been caused chiefly by a greater gain in per-capita productivity of the nonfarm population.

The "agricultural depression of 1922–1929" is defined as due to the fact that "agriculture as a whole apparently had a per-capita purchasing power equal to pre-war years, while the standard of living of the rest of the country had advanced about 25 per cent above that level." Income Parity for Agriculture, *ibid.*, Feb. 1936, p. 2.

3. The ratio of prices received by farmers to prices paid by farmers for the decade 1921–1930 averaged 92 per cent in terms of the 1909–1914 base (*ibid.*, June 1937, p. 31).

4. In February 1933 the above ratio was only 54 per cent (see F. C. Mills, *Prices in Recession and Recovery*, p. 104, 1936).

5. "It is hereby declared to be the policy of Congress: (1) To establish and maintain such balance between the production and consumption of agricultural commodities and such marketing conditions therefor, as will re-establish prices to farmers at a level that will give agricultural commodities a purchasing power with respect to articles that farmers buy, equivalent to the purchasing power of agricultural commodities in the pre-war period, August 1909–July 1914." (Section 2.)

6. The following is taken from Recent Changes in Production, *National Bureau of Economic Research Bulletin* 51, June 28, 1934.

INDEX OF PHYSICAL VOLUME OF PRODUCTION

	Agriculture	Manufacturing
1927	100	100
1929	103	116
1932	98	66
1933	94	74

7. G. C. Means in Notes on Inflexible Prices, *American Economic Review,* Supplement, March 1936, p. 29, presents the following contrast covering the period 1929 to 1933:

	Drop in price, per cent	Drop in production, per cent
Agricultural implements.............	15	80
Agricultural commodities.............	63	6

8. See Note 9 of chapter notes to Chap. V regarding the relatively small variations in the world's production and consumption of wheat between 1923 and 1936.

9. In the drought year 1934, the production of potatoes was well above average, that of rice exceeded 1933 and that of tobacco exceeded 1932. In the drought year 1936 the cotton crop was larger than in 1935.

10. See review by V. P. Timoshenko of George Brandan, Ernteschwankungen und wirtschaftliche Wechsellagen 1874–1913, in *Journal of the American Statistical Association*, June 1937, pp. 425–428.

11. Bratt relates the onset of the depression of 1837–1843 to wheat-crop failures in 1835 and 1936. On the other hand, recovery from the depressions of 1873–1879, 1890–1891 and 1895–1896 is related to the large wheat crops in the United States as against poor crops elsewhere (*Business Cycles and Forecasting*, pp. 181*ff*).

12. Exports of cotton during 1921–1930 represented 53.6 per cent of total production (see Table VIII in the Appendix).

13. This example is taken from W. P. Gee, *The Social Economics of Agriculture*, p. 96. An alternative method of attaining the objective of the McNary-Haugen Bill is by means of a processing tax, the proceeds of which are to be distributed among the farmers. As applied to this wheat example, it would result (*a*) in leaving the domestic price the same as the foreign price, *i.e.*, $1; (*b*) in collecting a processing tax of 42 cents per bushel on 600,000,000 bushels, or $250,000,000; (*c*) in distributing this sum in the form of a 30½ cents per bushel bonus to all wheat producers, netting them $1.30½ per bushel on the entire crop, the same as under the Equalization Fee plan.

This processing tax-bonus arrangement was introduced into Congress in 1932 as the Rankin Bill. It passed the Senate but died in the House. (See Geo. N. Peek and Samuel Crowther, *Why Quit Our Own?* pp. 51–54.) Support of this plan for cotton was strongly intimated by Secretary Wallace in his Memphis speech of Oct. 1, 1937. (*Wall St. Journal*, Oct. 2, 1937.)

14. The veto message and the Attorney General's opinion are given in full in *Chronicle*, Aug. 26, 1928, pp. 3236–3240.

15. For a discussion of the Export-debenture plan see Gee, *op. cit.*, pp. 98–107.

16. The act setting up the Farm Board was called the Agricultural Marketing Act of 1929 (for text see *Chronicle*, Apr. 20, 1929, pp. 2569–2570).

17. For text see *ibid.*, May 20, 1933, pp. 3415–3420, and Sept. 14, 1935, pp. 1657–1667.

18. For full text of majority opinion and excerpts from minority opinion, see *ibid.*, Jan. 11, 1926, pp. 201–205.

19. For text see *ibid.*, Mar. 21, 1936, p. 1590.

20. This date was originally Jan. 1, 1938 but it was postponed to 1942 by Act of Congress, June 28, 1937.

21. For a detailed account of these benefit payments, see report of Agricultural Adjustment Administrator Tolley, dated June 15, 1937. See also later summary in the *Wall Street Journal*, July 28, 1937.

22. Secretary Wallace appeared before the House Committee on Agriculture "in support of the bill." (Hearings on General Farm Legislation, May 27, 1935, p. 135.) President Roosevelt wrote to the chairmen of the Senate and House committees on agriculture, urging passage of the bill (*Chronicle*, July 17, 1937, p. 362).

However, Secretary Wallace criticized various features of the bill, as will be pointed out below. It cannot properly be said to represent the Department of Agriculture's views of a suitable Ever-normal Granary plan, and the measure to be worked out at the next session of Congress may be substantially different from the draft under discussion here.

23. Secretary Wallace has espoused the Granary principle for over 20 years, according to Prof. J. E. Boyle (That Ever-normal Granary, *Saturday Evening Post*, May 8, 1937, p. 14).

Chapter XV

1. Statement before the House Agricultural Committee, May 27, 1937.

2. S. 1397, passed the Senate Mar. 30, 1937. It was introduced in the House and favorably reported by Committee on Agriculture, but was not acted upon prior to adjournment in August 1937.

3. The Crop Insurance Bill states, "Such premiums shall be collected at such time or times, in such manner, and upon such security as the Board may determine." The suggestion that premiums be paid in years of large crops only is contained in the report of the President's Committee on Crop Insurance, December 1936, p. 14.

4. The report of the President's Committee on Crop Insurance contains a great deal of actuarial data based on the years 1930–1935, which include the great drought of 1934 (pp. 33–44).

5. The advantages of this arrangement are well illustrated by the situation of corn during 1937. The combination of a very short crop in 1936 and a very large indicated crop for 1937 resulted in the simultaneous price of 124¾ cents for July delivery (1936 crop) and 78½ cents for December delivery (1937 crop). Were the reservoir in operation it could have equalized both the supply and the price for the two delivery periods, through sales for July and corresponding purchases for December delivery.

6. The Agricultural Adjustment Act of 1937 has appeared before Congress in four different drafts: (1) the original version submitted on May 17, 1937 by the American Farm Bureau Federation; (2) The Flannagan Bill (H.R. 7577, dated June 18, 1937) which follows the original draft closely, with a few significant changes; (3) The Pope-McGill Bill (S. 2717, dated July 15, 1937) which is identical with the Flannagan Bill, except for a few additional provisions of minor importance; (4) The Jones Bill (H.R. 7972, dated July 22, 1937) which, while retaining intact a substantial part of the original draft, departs therefrom in many important respects.

The House Committee's hearings were held on the American Farm Bureau and the Flannagan drafts. The analysis and discussion in our text will accordingly be based on the Flannagan Bill. The important differences between this version and the Jones Bill will be summarized in Note 10 to chapter notes for Chap. XVI. As pointed out in Note 22 to Chap. XIV, the farm legislation to be enacted at the next session of Congress is likely to differ considerably from the Flannagan Bill. Our analysis should be useful, however, in considering whatever new legislation of this kind is proposed.

7. Average supply is computed by adding to average annual output the average carryover figures taken from records of the Department of Agriculture.

8. Secretary Wallace, however, opposed the flexible tariff provision in its entirety because "quickly variable tariff rates are disruptive to trade," and because the advances would not actually help the farmer while the reductions would hurt him (Hearings, p. 139).

9. Secretary Wallace recommended that the normal carryover, or reserve supply, be increased from 125 to 325 million bushels in the case of corn, and from 125 to 200 million bushels in the case of wheat (Hearings, p. 136). He contended, moreover, that "the most vital parts of this bill are those calling for the establishment of an ever-normal granary in the great food crops of corn and wheat" (*ibid.*, p. 135). Nevertheless, it seems undeniable that the Farm Bill of 1937, in all its various drafts, falls far short of realizing Secretary Wallace's ideal of a truly adequate granary.

Chapter XVI

1. For the full text of the Resolution see *New York Herald Tribune*, July 13, 1937.

2. Objections to the Farm Bill provisions similar to those advanced in this chapter are voiced in the leading editorials of the *New York Times* of May 18 and May 21, 1937. The latter is based in good part on the criticisms of Prof. J. E. Boyle in his article, That Ever-normal Granary in the *Saturday Evening Post*, May 8, 1937. See also a forceful editorial in the *Wall Street Journal*, July 27, 1937, entitled Consequences of a Granary.

3. The relative effect of the collapses of 1921 and 1932 upon the price of the farm and nonfarm components of our unit is shown in the following table:

| Year | Value of 100 commodity units | Per cent of this value represented by | |
		United States farm products	Other products
1920	183.0	66	34
1921	88.6	62.1	37.9
1926	100	66.7	33.3
1932	43.8	62.1	37.9

4. In June 1937 the value of the United States farm component of the unit rose to 75 per cent of the total, due chiefly to the high price of corn (see Table VI in the Appendix).

5. The farmer is to receive these parity payments "on the aggregate normal yield of his soil-depleting base acreage" (Section 5a).

6. As compared with the loan and bonus provisions of the proposed AAA of 1937, the government has actually agreed to loans at the rate of 9 cents per pound, and to a subsidy up to 3 cents per pound on a total of about 10,600,000 bales—provided the recipients agree to participate in the 1938 curtailment program (*Wall Street Journal*, Aug. 31, 1937).

7. The American Farm Bureau Federation presented estimates of the Department of Agriculture ranging between a minimum of 287 million dollars and a maximum of 766 millions, the "probable average" being set at 372 millions (Hearings, p. 12).

8. These are calculations of Marvin Jones, Chairman of the House Committee on Agriculture, given by him on p. 166 of the Hearings.

9. See references to this technique in the report of Agricultural Adjustment Administrator Tolley for 1936, dated June 15, 1937, particularly pp. 56–60.

10. As previously stated, the discussion in the text is based upon the Flannagan draft of the Farm Bill. The version later introduced by Chairman Jones involves the following significant differences:

1. Instead of parity payments at a prescribed rate, the cooperating farmer is to receive soil-conserving payments under the Soil Conservation Act. The amount is discretionary with the Secretary of Agriculture. There are to be no written contracts with farmers.

2. The penalty tax on marketings in excess of quotas is eliminated, the sole penalty being exclusion from all benefits during the following year. The flexible tariff provision is also omitted.

3. The granting and amount of Surplus Reserve loans are made largely discretionary with the Secretary. Marketing quotas can be imposed only if authorized by a two-thirds vote at a farmers' referendum.

4. There are new provisions for:

a. Imposition of a *processing tax* if the prospective supply exceeds "normal" by a prescribed percentage. The rate is 2 cents per pound on cotton; 10 cents per bushel on wheat and rice; and ¼ cent per pound on hogs in lieu of a tax on corn. There is a corresponding *producer's tax* of 20 per cent of the selling price in the case of tobacco (subject to a referendum for the guidance of Congress).

b. Reductions of payments to large producers.

c. Proceedings looking to lower freight rates on farm products.

d. Research to develop new uses and markets for farm products.

Chapter XVII

1. The Adequacy of Existing Currency Mechanisms, etc. *American Economic Review*, March 1937, p. 167.

2. See references to pronouncements on this point by the British Chancellor of the Exchequer in Leon Fraser, Recovery and Monetary Stabilization, *Proceedings of the Academy of Political Science*, May 1936, pp. 106, 108–109.

3. See Chap. IV, p. 56.

4. *Cf:* "The whole exchange problem can be stated very simply. It is not possibly to have both rigid prices and rigid exchanges." R. H. Stone, *Lloyds Bank Monthly Review*, June 1935, p. 350.

5. Import duties on the commodities in the proposed unit are shown in the Appendix, Table VIII. The aggregate duty on a commodity unit, if imported, would amount to 23 cents. Hence complete commodity units would have to be obtainable in the world market at 23 per cent less than the domestic price before they could be imported profitably.

6. Our gold stock of 12,189 million dollars on June 30, 1937 was over 50 per cent of the estimated total held by the central governments and treasuries of the world (*Federal Reserve Bulletin*, Aug. 1937, p. 768).

7. Tourist expenditures and immigrant remittances are important offsets in favor of foreign countries, but they have not been large enough to wipe out our annual credit balance on trade and investment account. Average annual figures for 1921–1930 are as follows:

Millions of Dollars

Net from	Debit	Credit
Merchandise trade.	. . .	767
Interest and dividends on investments, including war-debt receipts.	. . .	585
Tourist expenditures.	478	
Immigrant remittances.	325	
Shipping and other services.	68	
Net balance from above.		Cr. 481

These amounts are calculated from the table entitled The Balance of International Payments of the United States, 1919–1933, appearing in *The Index*, published by the New York Trust Company, September 1934, p. 204.

8. Typical of the caustic criticism of our foreign-debt policy is the following from a speech of Owen D. Young, delivered on May 15, 1933:

"They could only repay that debt by sending us their goods. To the extent which we would not accept sufficiently of their goods, they could only pay by sending us their gold. So having refused their goods we took their gold until we ruined the currency and banking system of the world, including our own, until international exchanges and trade were paralyzed." Quoted in *Chronicle*, May 27, 1933, p. 3626.

9. Compare the statement of Secretary Morgenthau in his radio address of May 13, 1935: "Loans in default are not very good backing for our currency. . . . If we must choose between the two, this Administration elects payment of international balances in monetary metal." Quoted in *Chronicle*, May 18, 1935, pp. 3321–3322.

Chapter XVIII

1. Quoted by Garet Garrett in the *New York Times*, July 16, 1922.

2. "Prices and price relationships almost completely dominate the economic life of the nation." Committee on Recent Economic Changes, quoted in the Introduction to *Prices in Recession and Recovery*, by F. C. Mills, 1936.

3. See also the kinds of money detailed by Adam Smith (*Wealth of Nations*, Vol. I, p. 33).

4. These tobacco receipts "were in general circulation and accepted unquestioningly." *Curious Currency*, Walter Longfellow & Company, Boston, 1913. In 1727 they were made current and payable for all tobacco debts in Virginia (Norman Angell, *The Story of Money*, p. 85).

The Chase Collection contains examples of paper money backed by cotton deposits; also of corn money, issued at the rate of 25 cents per bushel against corn stored in cribs (see account in *Clear Lake, Ia., Reporter*, Mar. 2, 1933).

5. A. DelMar, *History of Monetary Systems*, New York. He adds, "The Japanese used similar coins as late as 1866."

6. See Report of the Royal Gold and Silver Commission, 1888, recently republished with an introduction by R. W. Robey. Six of the twelve members recommended adoption of international bimetallism. Professor Alfred Marshall, the eminent economist, recommended the issuance of paper money against gold and silver combined in a fixed ratio. The advantages of this arrangement were acknowledged by all the members, but the suggestion was rejected because too much time would be needed to gain popular support (*ibid.*, pp. 126–127). Since from the monetary viewpoint our proposal may be defined as "symmetallism applied to basic commodities," it may be briefly denominated as commodity-symmetallism or, by contraction, "Commetallism."

7. See *Monetary Reform in Theory and Practice*, pp. 201–209.

8. See *Stabilizing the Dollar*, 1920.

9. Carl Snyder, The Stabilization of Gold, *American Economic Review*, June 1923, pp. 283–285.

10. See Commodity Prices versus General Price Level, *American Economic Review*, September 1934.

11. J. M. Keynes, *Monetary Reform*, 1924, pp. 201-213.

12. R. C. Hawtrey, *Monetary Reconstruction*, 1923, pp. 61–65.

13. See *Federal Reserve Bulletin*, June 1923, pp. 678–679.

14. This idea has been revived in the recent suggestion of the Bank for International Settlements (see Note 6 of the chapter notes for Chap. I).

15. G. N. Lewis, A Plan for Stabilizing Prices, *The Economic Journal*, March 1925.

16. See, *inter alia*, *Stabilizing the Dollar*, 1920; *The Making of Index Numbers*, 1922; *Booms and Depressions*, 1932. *Stable Money*, 1934, contains a detailed history of the movement, and describes many proposals not mentioned by J. S. Lawrence.

17. See Note 12 of the chapter notes for Chap. X.

18. For a severe criticism of the Fisher plan see B. M. Anderson, On the Practical Impossibility of a Commodity Dollar, *Chase Economic Bulletin*, Dec. 13, 1933. See also his article, A Planned Economy and a Planned Price Level, *The Chase Economic Bulletin*, June 9, 1933. On

p. 20, Dr. Anderson says, "I am very sure that no technique exists, even in theory, through which, *by means of credit and currency manipulation*, we could reach a particular price level and hold it" (italics mine).

The author agrees with Dr. Anderson on this point. It is the central feature of the plan here proposed that it does not involve credit and currency *manipulation*, but merely a physical equivalence between paper money and a commodity unit.

19. See reference in Note 15 above.

20. It may be proper to observe that the author's plan was devised in substantially its present form during the depression of 1920–1921 and was thus arrived at independently of both the Lewis and the Edison proposals.

21. I find that a plan resembling my own perhaps even more closely than that of Prof. Lewis was put forward by N. T. Bacon in an article entitled, Stabilizing Production by Means of Reserves, in the *American Economic Review* of March 1924. Bacon proposed that gold be replaced as the basis of money by stored basic commodities; that the government guarantee never to permit the value of the stored commodities to fall below a certain proportion of the circulation; that certain standard prices and relative quantities be established for individual commodities; that individual commodities be bought when their price fell 5 per cent below "the proportion scheduled for that commodity to the total value secured," and that the quantity held should be increased to a point inversely equal to the fall in price below the standard.

Mr. Bacon's suggestions were not put forward in complete and detailed form, but rather as a general idea. Hence it is not possible to consider them with any degree of thoroughness. The chief points of divergence from our own plan are that (1) the Bacon plan contains no basis for redeeming currency in stored commodities and (2) it endeavors to support the price of individual commodities by separate purchases.

22. See Frank A. Vanderlip, *Tomorrow's Money*, 1934.

23. H. R. 11499, 72d Congress, 1st Session. In 1936 and 1937 Representative Goldsborough introduced still another proposal, referred to as establishing the commodity dollar, but substantially embodying the "Social Credit" idea of Major Douglas (see *Journal of Commerce*, Jan. 13, 1937). In March 1937 Senator Thomas introduced a bill looking to the stabilization of the price level by means of a monetary authority (S. 1990).

24. Between Mar. 1 and July 18, 1933, Moody's Index of Staple Commodity Prices advanced from 80 to 149, over 85 per cent. Loans of reporting member banks actually declined during this period.

25. For a discussion of the peculiar elements entering into the Swedish stabilization, see B. Thomas, *Monetary Policy and Crises. A Study of the Swedish Experience.*

26. See the discussion of the Edison plan by Garet Garrett in the *New York Times*, July 16, 1922. Also criticism in the *Chronicle* editorial of May 27, 1922, p. 2789. A more recent account is that of Isaac Don Levine, *Today*, Jan. 13, 1934.

Chapter XIX

1. *The Nature of the State*, p. 160.
2. *New York Herald Tribune*, May 18, 1937.
3. "We know that depression is the enemy of democracy." Simeon Strunsky, *New York Times*, Magazine section, Dec. 27, 1936.

APPENDIX I

TABLE III.—VARIATIONS IN THE RELATIVE PRICES OF INDIVIDUAL COMMODITIES, 1911-1913

Range of prices in dollars and cents

	1911-1920			1921-1930			1931-1935			Average prices for single years				
	High	Low	Aver.	High	Low	Aver.	High	Low	Aver.	1913	1920	1921	1926	1932
Barley	203.	53.30	100.30	104.10	53.20	74.22	119.80	29.60	60.6	62.50	126.30	63.50	69.40	39.80
Coffee (No. 4 Santos)	23.	6.31	11.29	23.44	6.	14.06	10.91	5.35	7.82	11.13	11.98	7.19	18.39	8.06
Corn	236.	45.50	102.27	135.50	42.	82.21	111.	22.	51.90	61.40	139.70	56.50	73.30	30.50
Cotton	43.75	7.25	19.45	37.65	12.80	20.56	13.95	5.00	9.58	12.80	33.89	15.07	17.53	6.44
Cottonseed oil	27.10	5.20	11.86	15.64	5.90	10.38	11.40	3.16	6.28	7.22	15.33	7.90	12.17	3.84
Hides	52.	12.75	25.35	25.75	9.28	15.12	12.06	4.25	8.44	18.39	31.22	13.90	13.08	5.63
Lead	11.71	3.39	5.76	10.16	4.02	6.71	4.60	2.59	3.69	4.26	7.93	4.39	8.25	3.04
Oats	111.40	32.40	54.90	71.40	33.80	45.70	57.80	16.60	33.20	37.00	79.60	38.70	43.10	21.30
Petroleum, K.O.	3.50	0.40	1.54	3.40	0.85	1.48	0.98	0.22	0.75	0.93	3.41	1.71	1.89	0.83
Rubber	167.	16.	71.91	113.	7.50	28.85	15.83	2.50	8.13	82.	36.30	16.40	48.49	3.36
Rye	295.	55.	125.27	173.	45.	96.22	99.	30.	53.70	63.60	187.30	121.30	95.60	39.30
Silk	17.65	3.45	5.81	10.50	2.49	6.22	2.96	1.15	1.73	4.13	9.96	6.66	6.37	1.57
Sugar	22.47	3.72	7.17	9.90	4.41	6.15	5.30	3.76	4.51	4.27	5.45	6.16	5.65	4.08
Tin	100.	30.25	52.44	70.67	25.27	47.04	55.60	19.24	17.63	44.33	50.33	30.00	65.30	22.01
Wheat	350.	81.	160.	220.50	76.25	136.50	123.50	44.50	78.	95.	252.	144.	154.	53.
Zinc	22.14	4.81	8.27	8.73	4.06	6.18	4.86	2.53	3.81	5.61	7.77	4.67	6.82	2.88

Dollars and cents prices expressed as percentage of the 1921-1930 average

	1911-1920			1921-1930			1931-1935			Average prices for single years				
	High	Low	Aver.	High	Low	Aver.	High	Low	Aver.	1913	1920	1921	1926	1932
Barley	252.4	71.8	135.1	149.0	71.6	100	161.6	39.9	81.5	84.2	170.1	85.6	93.5	63.7
Coffee (No. 4 Santos)	163.4	44.8	80.2	166.8	42.7	100	77.7	38.0	55.6	79.4	85.3	51.5	130.5	57.1
Corn	287.0	55.2	124.5	164.5	51.0	100	135.0	26.8	63.1	74.5	169.9	68.7	89.1	37.1
Cotton	225.0	35.3	94.8	183.2	62.3	100	68.0	24.4	46.7	63.3	165.0	73.5	85.5	32.0
Cottonseed oil	265.0	50.2	114.4	150.9	54.9	100	110.1	30.4	60.7	69.6	148.1	76.2	117.5	31.2
Hides	344.1	84.3	167.3	170.0	61.2	100	79.8	28.1	55.4	82.4	206.2	92.1	86.3	37.2
Lead	174.7	50.6	85.8	151.5	59.9	100	68.6	38.6	55.0	63.5	118.0	61.1	122.8	45.2
Oats	239.9	70.9	120.0	155.5	74.1	100	126.6	36.4	72.7	80.8	174.1	84.6	94.4	45.4
Petroleum, K.O.	236.3	27.1	104.0	229.5	57.4	100	66.3	14.9	50.8	66.3	230.0	115.5	127.7	57.2
Rubber	580.0	55.6	249.1	382.0	25.9	100	54.8	8.7	28.2	284.0	125.2	56.8	169.5	11.7
Rye	307.0	57.2	130.5	180.1	46.9	100	102.9	31.2	55.9	61.3	195.3	126.3	99.4	41.6
Silk	260.0	50.7	85.5	154.5	36.8	100	43.6	16.9	25.4	66.6	160.1	107.1	102.5	25.2
Sugar	364.0	60.6	116.8	161.2	71.8	100	86.3	61.2	73.6	69.5	251.1	100.2	108.6	66.9
Tin	204.9	68.2	109.8	148.1	53.5	100	116.8	39.4	36.9	92.9	105.2	62.9	136.8	46.3
Wheat	255.3	59.3	117.1	164.7	53.5	100	90.6	32.6	57.2	69.6	184.6	105.4	112.8	38.8
Zinc	361.2	77.9	133.7	141.1	65.7	100	78.6	44.2	61.7	90.7	125.6	75.5	110.2	46.6

TABLE IV.—COMPOSITION OF PROPOSED COMMODITY UNIT
PRODUCTION OR CONSUMPTION BY YEARS (Quantities in Millions)

Commodity	Units	1921	1922	1923	1924	1925	1926	1927	1928	1929	1930	Average, 1921–1930	Quantity corresponding to 1 bu. of wheat
Wheat	Bushels	819	847	760	840	669	834	875	926	812	857	824	1.000
Barley	Bushels	131	154	159	166	193	164	241	331	280	304	212	0.257
Cocoa	Pounds	305	345	414	378	382	426	425	379	508	373	394	0.478
Coffee	Pounds	1,345	1,249	1,412	1,424	1,288	1,496	1,444	1,461	1,486	1,605	1,421	1.726
Corn	Bushels	2,912	2,688	2,860	2,305	2,853	2,575	2,678	2,715	2,535	2,060	2,618	3.175
Cottonseed oil	Pounds	1,186	827	858	1,057	1,345	1,478	1,592	1,331	1,451	1,458	1,258	1.525
Oats	Bushels	1,045	1,148	1,227	1,423	1,410	1,142	1,093	1,318	1,118	1,276	1,220	1.480
Rye	Bushels	61	105	54	58	40	33	52	38	35	45	52	0.063
Sugar	Pounds	11,179	11,780	11,292	13,080	13,296	13,936	13,136	14,384	12,730	12,784	12,670	15.380
Cotton	Pounds	3,977	4,878	5,070	6,814	8,052	8,989	6,478	7,239	7,414	6,666	6,588	8.000
Silk	Pounds	52	58	62	61	77	78	86	88	98	82	74	0.091
Wool	Pounds	300	313	311	250	252	254	259	233	253	201	263	0.319
Copper	Pounds	506	950	1,435	1,634	1,675	1,740	1,684	1,826	2,003	1,394	1,485	1.802
Lead	Pounds	898	1,066	1,236	1,380	1,534	1,598	1,594	1,562	1,550	1,286	1,370	1.665
Tin	Pounds	54	135	154	145	172	173	159	174	195	181	154	0.187
Zinc	Pounds	396	707	1,017	1,032	1,111	1,224	1,154	1,183	1,224	979	1,093	1.218
Cottonseed meal	Pounds	3,572	2,710	2,974	3,036	4,252	5,194	5,680	4,186	4,564	4,464	4,064	4.930
Flaxseed	Bushels	20	25	41	48	39	41	47	37	40	34	37	0.045
Hides	Pounds	800	1,195	1,085	945	975	955	955	915	870	795	949	1.152
Petroleum	Barrels	472	558	732	714	764	771	901	901	1,007	898	772	0.938
Rubber	Pounds	401	664	676	714	862	866	904	913	1,184	1,023	824	1.000
Tallow	Pounds	416	460	495	539	485	536	561	497	534	571	510	0.619
Tobacco	Pounds	1,095	1,254	1,518	1,245	1,376	1,289	1,211	1,373	1,537	1,647	1,346	1.635

TABLE V.—ANNUAL AVERAGE PRICES OF COMMODITIES IN PROPOSED UNIT, 1921–1930 (In Dollars)

Commodity	Unit	1921	1922	1923	1924	1925	1926	1927	1928	1929	1930	Weighted average, 1921–1930
Wheat.........	Bushel	1.30	1.15	1.09	1.31	1.59	1.45	1.32	1.18	1.21	0.87	1.240
Barley.........	Bushel	0.59	0.57	0.60	0.76	0.78	0.64	0.77	0.78	0.63	0.52	0.666
Cocoa.........	Pound	0.076	0.093	0.074	0.075	0.097	0.116	0.160	0.129	0.104	0.080	0.102
Coffee.........	Pound	0.107	0.129	0.135	0.175	0.223	0.216	0.185	0.213	0.204	0.131	0.172
Corn..........	Bushel	0.54	0.61	0.81	0.94	1.01	0.75	0.86	0.94	0.92	0.82	0.816
Cottonseed oil..	Pound	0.079	0.101	0.113	0.108	0.108	0.118	0.097	0.099	0.097	0.081	0.100
Oats..........	Bushel	0.37	0.38	0.43	0.50	0.45	0.41	0.47	0.53	0.47	0.39	0.443
Rye...........	Bushel	1.15	0.83	0.70	0.86	1.09	0.92	1.00	1.07	0.96	0.61	0.908
Sugar.........	Pound	0.062	0.059	0.084	0.075	0.055	0.055	0.058	0.056	0.051	0.057	0.061
Cotton.........	Pound	0.151	0.212	0.293	0.287	0.235	0.175	0.176	0.200	0.191	0.135	0.205
Silk...........	Pound	6.57	7.65	8.65	6.25	6.57	6.19	5.44	5.07	4.93	3.42	5.890
Wool..........	Pound	0.85	1.25	1.41	1.42	1.40	1.15	1.10	1.16	0.97	0.76	1.156
Copper.........	Pound	0.125	0.134	0.144	0.130	0.140	0.138	0.129	0.146	0.181	0.130	0.143
Lead..........	Pound	0.046	0.057	0.073	0.081	0.090	0.084	0.068	0.063	0.068	0.055	0.070
Tin...........	Pound	0.300	0.326	0.427	0.502	0.579	0.653	0.644	0.505	0.452	0.317	0.484
Zinc..........	Pound	0.047	0.057	0.066	0.063	0.076	0.073	0.062	0.060	0.065	0.046	0.063
Cottonseed meal	Pound	0.016	0.018	0.020	0.020	0.019	0.016	0.013	0.019	0.020	0.018	0.018
Flaxseed.......	Bushel	1.86	2.48	2.74	2.49	2.74	2.34	2.22	2.28	2.79	2.39	2.460
Hides.........	Pound	0.139	0.180	0.167	0.147	0.160	0.140	0.195	0.238	0.171	0.139	0.168
Petroleum......	Barrel	1.931	1.996	1.638	1.650	1.870	2.084	1.485	1.403	1.433	1.311	1.640
Rubber........	Pound	0.164	0.174	0.296	0.261	0.719	0.485	0.376	0.223	0.205	0.119	0.308
Tallow........	Pound	0.064	0.071	0.082	0.085	0.097	0.087	0.081	0.088	0.085	0.062	0.078
Tobacco........	Pound	0.220	0.253	0.215	0.215	0.193	0.204	0.232	0.225	0.211	0.154	0.210

TABLE VI.—UNITED STATES FARM PRODUCTS AND THE COMMODITY UNIT

Per cent of total for commodity	Commodity	Units	Amount of commodity in 100 one-dollar units	Weighted average price, 1921–1930	Value of commodity in 100 one-dollar units	Average price, June, 1937 (cents)	Value of commodity in 100 one-dollar units, June, 1937
	Major United States farm products:						
100.0	Wheat.....................	Bushels	8.44	$1.240	$10.47	123	$10.37
100.0	Corn.....	Bushels	26.80	0.816	21.88	120	32.20
100.0	Cotton..................	Pounds	67.48	0.205	13.80	12.7	8.59
	Total, three major crops....	......	.....	.....	46.15	....	51.16
	Other United States farm products:						
100.0	Barley.....................	Bushels	2.17	0.666	1.44	81	1.76
100.0	Cottonseed oil.............	Pounds	12.88	0.100	1.29	10	1.29
100.0	Cottonseed meal............	Pounds	41.60	0.018	0.73	1.6	0.67
50.4	Flaxseed..................	Bushels	0.19	2.460	0.47	192	0.36
79.8	Hides.....................	Pounds	7.76	0.168	1.30	16.8	1.30
100.0	Oats......................	Bushels	12.50	0.443	5.54	48	6.00
100.0	Rye......................	Bushels	0.53	0.908	0.48	99	0.53
47.2	Sugar....................	Pounds	61.22	0.061	3.74	4.6	2.82
100.0	Tallow...................	Pounds	5.22	0.078	0.41	8.0	0.42
100.0	Tobacco..................	Pounds	13.79	0.210	2.90	est. 25	3.50
71.9	Wool....................	Pounds	1.93	1.156	2.23	100	1.93
	Total.................	......	.....	.....	20.53	....	20.58
	Total United States farm products..................	......	.....	.....	66.68	....	71.74
	Other United States products:						
100.0	Copper....................	Pounds	15.22	0.143	2.16	13.8	2.08
93.5	Lead.....................	Pounds	13.12	0.070	0.92	6.0	0.79
91.6	Petroleum..................	Barrels	7.25	1.640	11.88	136	9.85
100.0	Zinc.....................	Pounds	10.27	0.063	0.65	6.8	0.70
	Total..................	......	.....	.....	15.61	....	13.42
	Total United States products..	......	.....	.....	82.29	....	85.16
	Imported products:						
100.0	Cocoa.....................	Pounds	4.04	0.102	0.41	7.4	0.30
100.0	Coffee....................	Pounds	14.55	0.172	2.50	10.9	1.59
49.6	Flaxseed..................	Bushels	0.19	2.460	0.46	192	0.36
20.2	Hides....................	Pounds	1.96	0.168	0.34	16.8	0.33
6.5	Lead....................	Pounds	0.92	0.070	0.06	6.0	0.05
8.4	Petroleum.................	Barrels	0.66	1.640	1.07	136	0.90
100.0	Rubber...................	Pounds	8.44	0.308	2.59	19.3	1.63
100.0	Silk.....................	Pounds	0.76	5.890	4.48	183	1.39
52.8	Sugar...................	Pounds	68.50	0.061	4.15	4.6	3.12
100.0	Tin.....................	Pounds	1.58	0.484	0.77	55.8	0.88
28.1	Wool....................	Pounds	0.76	1.156	0.88	100	0.76
	Total.................	......	.....	.....	17.71	....	11.31
	Grand total..............	......	....	.....	$100.0	......	$96.47

TABLE VII.—RELATIONSHIP BETWEEN STOCKS AND ANNUAL PRODUCTION OR CONSUMPTION, 1927–1936
(Quantities in Millions)

Commodity	Unit of quantity	Maximum stocks		Minimum stocks		Average stocks	Average annual production, consumption or imports, 1927–1936	Months supply, based on		
		Amount	Date	Amount	Date			Maximum stocks	Minimum stocks	Average stocks
Wheat	Bushels	378	July 1933	110	July 1927	236	752	6.04	1.76	3.77
Barley	Bushels	20.6	Oct. 1933	0.7	July 1928	10.5	234	1.06	0.04	0.54
Cocoa	Pounds	147	Mar. 1934	11	Jan. 1927	74	474	3.73	0.28	1.88
Coffee	Pounds	210	Aug. 1931	72	Jan. 1933	116	1,568	1.61	0.55	0.89
Corn	Bushels	386	Oct. 1933	65	Oct. 1935	200	2,307	2.05	0.34	1.40
Cottonseed oil	Pounds	843	Apr. 1934	160	Sept. 1928	482	1,318	7.68	1.46	4.39
Oats	Bushels	52	Aug. 1936	2	July 1928	25	1,043	0.60	0.02	0.29
Rye	Bushels	14.8	Sept. 1930	0.9	June 1927	9.2	36.5	4.87	0.30	3.03
Sugar	Pounds	2,040	May 1929	277	Dec. 1936	932	13,068	1.88	0.25	0.86
Cotton	Pounds	6,074	Nov. 1932	983	Aug. 1928	3,746	6,601	11.04	1.79	6.81
Silk	Pounds	12.8	Dec. 1933	3.9	Sept. 1936	6.8	79.5	1.93	0.59	1.03
Wool	Pounds	476	Dec. 1934	259	Dec. 1936	348	510	11.20	6.10	8.19
Copper	Pounds	1,004	Dec. 1932	114	Dec. 1928	442	1,353	8.90	1.01	3.92
Lead	Pounds	481	July 1934	84	Apr. 1930	349	804	7.18	1.25	5.21
Tin	Pounds	18.4	Jan. 1934	3.1	Oct. 1935	9.0	147.1	1.50	0.25	0.74
Zinc	Pounds	290	Nov. 1930	60	Jan. 1927	184	995	3.85	0.80	2.44
Cottonseed meal	Pounds	734	Nov. 1932	85	Aug. 1930	390	4,214	2.09	0.25	1.11
Flaxseed	Bushels	13.0	Dec. 1927	1.8	June 1933	4.3	29.7	5.26	0.73	1.74
Hides	Pounds	354	Dec. 1934	157	June 1927	226	865	4.92	2.18	3.14
Petroleum	Barrels	537	Sept. 1929	345	Dec. 1936	448	925	6.98	4.49	5.82
Rubber	Pounds	887	Mar. 1933	125	Nov. 1928	515	994	10.72	1.51	6.22
Tallow	Pounds	326	Dec. 1934	67	Dec. 1928	186	579	6.76	1.39	3.86
Tobacco	Pounds	2,434	Mar. 1934	1,612	Sept. 1929	2,036	1,326	22.02	14.60	18.44

NOTE: Wheat and corn figures are annual carryovers supplied by U. S. Dept. of Agriculture. Tallow data supplied by N. Y. Produce Exchange. Other figures taken from the *Monthly Survey of Current Business*.

TABLE VIII.—EXPORT AND IMPORT RATIOS AND IMPORT DUTIES, 1921–1930
(Quantities in Millions)

Commodity	Unit of quantity	Average annual production or consumption	Net exports	Net imports	Per cent of average production or consumption	Import duty per unit of quantity	Duty applicable to 100 one-dollar units
Wheat............	Bushels	824	177.0	......	21.5	$0.42	$ 3.55
Barley............	Bushels	212	28.5	......	13.4	0.20	0.43
Cocoa............	Pounds	394	.....	394	100.0		
Coffee............	Pounds	1,421	.....	1,421	100.0		
Corn.............	Bushels	2,618	48.5	......	1.8	0.25	6.70
Cottonseed oil.....	Pounds	1,258	29.6	......	2.3	0.03	0.39
Oats.............	Bushels	1,220	16.3	......	1.3	0.16	2.00
Rye..............	Bushels	52	24.2	......	46.5	0.15	0.08
Sugar............	Pounds	12,670	.....	6,690.0	52.8	0.01	1.30
Cotton............	Bales	13	7.0	......	53.6		
Silk..............	Pounds	74	.....	74	100.0		
Wool............	Pounds	263	.....	74.0	28.1	0.27	0.73
Copper...........	Pounds	1,485	221.5	......	14.9	0.04	0.61
Lead.............	Pounds	1,370	.....	89.1	6.5	0.02125	0.30
Tin..............	Pounds	154	.....	154	100.0		
Zinc.............	Pounds	1,003	36.4	......	3.6	0.0175	0.18
Cottonseed meal...	Pounds	4,064	568.0	......	14.0	0.003	0.13
Flaxseed..........	Bushels	37	.....	18.4	49.6	0.65	0.25
Hides............	Pounds	949	.....	191.7	20.2	10 % advalorem	0.15
Petroleum.........	Barrels	772	.....	64.7	8.4	0.21	1.66
Rubber...........	Pounds	824	.....	824	100.0		
Tallow...........	Pounds	510	.....	......	.....	0.005	0.03
Tobacco..........	Pounds	1,346	452.4	......	33.6	0.35 (min.)	4.83
Total...........	......	......	.....	......	.....	....	$23.32

TABLE IX.—VOLUME OF TRADING IN THE COMPONENT COMMODITIES ON THE
VARIOUS COMMODITY EXCHANGES
(Quantities in Millions)

Commodity	Unit of quantity	Year	Quantity traded	Average anual production or consumption, 1921–1930	Per cent of 1921–1930 average of total production or consumption traded
Wheat..............	Bushels	1929	18,777	824	2,279
Barley..............	Bushels	1929	89	212	42
Cocoa..............	Pounds	1929	1,416	394	360
Coffee..............	Pounds	1929	2,037	1,421	143
Corn..............	Bushels	1929	4,943	2,618	189
Cottonseed oil..........	Pounds	1929	1,210	1,258	96
Oats..............	Bushels	1929	1,002	1,220	82
Rye..............	Bushels	1929	91	52	175
Sugar..............	Pounds	1929	28,472	12,670	225
Cotton..............	Pounds	1929	57,889	6,500	890
Silk..............	Pounds	1929	29	74	39
Wool..............	Pounds	1936	12	263	4.57
Copper..............	Pounds	1935	437	1,485	29
Lead..............	Pounds	1935	28	1,370	2.04
Tin..............	Pounds	1935	0.4	154	0.26
Zinc..............	Pounds	1935	10	1,003	1.00
Cottonseed meal........	Pounds	1929	1,538	4,064	38
Flaxseed..............	Bushels	1929	48	37	130
Hides..............	Pounds	1935	763	949	80
Petroleum..............	Barrels	1935	0.1	772	0.01
Rubber..............	Pounds	1929	1,100	824	133
Tallow..............	Pounds	1936	30	510	5.88
Tobacco..............	Pounds	1936	1.6	1,346	0.19

TABLE X.—EXAMPLES OF PREMIUMS FOR NEAR OVER DISTANT DELIVERIES IN VARIOUS COMMODITIES DURING 1937

Date, 1937	Commodity	Near delivery		Distant delivery	
		Delivery month	Price	Delivery month	Price
June 1	Barley*	July	66¼	Oct.	57⅛
May 14	Coffee	May	11.42	Mar. '38	10.16
June 30	Corn	July	124¾	Dec.	78½
Apr. 5	Cotton	May	14.48	Sept.	13.84
Apr. 30	Cottonseed meal	May	39.50	Oct.	27.50
June 30	Cottonseed oil	July	9.15	Dec.	9.04
May 26	Oats	May	56⅛	Sept.	38¾
May 26	Rye	May	117½	Sept.	90
Apr. 5	Silk	Apr.	197	Nov.	190½
Apr. 5	Wheat	May	143½	Sept.	125⅝

* Winnipeg.

APPENDIX II

Notes re Establishment and Revision of the Commodity Unit

I. QUANTITY VS. PRICES

The central point in the composition of the unit is that the *price* of the various commodities has no bearing whatever upon their relative position in the unit. The ratio between the amounts, say, of wheat and of oats in the unit depends entirely upon their relative production, and is in no wise affected by the prices assigned to them. Nor have the base prices any influence whatever upon the price at which each commodity may sell in the future.

The base price taken for the several commodities enters only into the determination of the aggregate *price level*. In other words, it affects the size of the commodity unit made equal to a dollar. It follows that there is no need for absolute accuracy in the price computations, and it is quite sufficient to use price quotations which are reasonably representative of the various commodities. For any small inaccuracy is reflected merely in an extremely small variation in the general price level from the theoretical 1921–1930 average. But since the selection of this average as the standard is itself in part a matter of arbitrary choice, it follows that any variation of, say, 1 or 2 per cent in working out this standard level cannot be of great moment.

Because of this fact we are permitted to use the most representative and convenient price quotations for each commodity, instead of having to calculate laboriously the prices which would apply exactly to the entire volume of production and consumption, allowing for variations in grade. We have accordingly taken as many as possible of these quotations from the *Monthly Survey of Current Business*, published by the U.S. Department of Commerce, since these are official data readily obtainable. Some of the prices are obtained elsewhere, and for two of them adjustments are necessary to arrive at a representative futures trading price. The tabulation on page 280 shows the nature and source of the quotations used in *computing the average price level for the commodity unit as a whole.*

I have used refined sugar instead of raw, dealt in on the exchange, to reflect the United States beet-sugar production. Similarly I have used scoured wool, instead of the "wool tops" dealt in on the New York Cotton Exchange, because the former reflects more closely the entire consumption of apparel grades of wool. The 20 cents addition to the price of petroleum at the well represents the differential existing between the well price and the prices quoted on the Commodity Exchange, Inc., when there was

Commodity	Grade or designation	Source of quotation
Wheat.................	Weighted average six markets, all grades	Survey of Current Business
Barley.................	No. 2 Minneapolis	Survey of Current Business
Cocoa.................	Accra, N. Y.	Survey of Current Business
Corn...................	No. 3 Yellow, Kansas City No. 3 White, Chicago } Averaged	Survey of Current Business
Cottonseed oil..........	Prime yellow, refined, New York	Survey of Current Business
Oats...................	No. 3 White, Chicago	Survey of Current Business
Rye...................	No. 2 Minneapolis	Survey of Current Business
Sugar..................	Granulated, New York	Survey of Current Business
Cotton.................	Middling upland, New York	Survey of Current Business
Silk...................	Japanese 13–15, New York	Survey of Current Business
Wool..................	Raw, territory, scoured, Boston	Survey of Current Business
Copper.................	Electrolytic, New York	Survey of Current Business
Lead...................	Refined, New York	Survey of Current Business
Tin...................	Straits, New York	Survey of Current Business
Zinc...................	Prime western, St. Louis	Survey of Current Business
Flaxseed................	No. 1 Minneapolis	Survey of Current Business
Hides.................	Green salted, packers' heavy steers, Chicago	Survey of Current Business
Rubber.................	Smoked sheets, New York	Survey of Current Business
Petroleum..............	Kansas-Oklahoma (price at well plus 20 cents)	Survey of Current Business
Cottonseed meal........	Total production	Statistical Abstract of the United States
Tobacco................	Average farm price plus 10 per cent	Statistical Abstract of the United States
Coffee.................	Average import price	Statistical Abstract of the United States
Tallow.................	Inedible	New York Produce Exchange

fairly active trading in petroleum. Similarly the 10 per cent addition to the farm price of tobacco is intended to reflect the higher cost in a wholesale market. (Both of these adjustments are approximate, but as explained above, the effect of the error is inconsequential.) If the price of tobacco is to be based on trading on the New York Produce Exchange, a composite consisting of 70 per cent of the flue-cured type and 30 per cent of the burley type would be sufficiently accurate.

II. THE MATTER OF TENDERABLE GRADES

The commodities which will actually enter into the physical units will be limited to the grades tenderable under the standard contracts of the various commodity exchanges. Not all of the country's production or consumption of each commodity is of the tenderable grades. It will be found, however, that the weighting of each commodity by the total reported, instead of by the amount of tenderable grades only, will give both the simplest and fairest result. Statistics presented in Table XI herewith show that a large fraction of the total output or consumption is, in fact, tenderable under the standard contract, so that there is no problem of overemphasis involved in designating the deliverable grades as representative of the entire production as statistically reported.

TABLE XI.—PROPORTION OF TENDERABLE GRADES TO TOTAL PRODUCTION OR IMPORTS OF REPRESENTATIVE COMMODITIES*

Commodity	Approximate Per Cent
Cocoa	75 to 80
Coffee (Rio)	100
Cotton	90
Cottonseed meal	80
Cottonseed oil	80
Flaxseed	100
Hides	50
Rubber	80
Silk	90 to 95
Sugar	85
Tallow	75 to 80

* Data supplied by H. Hentz & Co., New York.

III. PERIODIC REVISION OF THE COMMODITY UNIT

No great difficulty should be encountered in arranging for (a) periodic revisions of the relative quantities (b) additions to the component commodities and (c) elimination of a commodity from the unit. The technique in each case may be summarized as follows:

a. Readjustment of Relative Quantities

Assume a decennial revision to be made on the basis of average production or consumption during the preceding decade, e.g., a revision in 1947 based on the 1937–1946 statistics. A new commodity unit is constructed in exactly the same way as our original unit, but based on the 1937–1946 average quantities and average prices instead of those for 1921–1930.

Compared with the old unit, the new dollar unit will be found to contain larger amounts of some items and smaller amounts of others. To transform the old relative amounts into the new it will be necessary to sell out in the open market the excess of those items which have diminished in importance and purchase the needed quantity of those that have expanded.

These open-market operations can be carried out over a period of time, if desirable. They may result in a cash loss or cash profit, depending on the price situation. It may be thought that a commodity that must be sold, because it has diminished in relative volume, will therefore have declined in price. This is by no means certain; on the contrary, those commodities which have increased in relative volume are perhaps more likely to be selling lower than before. (This is true of petroleum and rubber, comparing 1936 with 1913.) The sales and purchases to readjust the unit, whether they eventuate in a profit or a loss, must be regarded as a necessary but infrequent incident to the operation of the Reservoir plan. In the author's view the net financial result is not likely to be important one way or the other.

b, c. Additions to and Eliminations from the List

It may be satisfactory to change the items in the unit only at the time when the relative quantities are revised. If this rule is followed the general procedure becomes exactly the same as that just outlined. In the case of new commodities the full quantity in the revised unit will have to be purchased; and in the case of elimination the entire holdings will have to be disposed of.

An elimination because of an excessive price advance, as suggested in our text, may have to take place at some intermediate time. The procedure here is quite simple. Assume the commodity to be excluded represented 5 per cent of the unit on the basis of its dollar value during, say, the 1921–1930 period. The commodity is taken out of the units and sold, and concurrently 5 per cent of the commodity-unit currency is retired. Since such eliminations are to be made only in the event of an extraordinary price advance, it is clear that the stored product would be sold at considerably more than its former average price, so that the operation should yield a substantial cash profit.

If it is decided to add a commodity between general revision dates, the required technique would be just the opposite of that just outlined. If the new commodity had an aggregate dollar value in 1921–1930 equal to 5 per cent of the original unit, the appropriate quantity of the new product would be purchased and additional commodity-unit currency will be concurrently issued in an amount equal to 5 per cent of that previously outstanding. To guard against a loss on this operation it may be provided that new commodities will be added only when their current market price is less than their average value during the preceding base period.

Index

Page numbers followed by *n.* refer to Chapter Notes; *a.* refers to Appendix.

CPSIA information can be obtained
at www.ICGtesting.com
Printed in the USA
LVOW08s2227220617
539096LV00001B/60/P